ORGANIZATION THEORY IN AN OPEN SYSTEM:

A Study of Transferring
Advanced Management Practices
to Developing Nations

ORGANIZATION THEORY IN AN OPEN SYSTEM:

A Study of Transferring Advanced Management
Practices to Developing Nations

Anant R. Negandhi

University Press of Cambridge, Mass. Series
Consulting Editor: Eugene H. Nellen

DUNELLEN
New York • London

TO

PIA, AMIN, ERNY,

AND THE

PEOPLE OF THE THIRD WORLD

International Standard Book Number 0-8046-7075-7
Library of Congress Catalog Card Number 73-88807
Printed in the United States of America.

Distributed by
Kennikat Press Corp.
Port Washington, N.Y. 11050

CONTENTS

PREFACE

In the initial stage of this study, the primary concern was with the transferability of American management practices and know-how to industrial enterprises in developing countries. I was specifically interested in examining the potential of the managerial input in generating rapid economic and industrial developments and, consequently, higher standards of living for those people in the "have not" nations.

This project began in 1965 and during this period field research was conducted in a number of developing countries. As the field research progressed and data were analyzed, it became apparent that the field being studied is indeed broad. The transferability problem not only raised the issue of the sociocultural and environmental impact on management practices and effectiveness, but also provided the perspective to examine: (a) organizations in an open-system framework; (b) the validity and consequences of a closed-system approach in studying organizations; (c) the validity of universalistic approach in management, and (d) contributions of cross-cultural management studies to the organization theory discipline.

In this book, therefore, an attempt is made to unfold the above issues. More specifically, an endeavor is made to shed light on the following critical issues:

(1) The validity of the universality of organizational practices or so-called management-principles approach.

(2) The nature of similarities and differences in organizational practices and effectiveness of industrial enterprises in developing countries and developed ones.

(3) The applicability and utility of U.S. organizational practices to industrial enterprises in developing countries.

(4) The impact of socio-cultural and environmental variables on organizational practices and effectiveness.

(5) The nature of contributions of cross-cultural management studies to the general discipline of the organization theory.

No attempt is made pretending to have found answers to the various questions raised. However, it is hoped, that the attempts in this direction will further stimulate search for the answers of those critical questions raised in this volume.

The field study was conducted in six developing countries (Argentina, Brazil, India, the Philippines, Taiwan, and Uruguay) and the United States. A total of 126 industrial firms were examined, of which 56 were U.S. subsidiaries, 55 comparable local firms, and 15 were U.S. parent companies.

As the reader will recognize, a project such as this, cannot be conducted without the cooperation and help of many individuals, business firms, and funding agencies.

First of all, the project was initiated by the generous funding from the Ford Foundation, given through the Chancellor's Committee on International and Comparative Studies, at the University of California, Los Angeles. The Taiwan phase of the project was funded by the Council for International Economic Cooperation and Development, Taiwan, and the Research Council of Kent State University. The "desk phase" of the entire project (i.e., analyses of data and writing of this volume) was both morally and financially supported by the College of Business Administration through its Center for Business and Economic Research. The author owes a deep sense of gratitude to these organizations for their support.

A number of individuals were extremely helpful in the initiation and completion of this project. They are too numerous to list here. Only a few can be mentioned. Dr. Bernard Hall, former Dean of the C.B.A., Dr. Gail E. Mullin, and Dr. John K. Ryans, Dean and Associate Dean to the College of Business Administration, respectively, and Dr. John T. Doutt, Professor of Administrative Sciences, provided support and encouragement more than perhaps they realize. I am most thankful for their help and support. Professor Edward Rada, U.C.L.A., was particularly helpful for the research in Taiwan.

My long-time friend, colleague, and one-time co-author, Dr. Ben Prasad, Professor, Ohio University, provided much of the intellectual support and stimulation. I am greatly thankful to him for his contribution.

A number of my present and former doctoral students contributed more to my thinking than they realize. Of these, contributions of Dr. Bernard C. Reimann, Assistant Professor, Drexel University, and Dr. Krishna Shetty, Associate Professor at Utah State University, were immense. I am most thankful to all of them.

Mrs. Barbara Fisher, Publication Writer, Miss Catherine Dix and Miss Frances Bailey provided the necessary editing and typing help. I am grateful for their help.

A countless number of executive personnel and other employees of the firms studied, were extremely generous with their time. I owe all of them a deep sense of gratitude for their help and cooperation.

Lastly, my family, Pia, Amin, and Erny were the ones who provided moral encouragement, while at the same time bore loneliness with a smile, while I was preoccupied with the researching and writing of this volume. Without their understanding, this book would never have seen the light of day. As a token of appreciation, I have dedicated this volume to them, along with the people of the third world, who have courageously endured the pains of poverty with human dignity during the last half century or so.

Beechwood Inland
June, 1974

A. R. N.

CHAPTER 1

INTRODUCTION: ORGANIZATION THEORY IN AN OPEN-SYSTEM PERSPECTIVE

In this book are reported the findings of an empirical study of 126 industrial firms located in seven countries: the United States, Argentina, Brazil, India, the Philippines, Uruguay, and Taiwan. The study, which is a cross-cultural, comparative analysis of the organizational practices and effectiveness of those industrial firms, was conceived in an open-system perspective. The objective has been to ascertain the impact of contextual (size, technology, ownership, and location) and socio-cultural and environmental variables on organizational functioning, behavior, and effectiveness.

To provide a framework for the study, in the first chapter I will outline the salient characteristics of the closed and open systems and provide some illustrative examples of organizational studies undertaken in both perspectives.

CLOSED AND OPEN SYSTEMS

As Katz and Kahn have pointed out, "System theory is basically concerned with problems of relationships, of structures, and of interdependence, rather than with the constant attributes of objects."[1]

The systems approach to studying organizations can best be differentiated from the commonsense approach by noting the major characteristics of the system itself. *Webster's* defines a *system* as a "regularly interacting or interdependent group of items forming a unified whole," which "is in, or tends to be in, equilibrium."[2]

These attributes of a system—the interdependence and interlinking of various subsystems within a given system—and the tendency toward attaining a balance, or equilibrium, forces one to think in terms of multiple causation in contrast to the common habit of thinking in single-cause terms.[3]

Scholars utilizing the closed-system approach conceive of the units of their specific studies as being independent of environmental influences. As Emery and Trist have stated, "thinking in terms of a 'closed' system . . . allows most of its problems to be analyzed with reference to its internal structure and without reference to its external environment."[4]

In organizational studies undertaken from a closed-system perspective, one can discern the emphasis on such variables as size, technology, location, ownership, managerial strategies, and leadership style.

Research studies by Indik[5] and Caplow[6] (on the size variable), Woodward,[7] Pugh and his colleagues,[8] and Harvey[9] (on the technology variable), studies by Ohio State University[10] and by the University of Michigan Groups[11] (on leadership style) are examples of scholars using a closed-system approach. Although organization studies emphasizing closed-system variables are still much in evidence, many theorists have recently shown increasing concern for the impact of external environment factors on organizational structure and function. Such emphasis is generally known as an open-system perspective.

THE OPEN-SYSTEM THEORY

Von Bertalanffy[12] was perhaps the first to show us how to visualize the organization as an open system, but others such as Parsons,[13] Miller,[14] Emery and Trist,[15] Thompson,[16] Dill,[17] Thorelli,[18] and Katz and Kahn[19] have used an open-system approach in their studies. The following abstract from Katz and Kahn summarizes the salient characteristics of an open system:

> The open-system approach . . . begins by identifying and mapping the repeated cycles of inputs, transformation, output and renewed inputs which comprise the organizational patterns.[20] . . . Organizations as a special class of open systems

have properties of their own, but they share other properties in common with all open systems. These include the importation of energy from the environment, the through-put or transformation of the imported energy into some product form . . . the exporting of that product into the environment, and the re-energizing of the system from sources in the environment.

Open systems also share the characteristics of negative entropy, feedback, homeostasis, differentiation, and equifinality. The law of negative entropy states that systems survive and maintain their characteristic internal order only so long as they import from the environment more energy than they expend in the process of transformation and exportation.[21]

In characterizing the traditional management approach as a closed system, Katz and Kahn state:

Traditional organizational theories have tended to view the human organization as a closed system. This tendency has led to a disregard of differing organizational environments and the nature of organizational dependency on environment. It has also led to an overconcentration on principles of internal organizational functioning with consequent failure to develop and understand the processes of feedback which are essential to survival.[22]

As is stated above, some organization theorists have recently begun to focus their attention on the impact of the *external* environment on the *internal* functioning of social organizations. Emery and Trist, for example, provide a useful typology of environments for examining the connection between the external environment and various units within a given social organization. This typology of environment includes "placid-randomized," "placid-clustered," "disturbed-reactive," and "turbulent field."[23]

To simplify the analysis, Dill, Thorelli, and Thompson have advanced the concept of "task environment." Dill defines task environment as "that part of the total environment of management which was potentially relevant to goal setting and goal attainment." In attempting to find a relationship between the task environment and the autonomy found in managerial personnel, among two Norwegian firms, he identified the following factors as relevant task agents: customers, suppliers, employees, competitors, and regulatory groups.[24]

Thompson compared the concept of task environment with that of organizational domain. The domain, or task environments, identified the area of potential dependency for the organization; it posed both contingencies and constraints. Thompson suggested that "to attain any significant measure of self-control the organization must manage its dependency."[25]

In characterizing task environments as homogeneous-heterogeneous and stable-dynamic, Thompson further postulated:

> The organization whose task environment is relatively homogeneous and relatively stable to be relatively simple in the structure of its boundary-spanning components: This organization will have few functional divisions. . . . For the organization facing a heterogeneous but stable task environment, we would expect a variety of functional divisions. . . . When task environment become dynamic. . . . the organization faces contingencies as well as constraints. . . . When task environment is both heterogeneous and dynamic . . . we would expect boundary-spanning units to be differentiated functionally to correspond to segments of the task environment and each to operate on a decentralized basis. . . .[26]

Working primarily in the context of health and welfare organizations, Etzioni,[27] Eisenstadt,[28] Glasser and Strauss,[29] and Lefton and Rosengren[30] have explored the impact of client groups on organizational functioning. Lefton and Rosengren, for example, postulated that organizations with high longitudinal and lateral concern for clients tend to have decentralized structures, while those with low longitudinal and lateral concern may have relatively centralized structures.[31]

Burns and Stalker have examined how the management patterns in some 20 industrial firms in the United Kingdom were related to certain aspects of their external environments.[32] The specific environmental characteristics considered were the rates of change in the scientific techniques and markets of the selected industries. They found two distinctly different sets of management practices and procedures, which they classified as "mechanistic" and "organic." The "mechanistic" organizations consisted of highly centralized, bureaucratic structures, while the more flexible and decentralized "organic" organizations practiced many of the principles espoused by proponents of the "human relations" movement (Roethlisberger and Dickson[33]). Burns and Stalker's conclusion was that the "mechanistic" form of organization appeared to be most appropriate under relatively stable environmental conditions, while the "organic" form seemed best suited to conditions of change.

Finally, the recent study of Lawrence and Lorsch indicates that the formality of the effective organization's structure is related to the degree of certainty and stability of its market and technological environments.[34] Successful firms operating in relatively dynamic environments tend to be decentralized, while those facing more stable environments are relatively centralized. On the basis of their results, Lawrence and Lorsch have proposed a "contingency theory" of organization, in which the "optimum" organization form is regarded as being contingent on the demands of the organization's environment. Lawrence and Lorsch further propose that decentralization under stable environmental conditions and centralization under dynamic conditions may actually be dysfunctional. In other words, they argue that an organization must establish a "fit" between its internal structural arrangements and its external environmental demands.

THE CROSS-CULTURAL PERSPECTIVE

In recent years scholars working in cross-cultural and cross-national settings have added yet one more dimension to the open-system approach. This is the impact of socio-cultural variables on organizational practices and effectiveness. In contrasting this perspective with the closed-system approach, Oberg, for example, has argued:

> Cultural differences from one country to another are more significant than many writers now appear to recognize. . . . If management principles are to be truly universal . . . they must face up to the challenge of other cultures and other business climates. . . . The [Universalist claim] is hardly

warranted by either evidence or institution at this stage in the development of management theory.[35]

BOTH PERSPECTIVES

To a large extent, both closed and open-systems theorists have pursued their respective approaches separately. Closed-system theorists argue for the relevance of internal variables within the system, while open-systems theorists focus on external environmental variables. However, as Thompson[36] has shown, both perspectives are needed for the study of social organizations. As Maurer has indicated:

> At the technical level of the organization, it is necessary to reduce or eliminate uncertainty, and hence, the closed-system model is appropriate. At the institutional level or the organization-environment-interface, uncertainty is great, and hence, the open-system model is appropriate.[37]

The study which I am analyzing in this book is an attempt to utilize both closed and open-system perspectives in studying the specific organizational practices and effectiveness of industrial organizations. Of course, I make no claim that the book includes all of the pertinent variables found in closed and open systems. Only selected variables of both approaches are examined.

The variables I have discussed were conceptualized by viewing the environment as being divided into these specific layers: organization environment, task environment, and societal environment. This is shown in Diagram 1-1.

The organization environmental layer was conceived as existing within the "closed system," which marks the boundaries of a specific industrial firm. Particular variables examined in this layer are size, technology, ownership, and location.

The task environment was conceived in terms of the client groups, or publics, of the industrial organization. These include employees, consumers, stockholders, suppliers, distributors, government, and the community. Here the perception and attitudes of the decision-makers toward the publics were examined. In this book the variable is called "organizational concern toward publics."

Diagram 1-1

DETERMINANTS OF ORGANIZATIONAL
PATTERNS AND EFFECTIVENESS

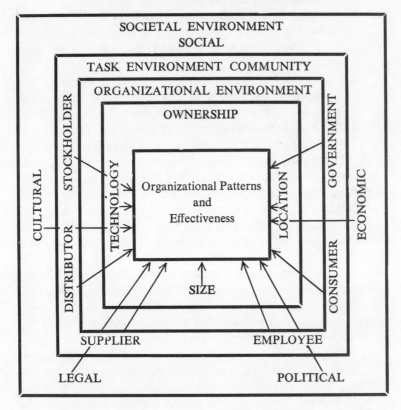

The societal environmental layer was conceived in terms of the macro environment of the firm. This layer includes socioeconomic, political, legal, and cultural variables.

The definition, conceptualization, and operationalization of variables, as well as related aspects of the research design and methodology are discussed in Chapter 2. In the remainder of this chapter, we will briefly look at the specific objectives pursued in this book, as well as its organization.

In this book I was guided by the following four specific objectives:

1. To test the universality of organizational practices, or "management principles."
2. To analyze the similarities and differences in organizational practices and effectiveness of industrial enterprises in a given country and among the firms in different countries.
3. To determine, on the basis of empirical evidence, the applicability and utility of U.S. organizational practices to industrial enterprises in developing countries.
4. To analyze the impact of both closed and open-systems variables on organizational practices and effectiveness.

As the reader will recognize, these objectives are not mutually exclusive; they are interrelated. For example, the universality and transferability of organizational practices are directly related to the nature and degree of the environmental impact on organizational practices. When the impact of such external variables is considerable, universality and transferability will be more difficult.

Realizing the strong interdependence of these objectives, I primarily focus on analyzing data in terms of transferring U.S. organizational practices to industrial enterprises in developing countries. Through these analyses we will be able to explore the other objectives mentioned above.

Chapter 2 details the research methodology and design-definition, conceptualization and operationalization of major variables, samples, and methods of data collection.

Chapters 3 through 8 provide a comparative analysis of management practices of the U.S. parent companies, the U.S. subsidiaries, and the comparable local firms in the seven countries.

In Chapter 3 the controlling function of management is examined. Elements of control investigated are: the nature and scope of policy-making, setting standards for production and clerical employees and for supervisory, cost, budgetary, and quality controls, time and motion studies, equipment maintenance, return on investment, profit and loss statement, and management audit systems. Finally, the environmental impact of controlling practices is examined.

In Chapter 4 we analyze the long-range planning practices of the U.S. parent firms, U.S. subsidiaries, and the local firms in the seven countries studied. Here the planning objectives, the nature and scope of planning the resultant plans, review procedures, and participation and information-sharing in the planning process are examined. Finally, the environmental impact on planning practices is examined.

Chapter 5 deals with the organizational set-up of the companies studied. The factors analyzed are: grouping of activities and departmentations, formalization and documentation of policies, authority definition and uses of organization charts, layers of hierarchy, delegation of authority, and the degree of decentralization in decision-making. Then the impact of environmental and socio-cultural factors on decentralization in decision-making is examined.

In Chapter 6 data on leadership practices and the impact of socio-cultural variables on leadership style are examined.

In Chapters 7 and 8 I discuss the manpower management practices of the U.S. parent companies, the U.S. subsidiaries, and the local firms in the seven countries studied. Here we have examined the nature of manpower planning and policies, organization of personnel functions, job analysis and appraisal systems, selection and promotion methods, training and development programs, compensation and motivation practices, and the impact of environmental and socio-cultural variables on manpower practices.

In Chapters 9 and 10 the managerial effectiveness of these firms is examined. In the last chapter, I have attempted to systematically evaluate the feasibility and utility of transferring advanced management practices to firms in developing nations. Also, in Chapter 11 I have examined the universality of management practices and principles.

Notes

1. Daniel Katz and Robert L. Kahn, *The Social Psychology of Organizations,* New York: Wiley, 1966, p. 18.
2. *Webster's Seventh New Collegiate Dictionary,* Springfield, Mass.: G. & C. Merriam Company, 1967, p. 895.

3. John A. Seiler, *Systems Analysis in Organizational Behavior,* Homewood, Ill.: Richard D. Irwin and Dorsey Press, 1967, pp. 1-21.

4. F. E. Emery and E. L. Trist, "Socio-Technical Systems," in *Systems Thinking,* ed. F. E. Emery, Harmondsworth, Eng.: Penguin Books, 1969, p. 281.

5. Bernard P. Indik, "Some Effects of Organization Size on Member Attitudes and Behavior," *Human Relations,* 16 (1963), 369-84.

6. Theodore Caplow, "Organizational Size," *Administrative Science Quarterly,* 1 (1957), 484-505.

7. Joan Woodward, *Industrial Organization: Theory and Practice,* London: Oxford University Press, 1965. See also a report on her recent research in "Technology, Managerial Control, and Organizational Behavior," in *Organizational Behavior Models,* ed. A. Negandhi et al., Kent, Ohio: Bureau of Economic and Business Research, Kent State University, 1970, pp. 21-31.

8. D. Hickson, D. S. Pugh, and D. C. Pheysey, "Operations Technology and Organization Structure: An Empirical Reappraisal," *Administrative Science Quarterly,* vol. 16, no. 3 (1969), 378-97.

9. Edward Harvey, "Technology and the Structure of Organizations," *American Sociological Review* (1968), 247-59.

10. See Ralph M. Stogdill, *Managers, Employees, Organizations,* Columbus: The Ohio State University Bureau of Business Research, 1965.

11. See Rensis Likert, *The Human Organization: Its Management and Value,* New York: McGraw-Hill, 1967.

12. L. von Bertalanffy, "The Theory of Open Systems in Physics and Biology," *Science,* (1950), 23-29.

13. Talcott Parsons et al., *Theories of Society,* New York: The Free Press, 1961, pp. 38-41.

14. J. G. Miller, "Toward A General Theory for the Behavioral Sciences," *American Psychologist,* 10 (1955), 513-51.

15. Emery and Trist, *op. cit.*

16. James D. Thompson, *Organizations in Action,* New York: McGraw-Hill, 1967, esp. pp. 70-82; J. D. Thompson and W. J. McEwen, "Organizational Goals and Environment: Goal-Setting as an Interaction Process," *American Sociological Review,* vol. 23, no. 1 (February 1968), 23-31.

17. William R. Dill, "Environment as an Influence on

Managerial Autonomy," *Administrative Science Quarterly,* 2 (June 1958), 409-43.

18. Hans B. Thorelli, "Organizational Theory: An Ecological View," *Proceedings of the Academy of Management* (1967), 66-84; A. R. Negandhi and S. B. Prasad, *Comparative Management,* New York: Appleton-Century-Crofts, 1970.

19. Katz and Kahn, *op. cit.*

20. *Ibid.,* p. 28.

21. *Ibid.*

22. *Ibid.,* p. 29.

23. F. E. Emery and E. L. Trist, "The Causal Texture of Organizational Environments," *Human Relations,* 18 (1965), 21-32.

24. Dill, *op. cit.,* p. 410.

25. Thompson, *op. cit.,* p. 38.

26. *Ibid.,* pp. 72-73.

27. Amitai Etzioni, *Modern Organizations,* Englewood Cliffs, N.J.: Prentice-Hall, 1964.

28. S. H. Eisenstadt, "Bureaucracy, Bureaucratization, and Debureaucratization," in A. Etzioni, ed., *Complex Organization: A Sociological Reader,* New York: Holt, Rinehart, and Winston, 1964, p. 276.

29. B. Glasser and A. Strauss, *Awareness of Dying,* Chicago: Aldine Press, 1965.

30. M. Lefton and W. R. Rosengren, "Organizations and Clients: Lateral and Longitudinal Dimensions," *American Sociological Review,* 31 (1966), 802-10.

31. *Ibid.* See also Mark Lefton, "Client Characteristics and Organizational Functioning: Interorganizational Focus," in *Organization Theory in an Interorganizational Perspective,* A. R. Negandhi, ed., Kent, Ohio: Center for Business and Economic Research, Kent State University, 1971, pp. 19-32.

32. T. Burns and G. M. Stalker, *The Management of Innovation,* London: Tavistock, 1961.

33. F. J. Roethlisberger and W.J. Dickson, *Management and the Worker,* Cambridge, Mass.: Harvard University Press, 1939.

34. Paul R. Lawrence and Jay W. Lorsch, *Organization and Environment: Managing Differentiation and Integration,* Boston: Division of Research, Graduate School of Business Administration, Harvard University, 1967, pp. 161-62.

35. Winston Oberg, "Cross-Cultural Perspectives on Management Principles," *Academy of Management Journal,* vol. 6, no. 2 (June 1963), 129-43.

36. Thompson, *op. cit.,* pp. 11-12.

37. John G. Maurer, *Readings in Organization Theory: Open-Systems Approaches,* New York: Random House, 1971, p. 6.

RESEARCH DESIGN AND METHODOLOGY

This study was guided by the following proposition, or hypothesis:

The organizational and enterprise effectiveness of an industrial firm in a given industry, with a given size and technology, are functions of management practices. Management practices are themselves functions of external environment and socio-cultural variables and of the firm's organizational concern toward its task agents or publics.

MAJOR VARIABLES

The theoretical proposition given above contains five major variables:

1. Organizational concern toward task agents or publics
2. External environmental factors in terms of socio-economic, political, legal, and cultural variables
3. Management practices
4. Organizational effectiveness
5. Enterprise effectiveness

As is seen in Diagram 2-1, the first two variables are conceived as independent variables, management practices as intervening or mediating variables, organizational effectiveness as a dependent variable, and enterprise effectiveness as an end-result variable.

Diagram 2-1

THEORETICAL MODEL AND MAJOR VARIABLES

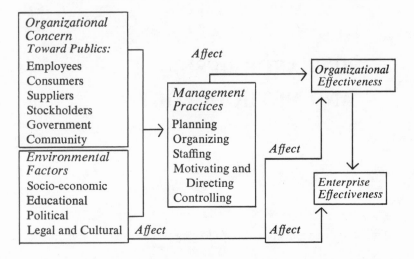

The organizational concern variable was conceptualized as attitudes and perceptions of decision-makers toward important task agents or publics. In business management literature, this type of variable has been called alternatively "management policy," "management philosophy," "management creed,"[1] etc. I myself have used these descriptive labels to identify this independent variable.[2] However, reader response to my previously published work indicates a great deal of confusion and misunderstanding which is created by using such words as "philosophy" and "policy."[3] At the same time, a recent analysis of the relationship between an organization and its clients offered by Lefton and Rosengren,[4] as well as studies by Dill,[5] Thompson,[6] and Thorelli,[7] indicate that it may be more appropriate to label this variable "organizational concern toward task environmental agents or publics."

The specific task environmental agents, or publics, examined in this research were consumers, employees, suppliers, distributors, community, government, and stockholders. Studies by Dill,[8] Thompson,[9] and Thorelli[10] have identified basically the same agents, but there are some differences between the approaches used in those studies and mine in this book. These authors emphasized the nature of interaction between an organization and its publics, whereas I concentrate on the attitudes of decision-makers toward their publics. My rationale is based on the premise that reality is not a unitary phenomenon. On the contrary, reality is in the eye of the beholder. As Graham indicated, "an individual's reaction within a situation is a function of his perception of the situation rather than his interaction with a solitary combination of 'real' stimuli and constraints."[11]

Likert has also assigned a central position to individual perception in his interaction-influence model.[12] He argues that the causal variables (structure, objectives, supervisory practices, etc.) interact with personality to produce perceptions, that it is only through perceptions that the relationship between causal and end-result variables may be explored.

March and Simon[13] have stressed the importance of the individual's perception and his cognitive limits in choosing alternatives and making decisions. Dill, too, recognized the importance of perception when he stated that "further studies . . . should put explicit emphasis on the cognitive activities of organizational participants as a link between environmental 'stimuli' and the participants' overt responses."[14]

I contend that the impact of the "true" task environment on a firm is not direct; rather, it is strongly mediated by how management perceives its task environmental agents.

INFERENCE AND MEASUREMENT

To examine the organizational concern toward these task agents, I interviewed top- and middle-level executives in my sample. On the average, I interviewed 15 to 20 executives in each firm, taking from one to three full working days for each interview. Group interviews were held in the preliminary sessions, followed by an intensive personal interview with each executive. Those interviewed held the following positions: chairman or president; board director; general manager; directors of marketing, sales, production, finance, and personnel; chief accountant or controller. The specific information sought in these interviews can be seen in the lists of factors outlined in Table 2-1.

Table 2-1

**Factors Evaluated to Infer Executives' Perceptions
toward Publics or Task Environmental Agents**

Task Agents	*Factors Evaluated*
Employees	a. top management's stated policy or philosophy—concerning employee development b. employee's perception of the company's concern toward individual development c. prospective employee's image of the company
Consumers	a. company's profit and service objectives implied, expressed and implemented b. consumer's image of the company and its products c. the employee's image of the company and of its profit objective d. suppliers' image of the company, its products, and its profit objectives e. distributors' image of the company, its products, and profit objectives f. stockholders' image of the company and its profit objective
Suppliers	a. company's policy statements concerning suppliers b. programs and procedures of purchasing department of the company c. purchasing agents' or executives' attitudes toward supplier d. supplier's evaluation of the company

Organizational concern for task agents was evaluated in terms of the degree of longitudinal and lateral interest in task agents that was evidenced by decision makers in each organization. Scores were derived from the intensity of concern shown. Three descriptive categories were created to rank the companies' concern toward their task agents, which are shown in Table 2-2.

Two persons were involved in the interviews, with each in-

Distributors	a. management policy statement concerning distributors
	b. marketing programs and procedures
	c. attitudes of marketing executives toward distributors
	d. distributor's attitude toward company
Stockholders	a. company's policy statement concerning stockholders
	b. stockholders' evaluation of company
	c. prospective investors' evaluation of company
	d. senior executives' attitudes toward stockholders
	e. actual programs and procedures of stock department of company
Community	a. programs and procedures of company's public relations department
	b. top executives' attitude toward community
	c. company's participation in community affairs
	d. company's contribution toward community chest, hospital facilities, and education
	e. evaluation of selected community leaders of company's community relations program
Government	a. top executive's attitude toward government
	b. company's participation in governmental affairs
	c. senior governmental officials' evaluation of company's programs
	d. program and procedure of company's public relation department
	e. speeches and press statements by company's executives on governmental affairs

dependently evaluating the information collected. The highest difference between the two interviewers did not exceed 8 out of a possible 100 points.

Environmental variables were conceptualized in terms of socio-economic, political, legal, and cultural settings in the countries studied. Here I used the Farmer Richman classification scheme as a checklist. Although environmental factors were conceived as

Table 2-2

**Ranking Scale for the Organizational Concern
toward Task Agents**

Employee	much or very much concern	some concern	little or no concern
	20	10	0
Consumer	consumer, the king	consumer, a necessary agent	consumer, passive agent
	20	10	0
Community	much or very much concern	some concern	little or no concern
	10	5	0
Government	good partner	necessary evil	government be damned
	10	5	0
Supplier	good relationship absolutely necessary	good relationship helpful	relationship a necessary evil
	15	7.5	0
Distributor	good relationship absolutely necessary	good relationship helpful	relationship a necessary evil
	15	7.5	0
Stockholder	owners, masters, good public relations personnel	owners, masters, only	profit-eaters
	10	5	0

independent variables, in actual field research they were treated as residual variables. In other words, my analysis of these factors and their specific impact on management practices and effectiveness fall short of establishing causal relationships.

Management practices variables were conceived in terms of managerial functions of planning, organizing, controlling, manpower management, directing, and leading. The following specific elements of management practices were examined:

Planning	(a) planning objectives
	(b) the nature and scope of planning
	(c) time horizons in planning
	(d) the resultant plans
	(e) reviews of plans
	(f) participation and informa-tion-sharing in planning
Organization	(a) authority-responsibility relationships
	(b) organization charts
	(c) degree of centralization and decentralization
	(d) span of control
	(e) degree of specialization
	(f) the use of informal organizations and manage-ment attitudes toward such groups
	(g) grouping of activities and departments
	(h) use of specialist staff and its relationship with line executives
Manpower Management	(a) methods used in appraising, selecting, and training personnel
	(b) promotion criteria used
	(c) management development practices used
Direction and Leadership	(a) the techniques used for motivating high-level manpower
	(b) the methods and techniques used for motivating workers
	(c) supervisory techniques used

Control   (a) control techniques used
                                    for different areas, i.e.,
                                    finance, production,
                                    marketing, etc.
                                (b) types of control standards
                                (c) information feed-back
                                    systems and procedures
                                    for corrective actions

Organizational and enterprise effectiveness were conceptualized in behavioral and economic or financial terms, respectively. Realizing the nature of market and economic conditions in
developing countries (for example, seller's market, shortage of
capital and consumer goods) and their input on the profitability
criterion,[15] I concentrated on the behavioral measures of effectiveness. The specific measures included the following factors:

Organizational Effectiveness

(1) management's ability to attract and retain high-level man-
    power
(2) employee morale and satisfaction in work
(3) employee turnover and absenteeism
(4) interpersonal relationships in organizational settings
(5) interdepartmental relationships
(6) the executive's perception of the firm's overall objectives
(7) utilization of high-level manpower
(8) organizational effectiveness in adapting to the external
    environments

Enterprise Effectiveness

(1) return on sales and investment
(2) growth in market share
(3) increase in sales
(4) growth in price of stock and P/E ratio
(5) unit cost
(6) utilization of plant facilities

Research Design

The research design utilized in this study consists of studying the management practices and effectiveness of U.S. subsidiaries and comparable local firms in each country. The rationale of the approach rests on the contention that the American subsidiaries in foreign countries are more progressive in their management practices and have been able to achieve greater effectiveness through their advanced management practices.[16] They are also in the advantageous position of learning the most effective management practices from their parent companies in the United States.

Examination of the management practices and effectiveness of U.S. subsidiaries in a given country will thus reveal the feasibility and limitation of transferring advanced management practices to given environmental-cum-cultural settings. An examination of management practices and effectiveness in comparable local firms, on the other hand, suggests the actual difference between what is feasible and what is not being done but could be done. Data from the U.S. parent companies were used to provide a comparative frame of reference for examining the nature of advanced management practices actually used by industrial firms in the United States.

Method of Data Collection and Sample

Data were collected from 56 American subsidiaries, 55 comparable local companies, and 15 U.S. parent companies. Background data were obtained from records and published sources. The information on organizational concern toward task agents, management practices, and organization and enterprise effectiveness was gathered by means of personal interviews. A total of 650 persons were interviewed.

Structured and nonstructured interview guides were prepared. Altogether, eight investigators conducted these interviews in the seven countries. Some were nationals of the country in question and others were fluent in the language of the country. Some interviews were repeated for clarification. The field interviews were conducted from January 1966 to December 1970. A 40-page interview guide was used to collect specific information.

Table 2-3 provides a breakdown of these firms by ownership, and location. Each American subsidiary was paired with a local firm on the basis of product, technology, and sales volume. The companies thus paired represented several industry categories. Table 2-3 illustrates this point.

Table 2-3

Industry Classification of the Companies in the International Sample (n=126)

Industry Group	Argentina			Brazil		India		Philippines		Uruguay		Taiwan	
	U.S. parent company	U.S. subsidiary	Local company	U.S. subsidiary	Local company	U.S. subsidiary	Local company	U.S. subsidiary	Local company	U.S. subsidiary	Local company	U.S. subsidiary	Local company
Chemicals and pharmaceutical	3	2	1	1	2	5	5	3	3	1	1	5	6
Petroleum	—	—	—	—	—	1	1	1	1	—	—	—	—
Light engineering	2	—	—	1	—	2	2	—	—	—	—	1	2
Heavy engineering	2	—	—	—	2	2	2	1	1	2	1	1	1
Electrical - consumer	2	—	—	—	—	1	1	—	—	—	—	2	2
Rubber tires	2	—	—	—	—	1	1	1	1	—	—	—	—
Soaps and cosmetics	2	1	2	3	1	2	2	1	1	1	1	—	—
Soft drinks, canned foods ..	1	1	1	2	2	2	2	2	2	2	2	—	—
Electrical-industrial	1	2	1	1	—	1	1	1	2	—	—	—	—
Totals	15	6	5	8	7	17	17	10	11	6	5	9	11

ANALYSES OF FINDINGS

In analyzing data collected in the seven countries, we will first look at the findings concerning the 15 U.S. parent companies. These will then be compared and contrasted with practices and effectiveness of the U.S. subsidiaries and local firms in the six other nations. Comparative analysis of findings will be undertaken at three levels: U.S. subsidiaries versus local firms in all six developing countries; U.S. subsidiaries in Latin America versus those in the Far East; and local firms in Latin America versus those in the Far East.

In discussing the findings, I will emphasize comparison by region rather than country. The rationale for choosing the regional approach is explained below.

There are considerable differences in the socio-cultural, political, and legal conditions between the Far East and Latin America. Also, these differences are quite apparent among the countries within a given region. Religious values and beliefs in Latin American countries, for example, are predominately Christian (Catholic, in particular). In contrast, religious values and beliefs in the Far East follow the traditions of Hinduism, Buddhism, and Confucianism, although a large number of people in Taiwan and the Philippines have firmly adopted Christianity. In addition, countries in Latin America are relatively less stable politically than those in the Far East.

In spite of these differences, socio-cultural behavior patterns, as well as economic conditions and behavior, are more similar than different in the two regions. For example, people in both hemispheres display the following socio-cultural and economic behavior patterns:[17]

close-knit families
distrust of "outsiders"
respect for age and authority
emphasis on political connections
sense of fatalism
dislike of impersonal relationships, preference for personal
  relationships

regard for social status and prestige in preference to material goods

faith and emphasis on words rather than actions

spirit of postponement

Economically, countries studied in both regions are marked by a shortage of foreign exchange, capital, and consumer goods, as well as by restrictive import and investment policies. The market condition in these countries can be characterized as a seller's market.

The impact of such similar socio-cultural and economic patterns on managerial practices and behavior was demonstrated in a large-scale international study by Haire, Ghiselli, and Porter. Similarly, the Myrdal study of South Asian countries shows the relevance of undertaking regional rather than country comparisons.[18] My observations of managerial practices and behavior and the examination of common problems faced by developing countries in general suggest that regional comparison may lead to higher levels of generalization and at the same time prove rewarding in analyzing the causal relationships between major variables investigated in this study. In brief, my attempts to undertake a regional comparison were guided by my desire to (1) focus attention on basic similarities in a given region, on the one hand, and similarities in developing countries as a whole, on the other hand; and (2) to explore causal relationships among major variables examined in the study.

Notes

1. For an excellent review of the various meanings assigned to the concept of management philosophy, see W. D. Litzinger and T. E. Schaefer, "Management Philosophy Enigma," *Academy of Management Journal,* vol. 9, no. 4 (December 1966) 337-43.

2. Anant R. Negandhi, "Determining Applicability of American Management Know-How in Differing Environments and Cultures," a paper presented at the annual meeting of the western division of the Academy of Management, San Diego, April 9, 1965. The published version of this paper (with B. D. Estafen)

appeared in the *Academy of Management Journal,* vol. 8, no. 4 (December 1965), 319-23.

3. For criticism on management philosophy concept see H. Koontz and Cyril O'Donnell, *Principles of Management: An Analysis of Managerial Functions,* New York: McGraw-Hill, 1972, pp. 102-103.

4. M. Lefton and W. R. Rosengren, "Organizations and Clients: Lateral and Longitudinal Dimensions," *American Sociological Review,* 31 (1966), 802-10.

5. William R. Dill, "Environment as an Influence on Managerial Autonomy," *Administrative Science Quarterly,* 2 (June 1958), 409-43.

6. James D. Thompson, *Organizations in Action,* New York: McGraw-Hill, 1967, esp. pp. 70-82; J. D. Thompson and W. J. McEwen, "Organizational Goals and Environment: Goal-Setting as an Interaction Process," *American Sociological Review,* vol. 23, no. 1 (February 1968), 23-31.

7. Hans B. Thorelli, "Organizational Theory: An Ecological View," *Proceedings of the Academy of Management* (1967), 66-84; A. R. Negandhi and S. B. Prasad, *Comparative Management,* New York: Appleton-Century-Crofts, 1970.

8. Dill, *op. cit.*

9. Thompson, *op. cit.*

10. Thorelli, *op. cit.*

11. G. H. Graham, "Correlates of Perceived Importance of Organizational Objectives," *Academy of Management Journal,* 11 (1968), 292.

12. Rensis Likert, *Human Organization: Its Management and Value,* New York: McGraw-Hill, 1967, esp. p. 212.

13. James G. March and Herbert A. Simon, *Organizations,* New York: Wiley, 1963.

14. Dill, *op. cit.,* p. 443.

15. For details on the impact of the seller's market on managerial behavior see A. R. Negandhi, "Advanced Management Know-How in Developing Countries," *California Management Review,* vol. 10, no. 3 (Spring 1968), 53-60.

16. Dunning's study of the U.S. subsidiaries in Britain also shows the greater effectiveness of the U.S. subsidiaries compared to the local British firms. See John R. Dunning, "U.S. Subsidiaries in Britain and their U.K. Competitors," *Business Ratios* (Autumn 1966).

17. See various articles on Asia and Latin America in Stanley Davis, *Comparative Management: Organizational and Cultural Perspectives,* Englewood Cliffs, N.J.: Prentice-Hall, 1971, pp. 127-324.

18. Gunnar Myrdal, *Asian Drama: An Inquiry into the Poverty of Nations,* New York: The Twentieth Century Fund, 1968, p. 39-47.

CHAPTER 3

POLICY-MAKING AND
CONTROL MECHANISMS

The concept of control carries negative and psychological con-
notations. Negatively, control implies some restrictive measures
and guidelines about what an individual must or must not do.
Psychologically, the exercise of control produces frustrating yet
satisfying consequences. Those individuals who are able to exercise some control over their own and others' activities may
experience satisfaction; those who are not able to exercise control
and who are, instead, *being* controlled by others may be dissatisfied and alienated from their activities.[1]

Yet some form of control is absolutely necessary for the
functioning of any organization, whether private or governmental,
profit or nonprofit. As Tannenbaum has said:

> Organization implies control. A social organization is an
> ordered arrangement of individual human interactions. Con-
> trol processes help circumscribe idiosyncratic behaviors and
> keep them conformant to the rational plan of the organization.
> Organizations require a certain amount of conformity as well
> as the integration of diverse activities. It is the function of
> control to bring about conformance to organizational require-
> ments and achievement of the ultimate purposes of the organi-
> zation. The coordination and order created out of the diverse
> interests and potentially diffuse behaviors of members is largely
> a function of control. . . . Control is an inevitable correlate of
> organization.[2]

CONTROL MEASURES

There are various measures of control suggested in management-organization literature. Evan, for example, has taken a broader perspective and suggests the following measures of control: span of control; the number of levels of hierarchy; the ratio of administrative to production personnel; "time-span of discretion" (maximum length of time an employee is authorized to make decisions on his own initiative which commit a given amount of the resources of the organization); the hierarchical level at which given classes of decisions are made; and the formal limitations that apply to the decision-making authority of management.[3] In their empirical studies, Tannenbaum and his colleagues at the University of Michigan's Survey Research Center have utilized some of these measures of control.[4]

As the reader will recognize, many of these measures are related more to the degrees of decentralization and participation in decision-making. As mentioned in Chapter 5, I have used some of these measures to evaluate the degree of decentralization in the companies I studied.

I conceived of control as a mechanism and process that enables an organization to achieve its goals and objectives with a minimum of deviation. Specifically, I collected data on the following control measures:

the nature and scope of policy-making
setting of standards for production and clerical employees and
   for supervisory personnel
cost control
budget control
quality control
time and motion studies
equipment maintenance
return on investment
profit and loss statement
management audit

In this chapter I will analyze data on the above control measures utilized by American subsidiaries and local companies in six developing countries—Argentina, Brazil, India, the Philippines, Taiwan, and Uruguay. Analysis of the data will be undertaken at four comparative levels:

1. comparative analysis of American subsidiaries and local firms in all six developing countries
2. American subsidiaries in Latin American countries and Far Eastern countries
3. local firms in Latin American countries and Far Eastern countries
4. the relationship between the firm's concern toward its publics and the nature of control measures utilized by the firm

Following these analyses, I will explore relationships between control measures, decentralization, and management effectiveness.* For this purpose, data from companies in India (both American subsidiaries and local firms) will be put to rigorous statistical analysis.

To provide a comparative perspective, however, we will first briefly review the control practices and techniques utilized by U.S. parent companies and other American companies in the United States.

Control Practices of Major U.S. Companies

Data collected from the 15 U.S. parent companies indicate that the large majority of these companies stress policy-formulation and use policy guidelines as overall control measures. For example, of the 15 companies, 14 have documented policies, and 12 have special policy committees to formulate, document, and communicate major policies. Generally speaking, such policies deal with relationships with the following important agents: consumers, suppliers, competitors, union, government, and community.

Although policies are made by either a policy committee or the top executives, senior- and middle-level executives are en-

*The terms management effectiveness and organizational effectiveness are used interchangeably throughout this book.

couraged to participate in discussions on formulating policies and devising guidelines to be implemented. In short, these policies are neither ivory tower nor authoritarian. Most of the executives interviewed showed involvement in arriving at the policies.

These parent companies also provide formal policy statements concerning major functional areas such as production, marketing, finance, distribution, purchasing, personnel recruitment, and promotion. In most of the areas, performance standards are firmly set and every attempt is made to adhere to these preset standards.

Among many other controlling measures, cost and budgetary controls, profit and loss statements, return on investment, periodical management audit, time and motion studies, statistical quality control, and inventory control are standard measures used by the U.S. parent companies studied. Holden, Pederson, and Germane,[5] in their study of large-scale U.S. companies, summarize their findings as follows:

1. The starting point in many companies studied (n=15) was the establishment of corporate objectives and policies.
2. The budget control was the most widely used control mechanism. In contrast to a similar study undertaken by the authors 25 years ago, when only half the participating companies were employing budgetary controls, the present study found universal application.
3. Profit and loss performance was another commonly used control.
4. Return on investment was a frequently used control device.
5. Control over pricing decisions and review of salaries and promotions was considered in many companies as the prime responsibility of top management.
6. "Periodic management audit" and control of corporate income were used by some of the companies studied.[6]

**Control Measures Used in Companies
in Six Other Countries**

As we have seen, the most basic controlling device used by many U.S. companies is the policy guideline. As Holden, Pederson, and Germane have pointed out, "corporate policies, when thoughtfully conceived and properly formulated, constitute one of the most effective instruments of overall control."[7]

Two types of information concerning the policy-making process were obtained: whether or not policies were formally stated and documented; and who was responsible for policy formulation.

My inquiries among American subsidiaries operating in Latin American and Far Eastern countries indicate that subsidiaries play a positive and constructive role in formulating and implementing major policies affecting their operations in those countries.

Approximately one-half of these subsidiaries (27 out of 56) formulate such policies on the basis of extensive consultation with their functional managers. Once the policies are made, they are documented and circulated among all levels of managerial and supervisory personnel.

In contrast to American subsidiaries, less than one-fourth of the comparable local firms in the countries studied formulate major policies concerning expansions, diversification, mergers, and so forth. A large majority of these companies (39 out of the total 55) prefer to undertake this task of policy-making on an ad hoc basis. In such a situation, documentation and information-sharing on major policies is a rarity. In many of the companies, even senior executives considered it a high privilege to know that such policies exist.

LATIN AMERICAN COMPARED TO FAR EASTERN COUNTRIES

Information on major policy-making in Latin America and the Far East shows some striking differences among the American subsidiaries, but not as much for the local firms. As is shown in Table 3-1, only one-fourth of the American subsidiaries in Latin America formulate and document their major policies, compared to more than two-thirds of the subsidiaries in Far Eastern countries. The proportion of local companies formulating and documenting such policies is also somewhat higher in Far Eastern nations than it is in Latin America.

To be sure, some of the American subsidiaries in the Far Eastern countries, especially in Taiwan, complained about the dominance of the parent companies, formulating the subsidiaries' policies. The general manager of a subsidiary in Taiwan echoed this: "We cannot decide anything: we are not allowed to do so. We do what they [executives of the parent company] tell us to do. It is fair to say we live like a king, but work like an educated peon." In spite of such complaints, there were significant differences between U.S. subsidiaries in Latin America and Far Eastern countries. The differences among American subsidiaries in the two regions can be explained in terms of distance and economic and political instability, as well as by the individual firm's orientations toward its clients.

Latin American countries, of course, are much closer to the United States than those in the Far East, which makes it easier for subsidiaries in Latin America to rely more on parent companies in the United States and for parent companies to dominate their subsidiaries.

ECONOMIC AND POLITICAL FACTORS

Economic and political situations in these two parts of the world differ considerably. Although price and wage spirals, and subsequent inflation, are serious problems confronting most of the developing countries, the level of price rise and degree of inflation in Argentina, Brazil, and Uruguay are much greater than those in India, the Philippines, and Taiwan. In Argentina the consumer price index rose from 100 in 1958 to 1,017 in 1966, to 3,003 in Brazil, and to 389 in Uruguay, compared to 159 in India, 137 in the Philippines, and 171 in Taiwan.[8]

Such rampant inflation in the Latin American countries affects future planning and policy-making. In addition to economic instability, Latin American countries are plagued by revolutions, dictatorships, and coups d'etat. Far Eastern countries are more stable politically. Obviously, political instability takes away necessary incentives for private enterprises to look ahead and formulate specific policies for future development of company activities. Davis found that this was true even in Chile, which was then more stable than other Latin American countries.[9] In Chile, Davis argues, businessmen are more concerned with survival than with policy-making, generating profits, and developing and coordinating the internal functions of an organization. Chilean businessmen, Davis reports,

[have] basically defensive and security-seeking orientations: how to hold out against the seemingly inexorable onslaught of those who would abolish the private enterprise system entirely . . . the struggle for existence of one economic system vis-à-vis another is basically a fight for power, not profit. The businessman who operates according to the belief that capitalism is fighting for survival in Chile sees the struggle as political, not economic in nature. . . . He [the Chilean businessman] believes that, in theory, there is a direct relationship between the effective direction of private corporate organizations and the strength of the private enterprise system; but, in practice, he does not apply this belief to planning, coordinating, and appraising the organization's activities.[10]

Aside from the impact of such an economic and political environment on managerial policy-making, one is still unable to explain, entirely on the basis of environmental factors, why some companies are sufficiently articulate in policy-making and others are not.

ORGANIZATIONAL CONCERN AND POLICY-MAKING

To explain the interfirm differences in various aspects of managerial activities, including policy formulation, I examined the impact of "organizational concern" variable on policy-making aspects. As was discussed in Chapter 2, this variable examined managerial attitudes toward consumers, employees, suppliers, distributors, stockholders, community, and the government. On the basis of information gathered through interviews with various levels of managers, I categorized all companies as follows:

much concern for publics
moderate concern for publics
little concern for publics

As can be seen in Table 3-1, approximately two-thirds of the American subsidiaries and local companies classified as having "much concern" for their publics pay considerable attention to major policy-making. In other words, these companies not only formally state and document their policies, but they also involve all levels of managerial and supervisory personnel in the formulation and information-sharing aspects of policy decisions. In

Table 3-1

Major Policies: Formulation and Decision-Making

Argentina, Brazil, Uruguay Organizational concern for its publics:

Nature of major policies:	Overall U.S. local		Much concern U.S. local		Moderate concern U.S. local		Little concern U.S. local	
Formally stated, documented, and formulated by committee	5	3	—	1	5	2	—	—
Formulated on ad hoc basis by chief executive /owner and not documented	13	11	2	—	11	10	—	1
Not discernible or available	2	3	—	—	2	3	—	—
Total	20	17	2	1	18	15	0	1

India, Philippines, Taiwan

Formally stated, documented, and formulated by committee	22	9	10	6	12	3	—	—
Formulated on ad hoc basis by chief executive /owner and not documented	11	28	—	5	8	14	3	9
Not discernible or available	3	1	2	—	1	1	—	—
Total	36	38	12	11	21	18	3	9

contrast, only 26 percent of the companies categorized as having "moderate" and "little concern" bother to state and document their major policies. To sum up, the analysis of the data just discussed and presented in Table 3-1 reveals four aspects:

Summary Comparisons

Item	U.S. subsidiary	Local firm	U.S. and local companies
	(N given in parentheses)		
Percent of firms that formulated and documented major policies with extensive consultations:			
In both regions	48% (56)	22% (55)	35% (111)
In Latin American countries	25% (20)	18% (17)	22% (37)
In Far Eastern countries	65% (36)	23% (38)	40% (74)
In "much concern" firms	71% (14)	57% (12)	65% (26)
In "Moderate" and "little" concern firms	45% (39)	16% (33)	26% (85)

1. A greater number of American subsidiaries seem to be utilizing major policies as guidelines and as an instrument of control.
2. Companies in Far Eastern countries have paid more attention to policy-making than those in Latin American countries.
3. Companies manifesting "much concern" for their publics tend to pay greater attention to policy formulation and documentation than do those categorized as showing "moderate" and "little concern."
4. Environmental factors (economic and political instability) seem to have greater impact on the companies in Latin America than those in the Far East.

    In addition to major policies, other control measures used by some of the companies include setting standards for production, clerical, and supervisory personnel, cost and budgetary controls, quality controls, and periodic management audits.

SETTING STANDARDS

An important tool available to management for controlling costs and assessing employee productivity is standards-setting. It is a yardstick by which organizations can measure the output and performance of each employee or group of employees.

Data concerning standards-setting were obtained for three levels of employees—production, clerical, and supervisory.

As one would expect, establishing standards for production employees is more popular than for clerical, supervisory, and managerial personnel. Approximately two-thirds of the companies studied have instituted standards for blue-collar or production employees, while only one-third have set standards for clerical and supervisory employees. This clearly reflects the nature of managerial orientation in underdeveloped economies. In other words, more emphasis is placed on production-manufacturing aspects than on developing manpower resources. This concern was aptly expressed by a Japanese executive in Taiwan: "What is important for us is production . . . we closely watch what is happening on the assembly line . . . for other employees, we do not worry . . . they do not produce anything."

In terms of intercompany and interregional comparisons, American subsidiaries and their local counterparts in the Far East set the pace in establishing standards for employees. As Table 3-2 shows, some 73 percent of the American subsidiaries, versus 52 percent of the local companies in all six countries, have established standards for their production employees. By region, however, 69 percent of the companies in the Far East have done so, compared to 55 percent of the Latin American firms.

The proportion of companies instituting standards for clerical and supervisory personnel is much lower than of those undertaking standards-setting for blue-collar employees. This proportion drops from 73 to 40 percent for the American subsidiaries and from 52 to 24 percent for the local companies.

ORGANIZATIONAL CONCERN AND STANDARDS-SETTING

There seems to be a positive relationship between a firm's concern for its publics and the nature of standards-setting. As the data in Tables 3-2 and 3-3 show, 87 percent of the firms categorized

---

Table 3-2
Standards-Setting for Production Employees

Organizational concern for its publics: Argentina, Brazil, Uruguay

How standards are set:	Overall	U.S. local	Much concern		Moderate concern		Little concern	
Formally done by committee								
Formally done by production manager	12	8	1	1	11	6		1
Ad hoc basis by chief executive/owner.	4	4			4	4		
Not discernible	4	5	1		3	5		
Total	20	17	2	1	18	15	0	1

Organizational concern for its publics: India, Philippines, Taiwan

	Overall	U.S. local	Much concern		Moderate concern		Little concern	
Formally done by committee	21	16	6	7	15	7	—	2
Formally done by production manager	9	5	4	3	5	2		
Ad hoc basis by chief executive/owner.	5	15	1	1	1	7	3	7
Not discernible	1	2	1	—	—	2	—	—
Total	36	38	12	11	21	18	3	9

Table 3-2, cont'd.

Table 3-2, cont'd.

Summary Comparisons

Item	U.S. subsidiary	Local firm	U.S. and local companies
	(N given in parentheses)		
Percent of firms in which standards-setting for the production employee was undertaken on a formal basis either by committee or production managers:			
In both regions	73% (56)	52% (55)	64% (111)
In Latin American countries	60% (20)	52% (17)	55% (37)
In Far Eastern countries	83% (36)	57% (38)	69% (74)
In "much cocern" firms	82% (14)	92% (12)	87% (26)
In "moderate" and "little" concern firms	73% (42)	44%(43)	58% (85)

as "much concern" set some sort of standards for their blue-collar, or production, employees; 60 percent of these firms have established standards for clerical and supervisory personnel. In contrast to the "much concern" firms, only 58 percent of those classified as "moderate concern" and "little concern" have established standards for their production employees, and a mere 24 percent make this provision for measuring clerical and supervisory personnel.

Moreover, the differences among the "much concern" and "moderate concern" and "little concern" firms are even more pronounced in the degree of sophistication employed in the standards-setting. Firms in the first category ("much concern") utilized time and motion studies and other engineering techniques (for example, linear programming, operations research, etc.) for establishing standards; firms in the "moderate concern" category rely mainly on either the gut feelings of their production managers and foremen or depend on machinery manufacturers' specifications. Firms in the "little concern" category operate largely on a random basis.

Table 3-3
Standards-Setting for Clerical and Supervisory Personnel

Organizational concern for its publics: Argentina, Brazil, Uruguay

How standards are set:	Overall U.S.	local	Much concern		Moderate concern		Little concern	
Formally done by committee	3	3			3	3		
Ad hoc basis by chief executive/owner	14	9	2	1	12	7	—	1
Not available, not done	3	5			3	5		
Total	20	17	2	1	18	15	0	1

Organizational concern for its publics: India, Philippines, Taiwan

	Overall U.S.	local	Much concern		Moderate concern		Little concern	
Formally done by committee	19	10	9	6	10	4		
Ad hoc basis by chief executive/owner	10	28	3	5	4	14	3	9
Not available, not done	7				7			
Total	36	38	12	11	21	18	3	9

Summary

Item	U.S. subsidiary	Local firm	U.S. and local
	(N given in parentheses)		
Percent of firms in which standards were set for clerical and supervisory personnel on formal basis by committee:			
In both regions	40% (56)	24% (55)	32% (111)
In Latin American countries	15% (20)	18% (17)	16% (37)
In Far Eastern countries	48% (36)	28% (38)	40% (74)
In "much concern" firms	65% (14)	50% (12)	60% (26)
In "moderate" and "little" concern firms	31% (42)	17% (43)	24% (85)

QUALITY, COST, AND BUDGETARY CONTROLS

In a competitive economy such as that of the United States, firms desiring an increase in the share of the market will stress improvements in the quality of goods and/or reduction in cost/ price. (Consider such advertisements of consumer goods as "New and Improved" or "Save 10¢.") In many instances such true or imagined claims are accompanied by rigorous quality and cost controls. Particularly, as we saw earlier, this is the case in many of the U.S. parent companies.

However, in a seller's market, there is no need to improve quality and/or reduce cost in order to expand sales. This situation is reflected in the orientations of the local enterprises in the six developing countries analyzed in this book. For example, only 25 percent of the firms undertake quality control, and only 37 percent have instituted cost and budgetary controls. But, the same is not true for the American subsidiaries and those firms categorized as manifesting "much concern" for their publics.

As can be seen in Table 3-4, 58 percent of the American subsidiaries undertake quality control, 62 percent cost control, and 52 percent budgetary control. The proportion of firms categorized as "much concern" utilizing these control devices is 77, 95, and 97 percent, respectively. In contrast, one-third or less of the local companies and those classified as "moderate" or "little concern" make use of such control devices.

Thus analysis of these data suggests a relationship between the organizational variables, the firm's concern for its publics, and the nature of the control mechanism used. The evidence indicates that the firms with positive attitudes toward internal and external agents (employees, consumers, suppliers, distributors, stockholders, community, and the government) are likely to use extensive quality, cost, and budgetary controls. In contrast, firms with negative attitudes are not likely to do so.

Most of these firms have some sort of maintenance controls. The degree of maintenance schedule, however, as well as the method of control, is more systematic in the American subsidiaries than in the local firms. The same holds true with regard to budgetary controls. To American subsidiaries, budgetary control implies a systematic income-and-loss statement, a periodic management audit, and detailed resource allocations for different departments. To many local companies, budgetary control means no more than income-and-loss statements at the end of the year (which, in fact, governments require for incorporated or limited companies in these countries).

Two significant questions emerge from the analyses of data presented above:

1. Are advanced control techniques and methods transferable to the industrial enterprises in developing countries?
2. Are advanced control techniques and methods useful, in terms of effectiveness, to the industrial enterprises in developing countries?

Answers to both of these questions seem to be affirmative.

It is clear from the evidence presented in this book that the large majority of American subsidiaries (percentages range from a low of 40 percent for standards-setting for clerical and supervisory personnel to a high of 73 percent for setting standards for operation employees) in the six developing countries are able to utilize major policies and other control devices. Other control devices include setting standards for blue-collar, clerical, and supervisory personnel, time and motion studies, and quality, cost, and budgetary controls. More importantly, the firms (U.S. subsidiaries and local companies) manifesting "much concern" for their publics are able to do so in increasing numbers (percentages range from a low of 71 percent utilizing major policies as an instrument of control, to a high of 97 percent utilizing budgetary control).

Of course, compared to the more sophisticated control techniques and methods (operations research, linear programming, queuing theory, management audit systems, behavioral and mathematical simulation techniques, and management information systems) utilized by large American companies in the United States, techniques and methods utilized by the subsidiaries and local firms are much less advanced and sophisticated. Nevertheless, considering the size of the companies and market sophistication in the six developing countries, the control techniques and methods being used represent a progressive step toward the

Table 3-4

Uses of Other Control Measures in
American Subsidiaries and Local Companies

Organizational concern for its publics: Argentina, Brazil, Uruguay

Type of control:	Overall	U.S. local	Much concern		Moderate concern		Little concern	
Quality Control								
Done formally	12	4	2	1	10	3	—	—
Done on ad hoc basis	7	12			7	12	—	—
Not done, not available	1	1			1	—	—	1
Total	20	17	2	1	18	15	0	1
Cost Control								
Done for all products	13	6	2	1	11	5	—	—
Done for new products	6	10	—	—	6	10		
Ad hoc basis, not done	1	1	—	—	1	—	—	1
Total	20	17	2	1	18	15	0	1
Budgetary Control								
Done for entire co.	6	4	2	1	4	3		
Done on ad hoc basis	14	13	—	—	14	12	—	1
Total	20	17	2	1	18	15	0	1

Organizational concern for its publics: India, Philippines, Taiwan

Type of control:	Overall	U.S. local	Much concern		Moderate concern		Little concern	
Quality Control								
Done formally	20	10	9	8	11	2	—	—
Done on ad hoc basis	5	16	3	3	2	13		
Not done, not available	11	12	—	—	8	3	3	9
Total	36	38	12	11	21	18	3	9
Cost Control								
Done for all products	22	14	11	10	11	4		
Done for new products	7	9	1	1	5	7	1	1
Done ad hoc, not done	7	15	—	—	5	7	2	8
Total	36	38	12	11	21	18	3	9
Budgetary Control								
Done for entire co.	23	17	11	10	12	7	—	—
Done on ad hoc basis	13	21	1	1	9	11	3	9
Total	36	38	12	11	21	18	3	9

Table 3-4, cont'd.

Summary Comparisons

Item	U.S. subsidiary		Local firm		U.S. and local firms	
	(N given in parentheses)					
1. Percent of the firms undertaking quality control in formal and systematic manner						
In both regions	58%	(56)	25%	(55)	42%	(111)
In Latin American countries	60%	(20)	26%	(17)	45%	(37)
In Far Eastern countries	57%	(36)	27%	(38)	41%	(74)
Categorized as "much concern"	80%	(14)	75%	(12)	77%	(26)
Categorized as "moderate" or "little" concern	50%	(42)	12%	(43)	31%	(85)
2. Percent of firms undertaking cost control for all products						
In both regions	62%		37%		50%	
In Latin American countries	65		36		51	
In Far Eastern countries	61		38		49	
Categorized as "much concern"	96		97		95	
Categorized as "moderate" or "little" concern	50		17		36	
3. Percent of firms undertaking budgetary controls for entire company						
In both regions	52%		37%		45%	
In Latin American countries	30		23		28	
In Far Eastern countries	67		45		55	
Categorized as "much concern"	97		97		97	
Categorized as "moderate" or "little" concern	39		24		31	

use of advanced management practices and know-how.

Such environmental factors as economic and political instability and a seller's market in these countries do affect a firm's willingness to use advanced management control techniques and methods. These factors by themselves, however, are not viewed as especially serious constraints, particularly by those firms which make use of control devices.

To explore the answer to the second question, "Are advanced control techniques and methods useful to the industrial enterprises in developing countries?", I examined the statistical relationship between the control techniques and methods being used and the organizational effectiveness.

In this analysis we will explore relationship between the control measures utilized and the organizational effectiveness among firms that were "decentralized" and "centralized."

For the purpose of this analysis, we will use a sub-sample of 30 firms in India (all but four, for which information was not available) to keep socio-cultural and environment variables as "constant."

The following research hypothesis was tested:

The more extensive the operations control devices in decentralized organizations, the greater the gain in organizational effectiveness.

The relationships explored are summarized in Table 3-5.

Table 3-5
Operations Control and Decentralization

| | | Extent of Decentralization | |
		High *(decentralized)*	*Low* *(centralized)*
	high	organizational effectiveness	organizational effectiveness
Extent of Operations Controls	medium	organizational effectiveness	organizational effectiveness
	low	organizational effectiveness	organizational effectiveness

VARIABLES AND MEASURES

Four factors were considered in determining the extent and sophistication of the firms' operations controls: (1) budget and resource allocation; (2) cost control; (3) maintenance control; and (4) quality control. The factors are representative of the various kinds of operations controls typically utilized by the firms under study. Although a number of other more sophisticated controls are used by the more progressive American firms (such as production control, inventory control, management audit), not many firms in the present sample have developed such controls to an appreciable extent.

Each factor is ranked from 1.0 (high) to 3.0 (low), depending on the extent to which the particular control has been developed and utilized by each firm. (See Table 3-6 for a detailed description of the ranking scheme.) A composite "Operations Control Index" was devised for each firm by computing the arithmetic mean of the four factors' rankings.

DECENTRALIZATION IN DECISION-MAKING

In order to evaluate the degree of decentralization in decision-making observed in the companies studied, nine factors were examined:

1. Layers of hierarchy—from top executive to the blue-collar worker
2. Locus of decision-making with respect to major policies (mergers, major expansions or suspensions, major diversification decisions)
3. Locus of decision-making with respect to sales policies
4. Locus of decision-making with respect to product-mix
5. Locus of decision-making with respect to standards-setting in production
6. Locus of decision-making with respect to manpower policies
7. Locus of decision-making with respect to selecting executives
8. Degree of participation in long-range planning
9. Degree of information-sharing

Table 3-6
Ranking Scale for Factors Evaluated
for Operations Control Index

Factors	*Points*

1. Budget and Resource Allocation
   Done for all departments by
   qualified personnel 1
   Done for few major departments
   by qualified personnel 2
   Not done, done randomly by
   unqualified personnel 3
2. Cost Control
   Done for all departments by
   qualified personnel 1
   Done for few major departments
   by qualified personnel 2
   Not done, done randomly by
   unqualified personnel 3
3. Maintenance Control
   Done for all departments by
   qualified personnel 1
   Done for few major departments
   by qualified personnel 2
   Not done, done randomly by
   unqualified personnel 3
4. Quality Control
   Done for all departments by
   qualified personnel 1
   Done for few major departments
   by qualified personnel 2
   Not done, done randomly by
   unqualified personnel 3

To arrive at a composite index for decentralization, I devised a three-point ranking scale for each of the factors evaluated (see Table 3-7). The final decentralization index for each company is obtained by averaging the scores for all nine factors. This gives us an index ranging from a minimum of 1.0 (highly decentralized) to a maximum of 3.0 (highly centralized).

Table 3-7
Ranking Scale for Factors
Evaluated for Decentralization Index

Factors	*Points*

1. Layers of hierarchy (top executive to blue-collar worker)
   (a) 3 to 6 1
   (b) 7 to 10 2
   (c) 11 or more 3

2. Locus of decision-making (major policies)
   (a) broad representation of executives and stockholders 1
   (b) top-level executive committee 2
   (c) chief executive or owner only 3

3. Locus of decision-making (sales policies)
   (a) executive committee with representation of all
       functional areas 1
   (b) chief executive with help from sales manager 2
   (c) top executive, owner only 3

4. Locus of decision-making (product mix)
   (a) executive committee with representation of all
       functional areas 1
   (b) chief executive with help from production/
       marketing manager 2
   (c) chief executive, owner only 3

5. Locus of decision-making (standards-setting in production)
   (a) executive committee with representation of all
       functional areas 1
   (b) chief executive with production manager—
       production manager only 2
   (c) chief executive only 3

6. Locus of decision-making (manpower policies)
   (a) executive committee with representation of all
       functional areas 1
   (b) chief executive with personnel manager 2
   (c) chief executive only 3

7. Locus of decision-making (selection of executive personnel)
   (a) executive committee with representation of all
       functional areas 1
   (b) chief executive with personnel manager 2
   (c) chief executive only 3

Table 3-7, cont'd.

Table 3-7, cont'd.

8. Degree of participation in long-range planning
   (a) all levels of executives—top, middle, lower 1
   (b) top level, with some representation of middle-
       level executives 2
   (c) chief executive, owner only 3
9. Degree of information-sharing
   (a) considerable—general memos on all major
       aspects of company's operation 1
   (b) fair—special reports on company's affairs
       distributed only to top-level and middle-level
       executives 2
   (c) little—all information kept secret from everybody
       except a few top-level executives 3

Organizational effectiveness is evaluated both in terms of behaviorally oriented measures and economic criteria. The behavioral factors examined are: (1) ability to hire and retain high-level manpower; (2) employee morale and satisfaction in work; (3) turnover and absenteeism; (4) interpersonal relationships; (5) interdepartmental relationships; and (6) utilization of high-level manpower. The economic, or financial, criteria examined are: (1) growth in sales and (2) net profits during the past five years.

Three descriptive categories have been created for evaluating the organizational effectiveness of each company studied, and a three-point ranking scale has been devised. Two effectiveness indices have been determined by averaging the appropriate factor scores, one for the behaviorally oriented measures and the other for growth in sales and profits. Again, this gives us indices ranging from a minimum of 1.0 (most effective) to a maximum of 3.0 (least effective). Details of this scaling are shown in Table 3-8.

ANALYSIS OF RESULTS

The 30 firms in our sample can be split into 17 relatively decentralized (index 1.8 or less) and 13 relatively centralized firms (index greater than 1.8). Each group can be divided into three sub-groups according to whether the operations control index is high (1.0), medium (between 1.0 and 1.4), or low (1.5 or higher).[11] This allows us to classify the firms in our sample according to the six categories illustrated by the 3 X 2 matrix in

Table 3-8
Ranking Scales for Factors Evaluated for
Organizational Effectiveness Indices

Factors   *Points*

Behavioral Measures

1. Ability to attract and retain high-level manpower
   (a) able to attract and retain highly trained personnel .. 1
   (b) able to attract and retain moderately trained
       personnel 2
   (c) not able to attract and retain even moderately
       trained personnel 3

2. Employee morale and satisfaction in work
   (a) excellent morale and highly satisfied 1
   (b) average morale and somewhat satisfied 2
   (c) poor morale and highly dissatisfied 3

3. Employee turnover and absenteeism
   (a) 0 - 5% 1
   (b) 6 - 11% 2
   (c) 12% or more 3

4. Interpersonal relationships in organizational settings
   (a) very cooperative 1
   (b) somewhat cooperative 2
   (c) not cooperative 3

5. Departmental relationships (subsystem relationship)
   (a) very cooperative 1
   (b) somewhat cooperative 2
   (c) not cooperative 3

6. Utilization of high-level manpower (what executives did)
   (a) policy-making and planning 1
   (b) coordination with other departments 2
   (c) routine work, day-to-day work, and excessive
       supervision of subordinates' duties 3

Economic Criteria

7. Sales growth (average of past five years)
   (a) phenomenal growth (50-100%) 1
   (b) moderate growth (49-25%) 2
   (c) declining or stagnant 3

8. Net profits on invested capital (average of past five years)
   (a) 25% or more 1
   (b) 15-24% 2
   (c) less than 15% 3

Table 3-5. Since none of the firms in our sample has a high operations control index with centralization, only five categories are left, each containing from four to nine firms. The average effectiveness scores in (1) behavioral and (2) economic terms have been computed for the firms in each category. These average effectiveness scores, along with the number of firms per category, are summarized in the appropriate cells of the matrix in Table 3-9. As can be seen, the most effective firms, by both criteria, are those that combine decentralization with a high operations control index. The least effective are those that are relatively centralized and that score relatively low on the control

---

Table 3-9
Operations Control and Decentralization

Operations Control	Decentralized (index = 1.0-1.8)	Centralized (index = 1.9-3.0)
High (index 1.0)	$N = 7$ $E_b = 1.28$ $E_e = 1.0$	$N = 0$
Medium (index 1.0-1.4)	$N = 6$ $E_b = 1.65$ $E_e = 1.5$	$N = 4$ $E_b = 2.08$ $E_e = 1.38$
Low (index 1.5 or higher)	$N = 4$ $E_b = 2.1$ $E_e = 1.5$	$N = 9$ $E_b = 2.52$ $E_e = 1.95$
Totals	$N = 17$ $E_b = 1.61$ $E_e = 1.30$	$N = 13$ $E_b = 2.38$ $E_e = 1.77$

N = number of firms in category

E_b = average of effectiveness (behavioral) scores for firms in the category

E_e = average of effectiveness (economic) scores for firms in the category

index. The two groups in the medium category for operations control have intermediate effectiveness (regardless of operations control, which is reported in Chapter 5).

Since the decentralized firms are of particular interest to me, the Kruskal-Wallis One-Way Analysis of Variance by Ranks has been used to determine the statistical significance of the observed differences in effectiveness between these three subgroups of the 17 relatively decentralized firms.[12] The results of the test indicate that the decentralized firms with extensive operations control are significantly more effective than those with medium or low operations controls (on the basis of both behavioral and economic criteria). Spearman's Rank Correlation Coefficient has also been computed for the operations control and effectiveness indices of the decentralized firms. The correlation coefficients for economic and behavioral criteria are both statistically significant ($p=.01$). The correlation between operations control and organizational effectiveness is substantially higher for the behavioral criteria ($r=0.80$) than for the economic criteria of effectiveness ($rs=0.58$). This result is not surprising in view of the seller's market in India.[13] Because of these market conditions, all the firms in our sample have little difficulty in increasing sales and profits. While some are more successful economically than others, none can be described as unsuccessful, and the variance in the economic criteria of effectiveness tends to be substantially smaller than the variance in the behavioral criteria. Analysis of the data thus lends considerable support to the research hypothesis given earlier (see page 44).

SUMMARY

In this chapter I have analyzed the policy-making and controlling aspects of managerial functions. Specific elements for which data were collected include: the nature and scope of policy-making; cost, quality, and budget controls; time and motion studies; equipment maintenance; return on investment; profit and loss statement; and a management audit. These data were collected and analyzed with respect to 56 U.S. subsidiaries and 55 comparable local firms in the six developing countries. The results show the following patterns:

1. A greater number of American subsidiaries seem to be utilizing major policies as guidelines and as an instrument of control.
2. Companies in Far Eastern countries have paid more attention to policy-making than those in Latin American countries.
3. A positive correlation is found between the firm's concern toward its publics, or task environemental agents, and the utilization of policy-making, both as a guideline and as an instrument of control.
4. The impact of environmental factors on policy-making is greater in countries in Latin America than those in the Far East.
5. A greater number of American subsidiaries have also successfully utilized other control devices such as setting standards, cost, quality, and budgetary controls.
6. Overall, results show that the advanced control techniques and practices are transferable to the industrial enterprises in developing countries and that the utilization of such techniques and practices does lead to higher organizational effectiveness.

Notes

1. Arnold S. Tannenbaum, *Control in Organizations,* New York: McGraw-Hill, 1968, pp. 3-28.
2. *Ibid.,* p. 3.
3. William M. Evan, "Indices of the Hierarchical Structure of Industrial Organizations," *Management Science,* 9 (April 1963), 468-77.
4. Tannenbaum, *op. cit.*
5. Paul E. Holden, C. A. Pederson, and G. A. Germane, *Top Management,* New York: McGraw-Hill, 1968.
6. *Ibid.,* pp. 22-36.
7. *Ibid.,* p. 27.
8. Figures for Argentina, Brazil, Uruguay, India, and the Philippines are from the *Monthly Bulletin of Statistics* (United Nations), vol. 21, no. 10 (October 1967), 27, 134, 160, 180, 190, 196. Figures for Taiwan are from *Taiwan Statistical Data Book,* Taipei: CIECD (June 1971), p. 121.

9. Stanley Davis, "Politics and Organizational Underdevelopment in Chile," *Industrial and Labor Relations Review,* October 1970, pp. 73-83, reprinted in his book, *Comparative Management: Organizational and Cultural Perspectives,* (Englewood Cliffs, N.J.: Prentice-Hall, 1971, pp. 188-209.

10. *Ibid.,* pp. 197-98.

11. This dichotomizing of decentralization index values was based on the procedure used in the nonparametric "Median Test." All the observed values of the independent variables are classified as "high" or "low" depending on whether they fall above or below the median value. Since there were several decentralization index scores equal to the median value of 1.8 in our data, 17 firms had scores on or below the median and were classified as "relatively decentralized." The other 13 firms, then, were, of course, "relatively centralized." The operations control index scores were split into three categories, mainly because the data lent themselves particularly well to this classification. Also, the relationships investigated were more clearly brought out than would have been possible with a simple dichotomy of "high" and "low."

12. For an excellent discussion of the Kruskal-Wallis test see Sidney Siegel, *Nonparametric Statistics,* New York: McGraw-Hill, 1956, pp. 184-94. I should also point out that my sample of firms was of necessity not randomly drawn from the population of all manufacturing firms, Indian or otherwise. Therefore, I cannot interpret this statistical significance in the usual sense to generalize only to manufacturing firms similar to the group in my sample. However, the sample of firms represents, in the judgment of the authors, a good cross-section of typical manufacturing firms in India, both local and American-owned. Therefore, the nonparametric statistical tests have been used in my data mainly to determine which of the observed relationships between variables have a significantly low probability (less than .05) of occurring due to chance alone (in my sample of manufacturing firms).

13. For the impact of the seller's market on management practices, see A. R. Negandhi, "Advanced Management Know-How in Underdeveloped Countries," *California Management Review,* vol. 10, no. 3 (Spring 1968), 53-60.

CHAPTER 4

LONG-RANGE PLANNING

The Soviet Union's experiment in economic development through national planning began in the 1920s. Since then, the concept of planning carries the connotation of governmental interference and control over economic enterprise.

In sharp contrast to this socialistic (or collective) approach to economic development, the United States is exemplified as a "free economy," working through the market-price mechanism. Accordingly, planning was once viewed with mixed feelings, if not contempt, by the U.S. government and the U.S. business community. More recently, this attitude has been changing. Mr. Willard F. Rockwell, chairman of the North American Rockwell Corporation, still opposed to socialistic planning, nevertheless admits that "our real fault lies in the fact that we've never really willed, as a people, an improved society as such, have never really launched an intelligent, concerted, planned, national attitude at all levels on the major problems that confront us. It's time we got started. It could be a great and exciting national experience."[1]

Among the business enterprises themselves, such ideas as "creating a world enterprise"[2] and "transnational enterprise"[3] have acquired a progressive and popular ring. It is still true, however, that even the major U.S. companies are far from considering the world as one market, and they undertake long-range planning accordingly. The notion of strategic planning, in which the world is viewed as one "common market," still remains primarily an ideal of academicians.[4]

Bruce Smackey has stated what is perhaps a realistic picture of current managerial thinking on long-range planning:

> Corporate executives have developed an increased concern about their corporate image and wish to present themselves as modern and forward looking by virtue of their possessing a formal planning group. Concurrent to these developments, executives, when queried off the "record," have stated that the functioning of such groups leaves much to be desired.[5]

Long-range planning is thus still a novel concept for many U.S. companies. As the recent study of Ringbakk indicates, "the formal long-range planning is mainly no more than 'ivory tower' planning by staffs to which line managers are unwilling to commit themselves."[6] Nevertheless, in recent years many U.S. companies have paid considerable attention to what is referred to in the literature as "operational, future-minded planning" of five- to ten-year duration. This is borne out in my study of 15 parent companies, as well as in findings reported in literature on the subject.

PLANNING ORIENTATION OF AMERICAN COMPANIES IN THE U.S.

My research on the 15 U.S. parent companies indicates that the large majority (13) undertakes comprehensive planning that involves all major activities such as finance, marketing and sales, production, plant capacity and equipment, organization, and manpower. The planning cycle is of a five- to ten-year duration. The resulting plans are detailed and systematic; plans are reviewed and revised, if necessary, on a quarterly or yearly basis, with all levels of line and staff managers participating.

Findings of other researchers in the United States correspond to the actual planning practices I observed in the 15 U.S. parent companies I surveyed. Holden, Pederson, and Germane's recent study of 15 large-scale U.S. companies, for example, indicates that planning is an accepted practice in all 15 firms:

> Although a five-year planning cycle is the prevailing pattern, some notable exceptions are found. . . . Companies that have

had successful experience in long-range planning and that are
cognizant of the need to extend the cycle for certain elements
are either moving rapidly to a ten-year program or are giving
serious considerations to that eventuality. . . . In contrast to
early corporate planning, the current practice is to develop
comprehensive projections involving product line, sales, facilities, research and development, manpower, organization,
structure and . . . finance. . . . The involvement of line management from bottom to top in the planning process is general
practice. . . . Chief executives devote from 25 to 70 per cent
of their time to long-range planning.[7]

A conference held at U.C.L.A. in 1962[8] to discuss long-
range planning practices of large U.S. companies and governmental agencies suggests these trends:

Long-range planning is an integral part of the operations in all
organizations that participated in the conference.

A number of companies and agencies represented at the conference have rather detailed five-year planning programs. In
some instances, coordinated strategic plans are made within
a ten-year time frame in addition to detailed five-year plans.

Strategic plans in the ten-year time span are sometimes revised
annually and sometimes only as the need seems to indicate.
Five-year plans usually are revised annually and extended
one year in time.

Plans cover the following major activities of the company:
production, manpower, finance, management, personnel,
sales, industrial relations, organization, marketing, public
relations, diversification, and research and development.

Structurally three sets of plans are made: (1) strategic long-
range plans; (2) intermediate-range five-year plans; (3)
operational plans.[9]

A committee of top managers in the functional areas assures
proper planning coordination. The primary responsibility for
planning rests with those responsible with operations.[10]

PLANNING ORIENTATIONS OF THE AMERICAN SUBSIDIARIES AND LOCAL COMPANIES IN LATIN AMERICAN AND FAR EASTERN COUNTRIES

My inquiry about the planning practices of American subsidiaries and local firms in Latin American and Far Eastern countries was directed mainly toward the nature and types of planning rather than at the exact procedures, methodology, and techniques used in the planning process. Specifically, I collected data on the following aspects of planning:

planning objectives (why do the companies plan?)
the nature and scope of planning
time-horizons in planning
the resultant plans
reviews of plans
participation and information-sharing in the planning process

In analyzing the data, we will undertake four levels of comparison:

1. American subsidiaries versus local companies in both regions (Latin America and the Far East)
2. American subsidiaries in the Latin American countries versus those in the Far Eastern countries
3. Local companies in the Latin American countries versus local companies in the Far Eastern countries
4. Firms (both American subsidiaries and local) with "much concern" versus those with "moderate" and "little concern" for their publics

In the concluding section I will raise and attempt to answer the questions: Are planning practices transferable to the industrial enterprises in developing countries? and Does long-range planning lead to higher organizational effectiveness?

Why do companies plan? Responses from those companies undertaking planning indicate three major objectives of the planning function: (1) long-term growth; (2) higher profitability; and (3) to provide a sense of direction for employees.

The following two quotations from executives in India by and large summarize the views of many executives interviewed concerning planning objectives:

It's true that our forecasts and targets will never be reached...
but if we don't plan for five or six years, our people (managers
and non-managers) will lose the sense of direction. As a
company we will never grow; our growth (30 percent annual
increase in sales during 1961-66) is largely due to our planning. . . . It gives us a sense of direction and a preview of the
problems which we will have to face.

Another Indian executive defended his company's need for planning in these words:

Planning for the future is one thing which we never underem-
phasized. Those who don't believe will keep on arguing against
it and point to the rising prices and government controls and
ask "why plan?" But they never realize that the damn government itself does this and pours out a lot of figures which
business houses can use to chart out their growth. . . . Let me
give you an example. You know ———— Company. Fifteen
years ago they were one of the biggest pharmaceutical companies here. Look where they are now. We moved in late but
we are going places. By their own system [referring to American management methods] we are giving them tough competition *and* winning.

In order to assess the nature and scope of a company's
planning, I inquired whether the firm's planning included all
aspects of operations (finances, product line, manpower, market,
new plants, etc.) or if it involved only one or two aspects of the
company's operation. The answers suggest that most American
subsidiaries (70 percent) in both Latin American and the Far
Eastern countries undertake systematic and comprehensive planning which involves financial, product-line, manpower, market,
and new plant considerations. In contrast to these, only one-third
of the comparable local companies in those countries undertake
systematic and comprehensive planning.

A larger number of local companies in the Far East undertake comprehensive planning, compared to those in Latin America
(40 versus 18 percent). The same is true among American subsidiaries located in the two regions; the difference in their proportion isn't that much, however. In the next section we will
explore these differences.

Organizational variables such as management concern toward consumers, employees, suppliers, distributors, stockholders, community, and government seem to be related to planning undertaken by companies. As is shown in Table 4-1, 70 percent of the firms manifesting "much" and "moderate concern" for their publics undertake systematic and comprehensive planning, which compares favorably with both the overall average of the companies undertaking planning and those firms categorized as "little concern." Some 52 percent of the firms studied pay systematic attention to the planning function, while none of the companies in the "little concern" category attempts planning of this sort. The proportion of local companies undertaking planning is much lower (40 percent in the Far East, 18 percent in Latin America) compared to both overall averages and firms categorized as "much" and "moderate concern."

Although a relatively larger number of companies consider various aspects of their operations in their planning (financial, plant, manpower, etc.), few formulate detailed plans. As is shown in Table 4-2, only one-third of the companies studied develop detailed plans. Of these, a greater proportion consists of the American subsidiaries, and many of them use computers in their planning.

There are no applicable differences between American subsidiaries in the two regions, which is not true in the case of local firms. Thirty-two percent of the local firms in the Far East formulate their plans in detail, while none of their counterparts in Latin America does so.

There seems to be a strong relationship between the organizational concern variable and the degree of sophistication in undertaking planning. For example, 77 percent of the firms categorized as "much concern" formulate their plans in detail, versus only 37 percent of the total number of firms (111). This striking difference is also seen between the firms in "much concern" and the "moderate" and "little concern" categories. Some 88 percent of the American subsidiaries and 66 percent of the local companies in the first category formulate their long-range plans in detail. This compares with 44 percent and 12 percent of the subsidiaries and local firms, respectively, in the

Table 4-1

Scope of Planning in Latin
American and Far Eastern Countries

Organizational concern for publics: Argentina, Brazil, Uruguay

Scope of planning:	Overall concern U.S. local		Much concern U.S. local		Moderate concern U.S. local		Little concern U.S. local	
Comprehensive*	13	3	1	—	12	3	—	—
Limited**	5	6	1	—	4	5	—	—
Financial only	2	3	—	1	2	2	—	1
No formal	—	5	—	—	—	5	—	—
Total	20	17	2	1	18	15	0	1

Organizational concern for publics: India, Philippines, Taiwan

Comprehensive*	27	15	12	5	15	10		
Limited**	3	9	—	5	2	4	1	
Financial only	4	7	—	1	2	4	2	2
No formal	2	7	—		2			7
Total	36	38	12	11	21	18	3	9

"moderate concern" category. None of the companies (American or local) in the "little concern" category makes detailed plans.

My third inquiry concerning the planning function was on the length of planning. As we will see in a later section, literature abounds with the suggestion that the people in the underdeveloped world have short-sighted perspectives, both toward life in general and organizational matters in particular. Such socio-cultural factors as fatalism and a belief in life after death are offered as possible reasons for the lack of long-range perspectives evi-

Summary comparisons

Item	U.S. subsidiary	Local firm (N given in parentheses)	Both
Comprehensive planning:			
In both regions	70% (56)	33% (55)	52% (111)
In Latin American countries	65% (20)	18% (17)	40% (37)
In Far Eastern countries	75% (36)	40% (38)	57% (75)
In "much concern" firms	94% (14)	43% (12)	70% (26)
In "moderate concern" firms	70% (39)	40% (33)	70% (72)
In "little concern" firms	0	0	0

* Includes financial, product, manpower, market, and new plants planning for the entire company.

** Includes only product or plant planning, besides financial.

---

denced by people in the underdeveloped countries. Although the data presented in Table 4-3 show that only 33 percent of the local firms in these two regions plan for a period of five to ten years (and only 6 percent in Latin America), empirical evidence concerning the impact of socio-cultural factors on planning practices is far from conclusive. Before discussing this issue at some length, however, let us first examine the time orientations in planning for American subsidiaries and firms with "much concern" for their publics.

As can be seen in Table 4-3, two-thirds of the American subsidiaries undertake long-range planning for five- to ten-year periods. This compares favorably with the number of comparable local firms, 33 percent, which also undertake five- to ten-year

---

Table 4-2

Resulting Plans in American Subsidiaries and Local Companies in Latin American and Far Eastern Countries

Organizational concern for publics: Argentina, Brazil, Uruguay

Resulting plans:	Overall		Much concern		Moderate concern		Little concern	
	U.S.	Local	U.S.	Local	U.S.	Local	U.S.	Local
Systematic and detailed	10	—	1	—	9	—	—	—
Systematic but limited	4	9	—	1	4	7	—	1
Randomly done, limited forecasts	4	4	1	—	3	4	—	—
No information	2	4	—	—	2	4	—	—
Total	20	17	1	1	18	15	0	1

Organizational concern for publics: India, Philippines, Taiwan

	U.S.	Local	U.S.	Local	U.S.	Local	U.S.	Local
Systematic and detailed	19	12	11	8	8	4	—	—
Systematic but limited	10	13	1	2	8	9	1	2
Randomly done, limited forecasts	6	7	—	1	4	5	2	1
No information	1	6	—	—	1	—	—	6
Total	36	38	12	11	21	18	3	9

planning. A difference between the American subsidiaries located in Latin America and the Far East is noticeable. The proportion of those in Latin American countries is higher than in the Far East (75 percent versus 62 percent, respectively). This is indeed a reversal of the situation observed in the local companies in these two regions. As indicated earlier, the larger number of local companies in Far Eastern countries (45 percent versus 6 percent in Latin America) plan for such long periods. It would seem that the lack of political and economic stability in Latin America has induced more American companies to plan ahead. If this is so, then their reaction to political and economic instability is dramatically opposite to that of local firms in these countries.

Summary Comparisons

Resulting plans: Systematic and detailed	U.S. subsidiary	Local firm (N given in parentheses)	Both
In both regions	52% (56)	22% (55)	37% (111)
In Latin American countries	50% (20)	0% (17)	28% (37)
In Far Eastern countries	52% (36)	32% (38)	40% (74)
In "much concern" firms	88% (14)	66% (12)	77% (26)
In "moderate concern" firms	44% (39)	12% (33)	28% (72)
In "little concern" firms	0% ((4)	0% (9)	0% (13)

Table 4-3

Time Orientation of Planning in American Subsidiaries and Local Companies in Latin American and Far Eastern Countries

Organizational concern for publics: Argentina, Brazil, Uruguay

Time Orientation of Planning:	Overall		Much concern		Moderate concern		Little concern	
	U.S.	Local	U.S.	Local	U.S.	Local	U.S.	Local
Short range (1-2 yrs.)	3	7	—	—	3	6	—	1
Long range (5-10 yrs.)	15	1	2	—	13	1	—	—
Nonspecific period	2	9	—	1	2	8	—	—
Total	20	17	2	1	18	15	0	1

Organizational concern for publics: India, Philippines, Taiwan

	Overall		Much concern		Moderate concern		Little concern	
	U.S.	Local	U.S.	Local	U.S.	Local	U.S.	Local
Short range (1-2 yrs.)	10	14	1	4	7	8	2	2
Long range (5-10 yrs.)	22	17	11	7	11	10	—	—
Nonspecific period	4	7	—	—	3	—	1	7
Total	36	38	12	11	21	18	3	9

ORGANIZATIONAL CONCERN AND LENGTH OF PLANNING

There seems to be a relationship between a firm's concern for its publics and its planning horizon. An overall 78 percent of the firms categorized as "much concern" plan for at least a five-year period, versus 50 percent and zero percent of the firms classified

Table 4-3, cont'd.

Summary Comparisons

Length of Planning:	U.S. subsidiary	Local firm	Both
Long range (5-10 yrs.):		(N given in parentheses)	
In both regions	66% (56)	33% (55)	50% (111)
In Latin American countries	75% (20)	06% (17)	44% (37)
In Far Eastern countries	62% (36)	45% (38)	53% (74)
In "Much concern" firms	95% (14)	60% (12)	78% (26)
In "Moderate concern" firms	62% (39)	34% (33)	50% (72)
In "Little concern" firms	0% (3)	0% (10)	0% (13)

as "moderate" and "little concern." When we analyze these data for American subsidiaries and local companies separately, we observe similar differences of proportion between "much," "moderate," and "little concern" firms. Particularly noticeable is the fact that 60 percent of the local firms categorized as showing "much concern" do plan ahead for a five- to ten-year period. Thus the general notion of a short-sighted perspective among industrialists in developing countries seems a weak argument.

PARTICIPATION AND INFORMATION-SHARING IN THE PLANNING PROCESS

There is considerable evidence in economics literature suggesting the positive value of greater employee participation and employee information-sharing in the planning process. As Ringbakk has demonstrated, ivory-tower planning by a specialized staff department, without the involvement of line and lower-level managers, is bound to suffer in its implementation.[11]

Similarly, a study of 15 large-scale U.S. companies by Holden, Pederson, and Germane, shows that successful companies tend to involve all levels of management in their planning.[12] In their experimental study, Bass and Leavitt[13] found that the employee morale and productivity were higher when they followed plans they had a hand in developing. Similar conclusions were also drawn from an experiment conducted in the General Electric Company.[14]

Of course, these studies refer to the situation in the American context. However, with respect to the developing countries, there are no research studies known to me that contradict these findings. There have been a number of studies undertaken in various developing countries which suggest broadly that employees prefer a consultative type of leadership. A survey undertaken among International Business Machines employees in 45 countries indicates that in general IBM employees prefer a consultative type of leadership.[15] Similar conclusions were drawn by Thiagarajan and Deep in their study of 12 countries.[16] On the other hand, as we will see in Chapters 5 and 6, there are a number of writers who argue that employees in underdeveloped countries prefer authoritarian leadership.[17] My own observations in the six developing nations do not support this view.

My inquiry revealed that in some 50 percent of the firms, both top- and middle-level executives participate in the actual planning process, regardless of the nature of the company's plans (for example, systematic versus ad hoc).[18] In these companies, planning information is provided through a general memo which is circulated to all levels of managerial, technical, and supervisory personnel.

Of course, as is shown in Table 4-4, a larger number of the American subsidiaries follow the practice of participation and information-sharing; two-thirds of American subsidiaries, versus one-third of their counterpart local firms, encourage such participation. There is no appreciable difference between local companies in the Latin American and Far Eastern countries, but the larger proportion of American subsidiaries (71 percent) in the Far East, compared to 55 percent in Latin America, encourage middle-management personnel to participate in the planning processes.

The relationship between the "organizational concern" variable and the degree of participation in planning seems much stronger in the case of local firms. Sixty percent of those local firms categorized as "much concern" involve their middle-level managers in planning. The corresponding percentage of the firms categorized as "moderate concern" was 37 percent. Among American subsidiaries, the respective percentages were 76 and 64. This shows that the American subsidiaries encourage participation regardless of their orientation toward client groups. Needless to say, none of the companies (American or local) classified as "little concern" encourages participation of middle-management personnel in planning activities.

The views toward participation and information-sharing in the planning process of firms with different orientations toward client groups are vividly brought out in the following expressions by executives in India:

> There are no secrets in our company. . . . We make every attempt to inform all our people where we want to go and how far we have gone. This is where our strength lies—in creating a well-committed manpower. [American executive in a "much concern" company]

In a similar vein, an Indian executive of a "much concern" company pointed to the need to share goals with the employees:

> We know where we are going and so do the employees. . . . It would be fatal for us if they did not know. . . . After all, they are the ones who have to work to reach the goals.

Compare these views with those of executives in "moderate" and "little concern" firms:

> Our company planning is done by the general manager and his staff. . . . No one else is expected to know. . . . Of course,

Table 4-4
Participation in the Planning Process

Organizational concern for publics: Argentina, Brazil, Uruguay

Participation:	Overall		Much concern		Moderate concern		Little concern	
	U.S.	Local	U.S.	Local	U.S.	Local	U.S.	Local
Top-level executives only	9	13	—	—	9	12	—	1
Top- and middle-level executives	11	4	2	1	9	3	—	—
Total	20	17	2	1	18	15	0	1

Organizational concern for publics: India, Philippines, Taiwan

	Overall		Much concern		Moderate concern		Little concern	
	U.S.	Local	U.S.	Local	U.S.	Local	U.S.	Local
Top-level executives only	11	23	3	5	5	9	3	9
Top- and middle-level executives	25	15	9	6	16	9	—	—
Total	36	38	12	11	21	18	3	9

I came to know about it through my own channels . . . that is the way it works. [assistant manager in an American subsidiary in India]

An Indian national, an assistant manager of a soft drink manufacturing company, expressed his total lack of knowledge of production-related figures when he said:

What planning figures? You will have to ask our managing director. I don't think even his own son [the plant manager in this case] knows what his father has in mind.

Table 4-4, cont'd.

Summary Comparisons

Participation:	U.S. subsidiary	Local firm (N given in parentheses)	Both
Top- and middle-level executives			
In both regions	66% (56)	35% (55)	50% (111)
In Latin American countries	55% (20)	36% (17)	41% (37)
In Far Eastern countries	71% '(36)	40% (38)	54% (74)
In "Much concern" firms	76% (14)	60% (12)	70% (26)
In "Moderate concern" firms	64% (39)	37% (33)	51% (72)
In "Little concern" firms	0% (3)	0% (10)	0% (13)

Management's concern and serious attitude toward the planning function also can be observed in their review procedures. In a sense, a periodic review of plans reflects management's desire to remain flexible and adaptable to the changing business environment. The positive value of flexible planning is reflected in a proposition advanced by Filley and House, which states: "Organizations with flexible plans are more effective than organizations that are fixed and stable."[19] There is some, though not much, evidence that supports this proposition. Filley and House cite two studies, one undertaken in the Virginia Electric and Power Company[20] and another, by Maier, in an unidentified manufacturing company.[21] Both studies indicate a relation between flexible planning and the effectiveness of organizational plans.

The business environment in developing countries is extremely dynamic in certain respects and stable in others. For instance, the market environment in most of the developing nations is much less competitive than in industrially developed countries. At the same time, governmental control of prices, the availability of raw materials and equipment, and imports and foreign exchanges make situations unstable, if not erratic, for a business firm.

Under such circumstances there may be a greater need for introducing higher flexibility into the targeted plans. A recent study by Wright, in Chile, seems to suggest such an imperative.[22] Wright argues that the managerial difference contributing to the greater success of the local Chilean firms is due to their flexibility in plans and policies. He cites two examples of the American subsidiaries' rigid planning policies which led to unprofitability, one concerning the brand-name policy of a pharmaceutical firm and another the product-line policy of an electronics company.[23]

Whatever may be the exact relationship between flexibility in planning and the success of such planning, on an intuitive basis it makes sense that some kind of systematic review of plans may be necessary in order to cope with environmental changes.

As the data presented in Table 4-5 indicate, progressive companies do take this facet of planning seriously. Of the 26 companies categorized as "much concern," only two do not review their plans in a systematic manner. As was the case with other aspects of planning, a higher proportion of American subsidiaries review their plans periodically.

THE ENVIRONMENTAL AND SOCIO-CULTURAL IMPACT ON THE PLANNING FUNCTION

Socio-Cultural Factors

As was mentioned earlier, many writers in cross-cultural, comparative management have advanced the thesis that socio-cultural factors in the developing countries are the main impediments to introducing advanced management—including those practices and know-how that concern the planning function—into those

Table 4-5
Frequency of Reviewing Plans
in Latin American and Far Eastern Countries

Organizational concern for publics: Argentina, Brazil, Uruguay

Time period:	Overall U.S.	Local	Much concern		Moderate concern		Little concern	
Monthly/ quarterly	9	6	1	1	8	5	—	—
Semi-annually	4	5	—	—	4	5	—	—
Annually	2	1	—	—	2	—	—	1
Ad hoc, when needed	5	5	1	—	4	5	—	—
Total	20	17	2	1	18	15	0	1

Organizational concern for publics: India, Philippines, Taiwan

Time period:	Overall U.S.	Local	Much concern		Moderate concern		Little concern	
Monthly/ quarterly	23	11	8	6	15	5	—	—
Semi-annually	3	1	1	1	2	—	—	—
Annually	4	4	3	2	1	2	—	—
Ad hoc, when needed	6	22	—	2	3	11	3	9
Total	36	38	12	11	21	18	3	9

countries.[24] However, systematic, empirical studies validating such a notion are lacking.

It is beyond the scope of this book to review in detail the sociological and anthropological literature concerning socio-cultural patterns in the developing countries.[25] For the analysis, I will mention the salient features of socio-cultural settings in these countries. Two examples are used for illustration, one from the Latin American countries in general and another reflecting Indian (Hindu) characteristics. I realize that there are considerable differences among individual countries, both in Latin America and the Far East, but the two examples cited below are offered as illustrations rather than as generalizations about the socio-cultural heritage of these societies.

Latin American Values

Anthropologist John Gillen has summarized the basic ethos on values of Latin American culture: "Personalism, kinship, hierarchy or stratification, materialism of special kind, transcendentalism or "interest in spiritual values," the high worth of inner states, and emotional expression and fatalism."[26]

In his study of businessmen in Puerto Rico, Thomas C. Cochran translated their socio-cultural traits into the following managerial attitudes and behavior. Entrepreneurs in Latin America, Cochran argues are:

1. More interested in inner worth and justification by standards of personal feelings thang they are in the opinions of peer groups;
2. Disinclined to sacrifice personal authority to group discussions;
3. Disliking of impersonal as opposed to personal arrangements, and generally preferring of family relations to those with outsiders;
4. Inclined to prefer social prestige to money; and
5. Somewhat aloof and disinterested in science and technology.[27]

Indian Values

Indian-born sociologist Dhirendra Narain has characterized the Indian character as having:[28]

1. absence of commitment
2. high passivity (identification with the mother rather than the father)
3. an attitude of dependence on authority
4. an inability to feel strongly
5. faith in words
6. lack of time-orientation
7. contradictions in ideals and performance

Commenting on the first characteristic (absence of commitment), which seems to have some implication for long-range planning, Narain writes:

There is a noticeable absence of commitment in contemporary Indian character, and absence of the total involvement that enables one to carry a task from start to finish through all trials and difficulties. It expresses itself at many levels. At the individual level, promises are freely made which are either not kept or incompletely kept; a great amount of initial enthusiasm may be shown, but it soon dissipates. At the collective level, faith in objectives is proclaimed, but the requisite amount of sustained effort is not forthcoming. . . . Character lacks definition, resulting in an incapacity to show forthrightness, determination, and doggedness. There is great patience, but little perseverence in the Indian character.[29]

On the charactertistic of "faith in words" Narain states:

Indians exhibit a peculiar faith in the efficacy and power of words. With others, language is employed to define issues; we use language to solve issues. Effort, sacrifice, postponement of immediate gratification recede into the background, and the words fill our pages and minds. . . . Lofty announcements are made from public platforms, not with a view to implementing them . . . but in the naive belief that this is somehow solving the problems and not a mere prelude to the solution.[30]

Finally, Narain argues that "the [Indian] attitude toward time is somewhat peculiar. The idea that time is measurable and irreplaceable is missing."[31]

These characteristics and values may indeed have implications for managerial attitudes, behavior, and practices. For example, the personalistic value in the Latin American culture described by Gillen[32] may deter the group discussion of issues, and in the present case, participation in the planning process, while the fatalistic trait may affect the planning horizon. Similarly, kinship and personalism may deter the reporting and information-sharing aspects of planning.

In the same way, the Indian traits of "lack of commitment" and "lack of time orientation" may affect planning implementation as well as the horizon of planning.

However, as was stated earlier, empirical evidence supporting such relationships between socio-cultural values and specific managerial functions unfortunately is lacking. To my knowledge, no systematic, empirical investigations have been carried out in *control situations* which could support these relationships. This is indeed a difficult, although challenging, task.

On the other hand, there seems to be evidence that negates the claims and arguments concerning the impact of socio-cultural variables on the economic development process in general and managerial behavior in particular. Sociologist David Mandelbaum, for example, writes on this point: "particularly misguided is the notion that there must be inherent contradictions between established customs and modern innovations."[33] Drawing from his comprehensive study of Indian villages, he states:

> . . . there has been considerable cultural continuity along with the modern social change.[34] . . . One of the ways of maintaining both persistence and change is through compartmentalization, the traditional mode of separating the standards of the work sphere from those of the domestic sphere.[35]

Referring to Milton Singer's[36] study of leading industrialists in Madras, India, Mandelbaum states:

> In their household behavior, members of these families tend to observe scriptural standards much more closely than they do in their activities outside the house. These industrialists separate the two spheres of action more sharply than was done in their boyhood homes. . . . This device . . . is not restricted to the industrial elite. Even the men who pull rickshaws in the streets of Lucknow [city in India] similarly separate their standards for conduct in their work domain from those followed in their homes.[37]

Similar behavior patterns are found in case studies of industrialists such as Torcuato Di Tella in Argentina.[38]

Economic, Political, and Legal Factors

The economic, political, and legal conditions in a given country can affect planning. Yet the impact of environmental factors on planning function has been noted only cursory in management literature. Although Steiner, in his comprehensive book on managerial planning,[39] mentions the impact of environmental factors on planning, none of the references he cites systematically report the nature of any relationship that may exist between environmental variables and planning activities.

However, in cross cultural management studies, such a relationship has been hinted at by a number of scholars. Davis,[40] in his study of Chile, Lauterbach,[41] in a number of Latin American countries, and Lauter,[42] in Turkey, have indicated a relationship between economic-political legal conditions and the planning function. Davis reports: "In answer to the question 'How far into the future does the formal planning in your enterprise extend?' More than half of those interviewed answer, 'that depends on how long it is before the next election.' "[43] In interpreting his findings, Davis says:

> It is not difficult to see why economic organization remains underdeveloped when systematic planning on the basis of anticipated requirements is replaced by the suspicion of major decision-making and planning on the basis of an unpredictable political environment. Planning for the efficient expenditure of resources is not likely to develop when it is not considered to bear any relation to profit-making, the future seems so uncertain, and when there is extreme difficulty in securing long-term credit.[44]

In inquiring about the impact of economic, political, and legal factors on planning, I asked the executives open-ended questions, asking them to identify the most important environmental variables affecting their long-range planning activities. To evaluate the importance of those factors, we carried out much follow-up discussion.

As can be seen in Table 4-6, a seller's market, governmental control of prices, the availability of raw materials, inflation, and the political situation were mentioned frequently by these executives. There are some differences in rank-order importance of these factors among different countries. Executives in the Latin American countries, for example, are more worried

Table 4-6

The Impact of Environmental Variables on Long-Range Planning Practices (interview response[1])

	Argen-tina[2]	Brazil	India	Philip-pines	Uruguay	Taiwan	Total
	n=65	n=90	n=272	n=77	n=66	n=27	n=597
Competition (seller's vs. buyer's market)	30 (46%)	47 (52%)	180 (66%)	38 (49%)	35 (53%)	17 (63%)	347 (58%)
Economic situation (inflation)	45 (69%)	75 (83%)	90 (33%)	48 (62%)	40 (67%)		298 (52%)
Govt. control of prices and the availability of raw materials	30 (31%)	32 (36%)	210 (77%)	30 (39%)	25 (38%)	10 (37%)	327 (56%)
Political situation	40 (62%)	50 (56%)	32 (12%)	10 (13%)	30 (45%)	1 (4%)	163 (28%)
Govt. attitude toward business	22 (34%)	35 (39%)	45 (17%)	20 (25%)	26 (39%)		148 (26%)

[1] Respondents included the senior- and middle-level executives of the companies studied. Figures in parentheses show the percentage of all respondents. Many respondents mentioned more than one factor; therefore the figures are not strictly additive.

[2] Data on Argentina, Brazil, India, the Philippines, and Uruguay are reproduced from A. R. Negandhi and S. B. Prasad, *Comparative Management*, New York: Appleton-Century-Crofts, 1971, p. 174.

[3] Data on Taiwan are reproduced from A. R. Negandhi, *Management and Economic Development: The Case of Taiwan*, The Hague, The Netherlands: Martinus Nijhoff's, 1973. Permission from both publishers is gratefully acknowledged.

---

about political instability and inflation, while those in the Far East show more concern over the existence of a seller's market.[45] Overall, my findings show that a large majority of the executives interviewed (58 percent) in Argentina, Brazil, India, the Philippines, Taiwan, and Uruguay indicate that the seller's-market condition in those countries makes planning less necessary for firms to achieve high profitability. In such a situation all firms are making high profits, regardless of their managerial practices. More or less the same proportion of executives (56 percent) point out that governmental control of prices and the unavailability of raw materials are factors inhibiting long-range planning. Inflation, the political situation, and government attitudes toward the business community were mentioned as additional factors that discourage firms from planning for the future.[46]

Hypothetical Propositions

Based on my findings, reported in Table 4-6, and on the findings of the researchers noted above, the following propositions can be stated as underlying the relationships between environmental variables and the planning function:

The greater the degree of competition, the greater will be the need for long-range planning by individual firms.

The greater the degree of economic and political instability, the lesser the likelihood that private industrial enterprises will undertake systematic long-range planning.

The greater the degree of governmental control of prices and the availability of raw materials, the lesser the likelihood that the firm will undertake systematic long-range planning.

The greater the governmental hostility toward the business community, the lesser the likelihood that a firm will undertake systematic long-range planning.[47]

TWO SIGNIFICANT QUESTIONS

In this final section we will raise two important questions about planning:

1. Is it feasible to introduce advanced management planning practices in underdeveloped countries?
2. Are advanced planning practices useful to industrial enterprises in those countries?

Let us explore answers to these questions in some detail.

Feasibility

If we conceived of advanced management practices concerning planning as those practices that involve the systematic review of

(a) the capacity of a firm to undertake planning; (b) the specification of corporate styles, objectives, and goals; and (c) the identification of corporate strengths, weaknesses, threats. and opportunities,[48] then large U.S. corporations are far from reaching these ideals.[49] For enterprises in underdeveloped countries, such activities are even more difficult to accomplish.

If we take a more charitable view and consider advanced management planning practices as those that involve a company undertaking systematic, future-minded operational plans of five- to ten-year periods, then my study shows that such a feat is not beyond the reach of industrial enterprises in developing nations.

Notwithstanding the impact of environmental (economic, political, legal) factors on planning, as discussed above, my results show that about 50 percent of the companies studied in the six developing countries are conducting this type of long-range planning. Moreover, the proportion of American subsidiaries and firms manifesting "high concern" for their publics is much higher. (See Tables 4-1, 4-2, and 4-3). Specifically, 66 percent of the American companies studied are undertaking long-range planning of five to ten years' duration, while 78 percent of the firms categorized as "high concern" are doing the same.

My findings show similar patterns with respect to other aspects of planning, such as participation in planning, scope of planning, review of plans, and so forth.

Long-Range Planning and Effectiveness

Studies undertaken in the U.S. context seem to indicate a relationship between long-range planning and the effectiveness of a firm. For example, the Stanford Research Institute has found that "in cases of both high growth and low growth companies, those that now support planning programs have shown a superior growth rate in recent years."[50]

Similarly, studies by Comrey et al.,[51] Thune,[52] Brown, Dobson and Thompson,[53] Thune and House,[54] and Herold[55] show a positive relationship between formal planning practices and more effectiveness.

Herold, for example, in cross-validating the previous study of Thune and House, showed that "companies which are actively engaged in formal long-range planning in the drug and chemical industries, significantly out-performed those which are not."[56] This study also indicated the relationship between research and development expenditure and performance.

My Results

In order to examine the relationship between formal planning and enterprise effectiveness, data from the sub-sample of 30 industrial firms in India were further analyzed. First, I constructed a *formal planning index* by examining the following elements of planning process:

the nature and scope of planning
the planning horizon
reviews of plans
participation in planning
information-sharing in the planning process

As is shown in Table 4-7, a three-point ranking scale was devised to evaluate these five elements of the planning process. The overall formal planning index was computed by adding the points for each element and dividing this total by the number of elements considered (five). This gave us a planning index ranging from a minimum of 1.0 (representing "most formalized and advanced planning practices") to a maximum of 3.0 (representing the ad hoc nature of planning practices).

Similarly, an *enterprise effectiveness index* was constructed by examining two of the financial measures of effectiveness, namely, (a) growth in sales during the last five years; and (b) net profits on invested capital during the last five years.

Spearman's rank correlation coefficient between the two indices of formal planning and enterprise effectiveness was 0.60, indicating a positive relationship between formal planning and a firm's effectiveness.

Thus my results provide further evidence in support of the utility of formal planning and show that advanced long-range planning contributes to a firm's effectiveness in developing countries.

Table 4-7

**Factors and Ranking Scale for Formal Planning
and Enterprise Effectiveness Indices**

Formal planning index

Factors	Points
Nature and scope of planning:	
comprehensive	1
somewhat comprehensive	2
no formal planning	3
Planning horizon:	
5 to 10 years	1
1 to 4 years	2
ad hoc basis	3
Reviews of plans:	
Periodic and systematic	1
ad hoc basis	2
Participation in planning:	
all levels of executives	1
top and middle levels only	2
only top level/owner himself	3
Information-sharing in planning:	
considerable—general memos	1
fair—special reports circulated restrictively	2
little—a great deal of secrecy is maintained	3

Enterprise Effectiveness

Sales growth (average of the last five years):	
phenomenal growth (50-100%)	1
moderate growth (49-25%)	2
declining or stagnant	3
Net profits on invested capital (average of the last five years):	
25% and more	1
15-24%	2
less than 15%	3

SUMMARY

In this chapter we have analyzed planning practices of the U.S. parent companies, as well as the American subsidiaries and local firms in the six developing countries. Six aspects of planning practices of companies studied were examined:

1. planning objectives
2. the nature and scope of planning
3. time horizons in planning
4. the nature of resultant plans
5. review methods
6. participation and information-sharing in the planning process

The results show that the U.S. parent companies undertook long-range planning of a five- to ten-year duration and that their resulting plans were detailed and systematic, involving all aspects of organizational activities. These companies also involved their line and staff managers in formulating long-range plans.

Data concerning the American subsidiaries and local companies in the six countries showed that a majority of the former companies followed the practices of their parent companies and undertook comprehensive long-range planning. In contrast, only one-third of the local companies did the same.

Region-wise, a larger number of American subsidiaries and local companies in the Far East undertook systematic long-range planning than those in the Latin American subsidiaries.

The results also indicate a positive correlation between a firm's planning practices and its concern for its publics.

Specific environmental factors affecting planning practices were the nature of competition, economic and political situations, and the governmental attitudes and controls on business activities.

The results of this study show that the advanced planning practices are transferable to industrial enterprises in developing countries and that such practices lead to higher organizational growth and profitability.

Notes

1. W. F. Rockwell, Jr., "Planning—The Golden Thread of Our National Fabric," *Managerial Planning,* vol. 19, no. 2 (September-October 1970), 8.

2. See G. H. Clee and A .D. Scipio, "Creating a World Enterprise," *Harvard Business Review,* 37 (November-December 1959), 77-89.

3. See R. Robinson, "The Global Firm-to-Be: Who Needs Equity," *Columbia Journal of World Business,* vol. 3, no. 1 (January-February 1968), 23-28.

4. Even a progressive and otherwise worldwide company such as IBM does not seem to have reached this ideal. For example, in a response to a question, "How important is planning at IBM?", Thomas J. Watson, chairman of IBM, said:

> Very important, but not as a formal function. We said to ourselves that we didn't have much planning, and we finally put a guy in charge of planning. It was a comfort to have him there, but he was hard to understand. So he decided we didn't care and left. Since then, we've had no organized planning, but we believe in planning. We do it in our conversations with the line executives and we measure what we do against our planning. "As I See It," *Forbes* (November 1, 1967), p. 62.

5. Bruce M. Smackey, "Research on Corporate Planning: A Case Study—Part 1," *Managerial Planning,* vol. 19, no. 3 (November-December 1970), 26.

6. Kjell-Anne Ringbakk, "Organized Corporate Planning Systems: An Empirical Study of Planning Practices and Experience in American Big Business," Unpub. Ph. D. dissertation, University of Washington, 1968.

7. P. E. Holden, C. A. Pederson, and G. E. Germane, *Top Management,* New York: McGraw-Hill, 1968, pp. 3-4.

8. The following companies and governmental agencies were represented at the conference: (1) Aerojet-General Corporation, (2) All-State Insurance, (3) American Airlines, (4) Atomic Energy Commission, (5) North American Aviation, (6) Bendix Corporation, (7) Continental Oil Company, (8) U.S. Department of Defense, (9) Federal Aviation Agency, (10) Ford Motor Company, (11) Glendale Federal Savings, (12) International Machine Corporation, (13) Lockheed Aircraft Corporation, (14) National Aeronautics and Space Administration, and (15) Southern California Edison Company.

9. In a sense, all three types of plans are interrelated. For a case study showing such interrelationships among strategic, tactical, and operational planning, see Bruce M. Smackey, "Research on Planning: A Case Study—Part III," *Managerial Planning,* vol. 19, no. 5 (March-April 1971), 7-13.

10. See George A. Steiner, ed., *Managerial Long-Range*

Planning, New York: McGraw-Hill, 1966, pp. 311-26.

11. Ringbakk, *op. cit.*

12. Holden, Pederson, and Germane, *op. cit.,* pp. 44-65.

13. B. M. Bass and H. J. Leavitt, "Some Experiences in Planning and Operating," *Management Science* (1963), PR=585, quoted in Allan C. Filley and Robert J. House, *Managerial Process Organizational Behavior,* Glenview, Ill.: Scott, Foresman, 1969, p. 204.

14. General Electric Company, "A Comparison of Work Planning Program with the Annual Performance Appraisal Interview Approach," *Management Development and Employee Relations Services* (1964), quoted in Filley and House, *op. cit.,* p. 205.

15. David Sirota and J. Michael Greenwood, "Understand Your Overseas Work Force," *Harvard Business Review,* vol. 49, no. 1 (January-February 1971), 53-60.

16. K. M. Thiagarajan and S. D. Deep, "A Study of Supervisor-Subordinate Influence and Satisfaction in Four Cultures," *Journal of Social Psychology,* 82 (1970), 173-80.

17. See, for example, R. Meade, "An Experimental Study of Leadership in India," *Journal of Social Psychology,* vol. 72, pp. 35-43.

18. To the Western reader this may not amount to a high degree of participation, but we must realize that in developing countries a firm's organizational hierarchy is simple and falls rather quickly. In other words, middle-level executives represented in this case are the college-educated and technically-trained personnel. The next level was clerical, which included such personnel as storekeeper, file clerk, and typist.

19. Filley and House, *op. cit.,* p. 208.

20. *Ibid.,* pp. 208-11.

21. N. R. F. Maier, *Problem-Solving Groups and Discussions,* New York: McGraw-Hill, 1963.

22. Richard W. Wright, "Organizational Ambiente: Management and Environment in Chile," *Academy of Management Journal,* vol. 14. no. 1 (March 1971), 65-74.

23. *Ibid.,* pp. 72-73. It may be mentioned, however, that Wright, in this particular publication, does not provide hard data on profitability. Also, his considerations may involve "short-range" versus "long-range" profitability.

24. For such discussion see R. N. Farmer and B. M. Richman, *Comparative Management and Economic Progress,* Home-

wood, Ill.: Richard D. Irwin, 1965; various articles in Stanley M. Davis, *Comparative Management: Organizational and Cultural Perspectives,* Englewood Cliffs, N.J.: Prentice-Hall, 1971; and Ross Webber, *Culture and Management,* Homewood, Ill.: Richard D. Irwin, 1969.

25. For a brief review of Latin American culture, see John P. Gillin, "The Middle Segments and Their Values," in Richard N. Adams et al., eds., *Social Change in Latin America Today,* New York: Random House, Vintage Books, 1960, pp. 28-37, reprinted in Davis, *op. cit.,* pp. 130-44. For Brazilian culture particularly, see Fernando de Azevedo, *Brazilian Culture: An Introduction to the Study of Culture in Brazil,* New York: MacMillan, 1960. For Indian culture see Dhirendra Narain, "Indian National Character in the Twentieth Century," *Annals,* March 1967, pp. 124-32, reprinted in Davis, *op. cit.,* pp. 245-54.

26. John P. Gillin, "The Middle Segments and Their Values," in *Social Change in Latin America Today,* ed. Richard N. Adams et al., New York: Random House, Vintage Books, 1960, pp. 28-37, quoted in Davis, *op. cit.,* p. 130.

27. Thomas Cochran, *The Puerto Rican Businessman: A Study in Cultural Change,* Philadelphia: Univ. of Pennsylvania Press, 1959, p. 131.

28. Narain, *op. cit.,* pp. 245-54.

29. *Ibid.,* pp. 248-49.

30. *Ibid.,* p. 253.

31. *Ibid.*

32. Gillin, *op. cit.*

33. David G. Mandelbaum, *Society in India,* Vol. 2: *Change and Continuity,* Berkeley: Univ. of California Press, 1970, p. 641.

34. *Ibid.*

35. *Ibid.,* p. 645.

36. Milton Singer, "Indian Joint Family in Modern Industry," in *Structure and Change in Indian Society,* ed. Milton Singer and Bernard S. Cohn, Chicago: Aldine Publishing Company, 1968, pp. 423-52.

37. Mandelbaum, *op. cit.,* p. 645.

38. T. C. Cochran and R. E. Reina, *Entrepreneurship in Argentine Culture,* Philadelphia: Univ. of Pennsylvania Press, 1962.

39. Steiner, *op. cit.*

40. Stanley M. Davis, "Politics and Organizational Underdevelopment in Chile," *Industrial and Labor Relations Review,* October 1970, 70-83, reprinted in his book, *Comparative Management,* pp. 188-209.

41. Albert Lauterbach, *Enterprise in Latin America,* Ithaca, N.Y.: Cornell Univ. Press, 1966.

42. G. Peter Lauter, "Advanced Management Processes in Developing Countries: Planning in Turkey," *California Management Review,* vol. 13, no. 3 (Spring 1970), 7-12.

43. Davis, *op. cit.,* p. 199.

44. *Ibid.*

45. In the case of Taiwan, executives mentioned excessive competition instead of a seller's market. For a detailed discussion on this point, see A. R. Negandhi, *Management and Economic Development in Taiwan,* The Hague: Martinus Nijhoff's, 1973, chap. 2.

46. Stanley Davis mentioned similar factors in the case of Chile, although he has argued that the political instability seems more important. My findings do not necessarily contradict his results. See Davis, *op. cit.,* pp. 192-99.

47. For a detailed discussion of these propositions, see A. R. Negandhi and S. B. Prasad, *Comparative Management,* New York: Appleton-Century-Crofts, 1971, pp. 171-74.

48. Smackey calls this "strategic planning" versus "tactical and operational planning." See Bruce M. Smackey, "Research on Corporate Planning: A Case Study—Part III," *Managerial Planning,* vol. 19, no. 5 (March-April 1971), 8.

49. *Ibid.,* pp. 9-10.

50. Quoted in George Steiner, "Does Planning Pay Off?", *California Management Review,* vol. 5, no. 2 (Winter 1962), 37.

51. A. L. Comrey, W. High, and R. C. Wilson, "Factors Influencing Organizational Effectiveness, VI, A Survey of Aircraft Workers," *Personnel Psychology,* 8 (1955), 79-99.

52. S. Thune, "An Investigation into the Effects of Long-Range Planning in Selected Industries," Unpub. M.B.A. thesis, Bernard M. Baruch School of Business, City University of New York, 1967.

53. H. J. Brown, S. C. Dobson, and G. C. Thompson, "Company Growth: Mostly Planned But Sometimes Painful," *The Conference Board Record,* October 1966, pp. 7-15.

54. S. Thune and R. House, "Where Long-Range Planning Pays Off," *Business Horizons,* vol. 13, no. 3 (August 1970).

55. David M. Herald, "Long-Range Planning and Organizational Performance: A Cross-Valuation Study," *Academy of Management Journal,* vol. 15, no. 1 (March 1972), 91-102.

56. *Ibid.,* p. 100.

CHAPTER 5

ORGANIZATION

Management literature contains many definitions of *organization*. It has been viewed as (a) a system of communication, (b) a means of facilitating decision-making, (c) a social system involving interpersonal relationships, and (d) a managerial function of organizing which involves grouping of activities, establishing authority-responsibility relationships, coordination of different functional activities in pursuit of achieving overall organizational objectives and goals, and delegation of authority.[1]

There seems to be a dividing line between the organization theorist and the management theorist regarding how organization is conceived of and studied. Organization theorists place greater emphasis on studying interpersonal relationships among people within a given organization; they use their observations as a "springboard to observe all other activities of an organization."[2] Management theorists advocate multiple functions of management, of which establishing cooperative interpersonal relationship is only one of many activities. To them, organizational activity or function represents the grouping of activities, departmentalization, providing a system of coordination for different activities, and establishing authority-responsibility relationships among people working in a given organization.[3]

Organization and management theorists, as well as practicing managers, however, have paid concerted attention to one common issue: the delegation of authority and decentralization in decision-making. Particularly in the last two decades or so, management concepts such as "participative or consultative management," "Y-theory," and "management by objectives" have become catchall expressions among theorists and practitioners. All of these concepts essentially convey the same message of delegating authority and pushing decision-making power to the lower levels.

Even among cross-cultural management researchers the issue of decentralization in decision-making seems to be a major concern. As we will see in a later section, the overall conclusion of these researchers is that participative management is a special case applicable to more developed countries such as the U.S. and it is dysfunctional (has negative consequences) in underdeveloped nations.

In this book I view organization as one of the managerial functions involving both structuring of task and grouping of activities, as well as structuring of the authority system within a firm. Specifically, data for the following aspects were collected from the companies studied in Latin America and the Far East:

1. grouping of activities (departmentalization)
2. formalization and documentation
3. authority definition and uses of organization charts
4. layers of hierarchy
5. delegation of authority and decentralization in decision-making
6. decision-making concerning major and functional policies

To provide a comparative perspective, we will first briefly review the organizational practices of the American companies in the United States. This information is drawn from my study of 15 U.S. parent companies and from the findings of other researchers.

ORGANIZATIONAL PRACTICES OF THE AMERICAN COMPANIES

Findings Concerning 15 Parent Companies

Data collected from the 15 U.S. parent companies indicate that the majority of these companies are organized on the basis of business functions—production, sales, accounting, finance, etc. Organization through product line is evident in a few of the companies studied, but interviews of their executives indicate a trend in this direction.

The U.S. parent companies examined were all large-scale firms employing from 500 to 180,000 persons; therefore, data on the layers of hierarchy are not strictly comparable. The highest number of layers in the organization structure of these companies is 11, while the average is seven.

Thirteen out of 15 companies have revised and updated organization charts, with authority specified for each organization position shown in the charts. A majority of the companies do more than pay lip service to the delegation of authority. Decision-making in many instances is a group process, making extensive use of committees and conferences. In all the companies studied, there are service and staff departments.

Findings of Other Studies

Ernest Dale, in comparing his 1952 study of U.S. corporations[4] with that of a 1967 study of 100 large and 60 medium-sized U.S. companies,[5] noted these trends:

1. The problem of executive distance has been increased and in future years may be further aggravated.
2. There is a trend toward greater divisionalization, each division itself becoming larger and more autonomous.
3. The top management is taking the character of group management (evidence of higher desire of decentralization in decision-making).
4. Better communication lines make it possible to require a higher degree of accountability for each unit/person.
5. There is a higher degree of delegation of authority and decentralization in decision-making.
6. The role of technical and scientific staffs has increased and will further increase in future years, which may lead to a corresponding decrease in power and influence of generalist line managers.

Holden, Pederson, and Germane,[6] who studied large companies in the U.S. during 1941 and 1968, found these trends in their organization set-ups:

1. Relative stability of organization structure.
2. Changing attitudes toward committees; fewer standing committees and more ad hoc task forces.
3. Grouping of activities on the basis of product and geographical divisions versus functional aspects of business.
4. Emergence of product and program managers as new elites.
5. Increased number of vice presidents with a consequent decrease in span of control for the chief executives.
6. No change in the role and function of boards of directors; the board member is merely vested with the trusteeship function.[7]
7. A trend toward adherence to the decentralization philosophy, although changes in environmental factors, growth, complexity, and greater interdependence of divisions resulted in greater centralized controls for such activities as setting corporate objectives, strategic planning, determination of basic policies, finance, accounting systems, basic research, bargaining with unions, and public relations work.

Empirical investigations have been accumulated to pinpoint the specific advantages and disadvantages of work division, specialization, departmentalization, and delegation of authority. On the basis of various studies, Filley and House[8] recently formulated the following propositions, or hypotheses, concerning these relationships:

1. Division of labor leads to decreased job satisfaction, but increased productivity.
2. Departmentalization by product or customer will result in less attention to professional or functional skill, and more attention to client needs, than departmentalization by function or process.
3. A clear definition of roles is requisite for effective delegation of responsibility and authority and acceptance of accountability.

4. Responsibility and authority for decision and task accomplishment should be delegated to the lowest level in the organization at which there is sufficient competence and information for effective decision-making or task performance.

5. Organizations with a clear and single flow of authority (unity of command) to the bottom are more satisfying for their members and realize more effective economic performance and goal achievement than do organizations without a single clear flow of authority.

6. Role conflict is associated with decreased satisfaction and decreased organizational effectiveness.

ORGANIZATIONAL PRACTICES OF AMERICAN SUBSIDIARIES AND LOCAL FIRMS

Grouping of Activities: Departmentalization

My initial inquiry concerning the organizational set-up in companies studied in Latin America and the Far East was about the grouping of activities. Various researchers have noted the trend toward greater divisionalization among the American companies in the United States. More and more companies in the U.S. seem to be organizing their divisions and departments on a product or regional basis. The aerospace, electric, and other complex technology-oriented industries have gone one step further by organizing on a *project basis*.

Traditionally, when firms were smaller and technology less complex, many firms organized their activities on the basis of business functions—for example, production, finance, accounting, purchasing, marketing. As was noted earlier, this is still a popular basis for organizing departments among many companies, but the trend is rapidly shifting to product, regional, and project orientations.

American subsidiaries and local companies in Latin America and the Far East are still organizing on the basis of traditional business functions, with rare exceptions. To some extent, this reflects the relatively small size and less complex technological orientation of the companies in the two regions.

Although there are a number of larger companies (those employing 2,000 or more) in my sample with advanced technologies, such as petrochemical and electronics, these companies continue to follow traditional methods of grouping organizational activities.

There were, however, considerable differences among the American subsidiaries and local firms in their emphasis on the organization of different units. In American subsidiaries, departments that affected the cost and quality of products and the productivity of employees were well organized and staffed with qualified and trained personnel, while in the local companies, more emphasis was placed on the production of goods. Accordingly, the former firms have had well-organized cost, quality control, budgeting, personnel, sales, purchasing, and production departments. In the latter, only the production departments received some consideration. In other words, the organizational pattern of American subsidiaries reflects a mentality of competitive-market situation, while that of the local companies underscores the existence of a seller's-market condition. Among local companies, the personnel department especially was the least organized.

The Staff and Service Department

The degree of organizational sophistication can also be seen in the existence of service and staff departments. During the last 20 years there has been a growing trend among U.S. companies to utilize specialized and expert knowledge through staff and service departments. In many of the U.S. companies, such personnel play a pivotal role in policy-making and the company's long-range plans.

My inquiry into this aspect revealed that the American subsidiaries in the Far Eastern countries use more staff and specialized personnel. The number of staff positions in these firms varies from a minimum of three to a maximum of eight. In contrast, less than one-half of the American subsidiaries in the Latin American countries have three or more staff personnel. Most of the local companies in both regions operate entirely with line-type organizations. Fewer than 15 percent have two to three staff positions.

Some kind of service department was found in most of the American as well as the local companies. In the former, however, service departments are customer- and cost-oriented, while in the latter, the main function of the service department is either to carry out maintenance activities or to use it as a dumping ground for "trouble maker" employees.

Formalization and Documentation

In the American companies in the United States, much emphasis is placed on formalizing and documenting organizational rules, policies, procedures, and processes. "Organizational manuals" are as common as water coolers. A recent study of American and British firms by Inkson et al.[9] indicates that the American firms are considerably more formal than their counterpart British firms.

Richardson[10] provides interesting insights into the higher level of formalization and documentation in the American organizations. Referring to his findings concerning the organizational patterns of American and British ships, he states:

> Comparison of British and American crews suggests that the British realize and accept the authority of competent persons and are not as fearful of the misuse of authority as Americans. The acceptance of authority is closely related to acceptance of social stratification and the symbols of these differences. Status symbols function as cues for self-regulation. . . . British seamen are conditioned before going to sea to accept authority, and consequently the change in attitudes required when a man becomes a seaman is slight. . . . [in contrast] Among American crews a far greater fear and suspicion of authority appears to exist. Social stratification is not widely accepted and often denied. . . . If the symbols of social stratification are ineffective, alternative procedures are necessary . . . for maintaining the necessary social system. The alternative procedure has been a far greater formalization of the social system than the British.[11]

Whatever the basic reasons for a higher level of formalization and documentation in the American firms, a clear-cut definition of roles seems to be a prerequisite for organizational effectiveness.

Higher levels of formalization and documentation are evident among the American subsidiaries in the Latin American and Far Eastern countries. Many subsidiaries have prepared comprehensive organizational manuals for different activities, such as employment, hiring and dismissal, employee selection, promotion procedures, and accounting methods and procedures. By and large, the average employee in these companies knows his obligations, rights, responsibilities, as well as the appeals procedures.

Authority line itself is clearly spelled out in manuals and organizational charts. There are very few instances of "authority overlaps" and "authority bypassing" among the American subsidiaries. In short, formalization and documentation in many of the American companies is so detailed that they irritate some of the local employees who otherwise are accustomed to more informal, personal relationships. One of the employees in an Argentine subsidiary commented: "Americans live by the book . . . you know, we are human beings . . . we need some personal touch."

In contrast to the American subsidiaries, local firms in both regions rely on verbal communication. Formalization and documentation appear only in labor contracts. Other organizational matters such as rules, policies, and procedures are informally and verbally communicated.

Authority line is not clearly spelled out; in more than half the local companies, organization charts don't exist. Even among companies boasting the preparation of such charts, the charts are not used as a mechanism for communicating authority relationships. These charts, if they exist, are considered top secret. A company in Taiwan, although a somewhat extreme case, typifies local concern in this respect. When I asked the president of a local company in Taiwan about the organization chart, he stood up, locked the office door, opened his safe, pulled out the organization chart, and then said, "This is a treat for you. . . . I have not shown this chart to anybody, not even my vice-president."

In answer to the general question, "How do you know what your authority is?", the supervisors and middle-management personnel in local companies indicated that they know their authority from verbal conversation with their superiors. Authority overlap and bypassing are much in evidence. In this respect, my findings substantiate those of Stanley Davis in Mexico, who reports:

> Bypassing is an extremely common phenomenon in Mexican organizations. It is particularly widespread in traditional systems of enterprise, which are small in size, and characterized by an informal and personal system of management. Here, it is easy for the head of the company to communicate directly with someone at any level, without the implication of thereby criticizing his immediate subordinate(s). The informal and largely unstructured quality of lines of authority depends almost entirely on the discretion of the man at the top and his subordinates' personal loyalty to him.[12]

I found more instances of overlap in authority and bypassing in the local companies in Latin American countries than in their Far Eastern counterparts.

According to some writers, the lack of authority definition, overlap and bypassing in authority, and preference for verbal communication may reflect the socio-cultural characteristics of personalism in Latin American countries and particularism and collective orientations in Far Eastern countries.[13]

Although Japan seems to use such collective orientation positively and efficiently[14] it is doubtful whether such orientations in Latin American and Far Eastern countries are necessarily more effective. Indeed, I am still unsure that socio-cultural variables alone explain everything. My interviews with top- and middle-level executives in both regions, especially in the local firms, indicate that diffuseness in authority structure is used by top managers (who are largely owner-managers) to exercise close control over subordinates and to foster nepotism within their firms rather than to provide satisfaction for average employees who want personal contact with top-level authorities.

DELEGATION OF AUTHORITY AND DECENTRALIZATION IN DECISION MAKING

As was mentioned above, the concepts of delegation of authority and decentralization in decision-making are the most discussed issues in the management-organization literature. Starting from the now-famous Western Electric experiment,[15] concepts such as "participative management," "consultative management," "theory Y," "humanistic approach," etc., have become catchall expressions for many theoreticians and practicing managers. To such researchers as Likert and the late McGregor,[16] participative, or democratic, management is a kind of "universal principle" of management, being more effective in all organizations regardless of their size, the nature of their technology, or their environmental and cultural setting.

Only in the last few years have such claims been moderated by empirical studies of environmental setting and organizational functioning. Woodward's study[17] in Midland, England suggests that the levels of authority (measure of the degree of decentralization) were positively related to the kind of technologies used. In classifying the nature of a firm's technology into three categories—unit or small batches; large batches and mass production; and continuous processes—she found significant differences between three groups of firms:

> Among the 24 small batch and unit production firms, the median number of levels of management authority was only three, with a range from three to eight. Among the 25 companies in the process production group, the median was six, and the range from two to seventeen.[18]

Also in recent years, such researchers as Burns and Stalker[19] and Lawrence and Lorsch[20] have shown the impact of environmental conditions (market and technology changes) on the authority structure. Burns' and Stalker's study indicates that the firm in a dynamic market condition will be more effective under decentralized authority, while the firm in a stable market will be more effective under centralized authority.

Impact of Socio-Cultural Factors

Cross-cultural management researchers themselves have added another dimension to the issue of decentralization in decision-making. Basically, there seems to be a broad consensus among these writers that the authority structure of industrial enterprises (and, for that matter, governmental agencies and other social organizations) in developing countries is highly centralized. Among others, studies by Harbison and Myers in a number of developing countries,[21] Davis in Mexico and Chile,[22] Lauterbach in Latin American countries,[23] Lauter in Turkey,[24] Fillol in Argentina,[25] Flores in the Philippines,[26] Whyte in Peru,[27] and Jain in India[28] support the belief in centralized authority. In referring to his findings in Mexico, Davis describes the typical findings of many researchers in other developing countries:

> The most characteristic feature of the authority system is its centralization. In more traditional Mexican firms, it is the centralization of all power in the one top man who is simultaneously organizer, owner, manager, and the sole decision-maker. Here, management is a person, not a position, concept, or function. Authority, likewise, resides in this person and is not spread throughout a managerial organization for, indeed, no such organization exists. . . . The Mexican manager [says Davis's interviewee] . . . would delegate work but not authority.[29]

The influence of sociological, economic, cultural, and psychological factors in bringing about such a high degree of centralization has been underscored by many cross-cultural researchers. Among the factors identified, the following are mentioned frequently:

the owner-manager situation
the lack of trust and confidence in subordinates
the low level of education among subordinates
child-parental relationships
the psychological make-up of the people in developing countries (more authority-dependent, as well as particularistic and less achieving motivation)

Referring to the owner-manager situation in Mexico, Davis reports:

> No matter how highly placed a traditional employee may be, he still lacks the functional prerequisite to his office, namely,

authority of his own. This is because of the intimate bond
between ownership and authority in Mexican enterprise. The
notion was well expressed by one engineer who simply said,
"If the men who give the orders were not the owners, they
could not give the orders." The owner is the ultimate and often
only source of authority in the firm.[30]

Similarly, McMillan's study in Brazil indicates:

> [The] Brazilian industrialist of the mid-twentieth century is
> the family owner-manager . . . he is less a promoter of his
> business interests and more a defender of his aristocratic
> class.[31]

Lauter, explaining the reasons for the high level of centralization
in Turkish industrial enterprises, states:

> Historically, the Turkish society has always been very authori-
> tarian. The authoritarian atmosphere permeated every phase
> of life from the family through the school to the government.
> It was probably the result of many divergent forces acting
> simultaneously. A Turkish psychiatrist, for example, hypothe-
> sized that over-protection, thus lack of independence in child-
> rearing practices in the family, could lead to passivity and
> dependence in adult life.[32]

Other social scientists, probing into the psychological characteristics of people in developing countries, have reinforced such
conclusions. Zurcher, using the Stouffer-Toby Role Conflict Scale
among 230 bank employees in Mexico, concluded that Mexicans
are significantly more particularistic than Mexican-Americans
who, in turn, are more particularistic than Anglo-Americans.[33]
Administrating the Thematic Apperception Test (TAT)
to subjects from industrially developed and underdeveloped countries, Josh found that subjects from industrial countries were more
insecure, non-conforming, experimental, and progressive, while
those from the underdeveloped countries were more secure, con-
forming, tradition-bound, conventional, and resistant to change.[34]
Sharma found that male Indian students were less dominant
(hence more dependent on authority) than were the Caucasian

Americans.[35] Similarly, Narain argues that Indian men are passive and submissive to authority.[36]

In my interviews with top- , middle- , and lower-level executives of American subsidiaries and local companies in the six developing countries studied, the impact of the following factors on centralization was frequently mentioned: the owner-manager situation; the seller's-market condition; the governmental interference and controls on imports of raw materials, machinery, foreign exchange, etc.; and the lack of experience with the delegation of authority.

The influence of the owner-manager situation has already been discussed, and the typical mentality of an owner-manager is well expressed by an executive in Uruguay: "I do not believe in anybody having anything to do with management except my own family. There is a clear distinction in my organization. My family is on one side, and the rest of the salaried and hourly personnel [are] on the other side."

Oberg has reported similar situations with respect to Brazil: "The family idea . . . is strong. You get a young fellow with ability and he works hard expecting to get ahead, and then comes the 20-year-old son of the owner and he is the boss."[37]

Coupled with the owner-manager situation, the seller's market provides much less incentive to the owner-manager to delegate authority to specialized and qualified employees. Under such a condition, huge profits are made regardless of cost and quality of products. However, the owner-manager takes this positive profit picture as a sign of his success as a manager or decision-maker. And why shouldn't he? After all, in a capitalist economy we preach that the primary role of the business enterprise is to "serve" its stockholders (the owner). As a sole stockholder, the owner-manager exactly does this. His only mistake is that he has not learned to distinguish between short-run and long-term profitability. Unfortunately the seller's market itself seems to be a "long-term" proposition in many of the developing countries.[38] To this matter, it is doubtful that, under a similar (seller's) market condition, the counterpart owner-manager in industrially developed countries will be able to distinguish between short-term and long-term objectives. (Consider the attitudes and pricing policies of a storekeeper in a small college town in the United States.)

In my opinion, the impact of the seller's market on managerial decision-making seems greater than any other environmental-cum-cultural factors mentioned by other writers.

Excessive governmental interference and control of pricing; the availability of foreign exchange, raw materials, machinery, and imports; and the subsequent need for centralization in decision-making in business enterprises in developing countries have been mentioned by many scholars. Notwithstanding the impact of certain environmental and cultural variables on decision-making, these factors by themselves cannot fully explain the high degree of centralization in industrial enterprises in underdeveloped countries.

A number of scholars have argued against overemphasizing this socio-cultural explanation. England, for example, has shown that managers per se are similar in their values in different countries; they are pragmatic rather than idealistic.[39] Haire's, Ghiselli's, and Porter's study of 14 countries indicates that managers desire more autonomy than they are presently given.[40] Especially with respect to developing countries, they found that managers in Argentina, Chile, and India were the most dissatisfied when it came to fulfillment of their autonomous needs. Sirota and Greenwood, in their large-scale study of industrial workers in 25 countries, report similar conclusions.[41] Commenting on the overemphasis on socio-cultural factors, they state:

> It is not only Americans who want money or Frenchmen who want autonomy or Germans who want their work skills utilized and improved. A management whose policies and practices reflect these stereotypes should be prepared to suffer the consequences of managing a frustrated and uncommitted work force whose apathy and anxieties it helped nurture.[42]

They go on to say:

> In this respect, it would be interesting to determine how much of the difficulty experienced in managing employees in other countries is due not to cultural differences at all, but rather,

to the automatic and psychologically self-serving assumption of differences that, in reality, may be minor or even non-existent.[43]

My findings suggest considerable interfirm differences in their decision-making processes. We will examine these findings in more detail in following sections.

Measures of Decentralization

To probe further into the actual decision-making process and the degree of decentralization observed in those companies studied, I collected specific information on a number of items: layers of hierarchy; the locus of decision-making with respect to major and functional policies and standards-setting for production supervisory and clerical employees; and the participation and information-sharing in the planning process. Let us examine these data in some detail.

Layers of Hierarchy

The layers-of-hierarchy measure corresponds with what many writers refer to as "levels of management." Hierarchy levels are counted from the operative level to the chief executive level. The number of levels were inferred from the organization charts of the companies. Whenever such charts were not available, I asked the high-level (top of high-middle level) executive to write out such an authority-structure chart for me.

I fully realize that this factor by itself is a crude measure for inferring the degree of decentralization in decision-making. Combined with other factors discussed below, however, it does provide insight into the amount of decentralization among the companies.

To carry out my overall analyses, I first grouped the hierarchical levels into two categories: (1) 4 to 7 layers and (2) 8 to 15 or more layers.

Data presented in Table 5-1 show no striking differences between American subsidiaries in Latin American and Far Eastern countries.[44] More than two-thirds of the firms in both regions

Table 5-1

Organizational Structure

Organizational concern for publics: Argentina, Brazil, Uruguay

Structure of hierarchy:	Overall		Much concern		Moderate concern		Little concern	
	U.S.	Local	U.S.	Local	U.S.	Local	U.S.	Local
4 to 7 layers	15	15	1	1	14	13	—	1
8 to 15 more layers	5	2	1	—	4	2	—	—
Total	20	17	2	1	18	15	0	1

Organizational concern for publics: India, Philippines, Taiwan

4 to 7 layers	30	21	12	9	17	11	1	1
8 to 15 more layers	6	17	—	2	4	7	2	8
Total	36	38	12	11	21	18	3	9

have 4 to 7 layers of hierarchy. There seems to be a significant difference between local companies in the two regions. Approximately 90 percent of the local firms in Latin America claim to have 4 to 7 layers, compared to 60 percent of these in the Far East.

Strictly interpreted, these results indicate that the local firms in Latin American countries are as decentralized as their American counterparts and more decentralized than local firms in the Far East. However, my interviews with lower levels of personnel in the two regions suggest, first, greater degrees of authority differences, and second, authority overlap among local companies in Latin America. Thus a "flat" structure in those companies apparently does not mean more delegation of authority.

Furthermore, the owner-manager situation is somewhat stronger among the local Latin American companies. As was discussed above, the owner-manager tends to retain the decision-making power in his own hands.

Decentralization Indices

In order to better understand the actual decentralization in decision-making practiced by the American subsidiaries and local firms in both the Latin American and Far Eastern countries, I devised two different decentralization indices: an overall decentralization index for all companies studied, regardless of size, technology, and industrial category; and an index for American subsidiaries and local firms in a single country, namely India.

The first decentralization index is used to gain an overall perspective regarding the degree of decentralization practiced in American subsidiaries versus that practiced by the local firms in both regions. This index is also useful in examining differences between "high concern," "moderate concern," and "low concern" firms.

The second index is used to probe further into the impact of technology, size, ownership, and "organizational concern" variables on the degree of decentralization. This index is then used to examine the relationship between the degree of decentralization in decision-making and a firm's effectiveness.

Overall Decentralization Index

Five factors were evaluated in computing the index:
1. major policy-making
2. participation and information-sharing in the planning process
3. decision-making in the selection and promotion of managerial and supervisory personnel
4. decision-making in setting standards for production employees
6. decision-making in setting standards for clerical and supervisory personnel

To gain a comparative perspective on the degree of decentralization practiced in different firms, a simple scaling of the above factors was undertaken. I categorized decision-making into two groups, consultative and nonconsultative.

A consultative type of decision-making simply means some sort of involvement of functional managers and lower-level employees in decision-making, whether in the form of a committee or individually. A nonconsultative type means that, by and large, the chief executive or owner-manager keeps decision-making in his own hands.

For the consultative type I gave a score of 0, and for the nonconsultative type a score of 1. Then the percentage of the firms under both categories was multiplied by the respective scores. The sum of these five factors was added to give an overall score of decentralization, the overall score ranging from a minimum of 0 to the maximum of 500. Obviously the lower the score, the higher the degree of decentralization in decision-making, and vice versa.

Judging from the data presented in Table 5-2, it is clear that neither the American subsidiaries nor the local firms as a group reach the level of "most decentralized." These data, then, confirm the overall observation of many cross-cultural management researchers—that industrial enterprises in underdeveloped countries are centralized.

My data, however, also show some interfirm differences. Looking at the total score in Table 5-2, we find that the American subsidiaries in Far Eastern countries are relatively more decentralized than their counterparts in Latin America, while the local firms are relatively more centralized in both regions.

Second, these data also show that firms having "high concern" for their publics are relatively more decentralized than those showing "moderate" and "low concern." Interestingly, the most centralized firms are those with "low concern" for their publics. Put differently, my results indicate that the degree of decentralization in a firm is more a function of managerial policy than a culturally stimulated phenomenon.

THE IMPACT OF SIZE, TECHNOLOGY, AND MARKET CONDITIONS ON DECENTRALIZATION

As was noted earlier, several writers seem to have demonstrated the influence of size, technology, and market conditions on the

Table 5-2
The Decision-Making Process

Items	Latin American countries		Far Eastern countries		Organizational concern for publics		
	U.S. %	Local %	U.S. %	Local %	Much %	Moderate %	Little %
1. Major policy-making:							
Consultative	25	18	65	23	65	30	0
Non-Consultative	75	82	35	77	35	70	100
2. Participation and information-sharing in planning process:							
Consultative	55	36	71	40	70	52	0
Non-Consultative	45	64	29	60	30	48	100
3. Selection and promotion of managerial and supervisory personnel:							
Consultative	35	52	33	40	58	37	18
Non-Consultative	65	48	67	60	42	63	72
4. Standards-setting for production employees:							
Consultative	60	52	83	57	85	54	24
Non-Consultative	40	48	17	43	35	46	76
5. Standards-setting for clerical and supervisory personnel:							
Consultative	15	18	48	28	60	28	0
Non-Consultative	85	82	52	72	40	32	100
Total score of 5 items rank*	310	326	200	312	202	299	438

*The total score is derived by multiplying "consultative" percents for each item by 0 and "nonconsultative" percents by 1 and adding up the score of all items given in the table.

level of decentralization in decision-making.[45]

To explore the relationships among these factors, I undertook a detailed analysis of 15 closely paired American subsidiaries and local firms in a single country—India.

First, the firms were divided according to Woodward's technological classifications of process, mass, and unit production.[46] A comparison of decentralization indices for the three types of firms showed no significant differences, according to the Kruskal-Wallis test.

Firm size, as measured by the number of employees, was found significantly related to the degree of decentralization practiced. Spearman's rank correlation coefficient between these two variables was 0.50.

Market Condition, Decentralization, and Organizational Effectiveness[47]

To examine the influence of market conditions on decentralization and organizational effectiveness, I first divided my sample of 15 American subsidiaries and 15 Indian firms into three categories according to the competition faced by each firm. The following information was collected for this purpose:

1. the degree of price competition among manufacturers of similar products
2. the degree of delay in securing a product
3. number of alternatives available to the consumer

On the basis of this information, the following three descriptive categories were created to represent the different degrees of market competition in which the various firms in my sample were operating: highly competitive market; moderately competitive market; seller's market or noncompetitive market.

Firms operating in a highly competitive market faced severe price competition from other manufacturers of similar products. At the same time, the consumer did not experience any delay in securing needed products (the products could be picked from the shelves), and the number of alternatives available to the consumer varied from five to 20. Firms in this category manufactured pharmaceutical products, sewing machines, and soft drinks.

Firms operating in a moderately competitive market experienced little price competition. There was no delay in securing the product, and the consumer had two to four substitutable products available in the same marketplace. Firms facing this market condition were manufacturing cosmetics, electric bulbs, and canned products.

Firms operating in a seller's market experienced no price competition, the consumer (in most cases, industrial consumers) had to wait for six months to two years to secure the product, and there were no real alternatives available to him. Firms operating in this market condition were manufacturing automobiles, trucks, and heavy industrial machinery.

To explore the impact of decentralization on the organizational effectiveness of the firms under differing market conditions, I first classified the firms in my sample according to (1) the competitivenes of their markets and (2) their degrees of decentralization, resulting in the 3 × 3 matrix shown in Table 5-4. The effectiveness indices (both behavioral and economic) were then averaged for the firms in each of the nine resulting categories. The average index is listed in the appropriate cells of the matrix, along with the number of firms used in computing them. As may be seen from this matrix, the relatively decentralized firms operating in highly competitive markets were relatively effective (average index of 1.32 and 1.00 in behavioral and economic terms, respectively). On the other hand, the relatively centralized firms in highly competitive markets were considerably less effective (average index of 2.60 and 2.25). Under these competitive conditions, firms with an intermediate degree of decentralization were in between the above two extremes on effectiveness. These results lend considerable support to the contention that, under relatively competitive market conditions, decentralized firms are likely to be more effective than centralized ones.

Contrary to my expectations, however, a similar pattern was found operating under noncompetitive market conditions. As may be seen from the third column of the matrix in Table 5-4, the average organizational effectiveness index (both behav-

Table 5-3

Market Competitiveness, Decentralization, and Effectiveness

Firm no.	Market Conditions	Decentralization Index	Effectiveness: behavioral	economic
1	highly	1.2	1.1	1.0
2	competitive	1.6	1.4	1.0
3		1.2	1.1	1.0
4		1.8	2.1	2.0
5		1.9	1.9	1.5
6		2.0	2.5	2.5
7		1.7	2.0	1.5
8		2.8	2.5	3.0
9		1.4	1.9	1.0
10		2.4	2.7	1.5
11		1.2	1.1	1.0
12		1.3	1.1	1.0
29		1.7	1.9	2.5
30		1.8	1.7	1.0
13	moderately	1.8	1.9	2.0
14	competitive	3.0	3.0	2.0
15		2.9	2.5	2.0
16		3.0	2.9	2.0
27		2.1	2.0	2.0
28		1.6	2.0	1.5
17	non-	1.6	1.4	1.0
18	competitive	2.5	2.5	1.5
19		1.8	2.4	1.5
20		1.8	1.3	1.0
21		2.2	2.3	1.0
22		1.1	1.1	1.0
23		1.5	1.6	1.0
24		2.2	2.1	1.0
25		2.3	2.1	1.5
26		2.0	2.0	1.5

ioral and economic) was again greatest in decentralized firms. However, these differences in effectiveness between centralized and decentralized firms were noticeably smaller than under competitive market conditions.

A similar increase of effectiveness accompanied increasing decentralization under moderately competitive conditions, al-

Table 5-4

Relationships Between Indices of Market
Competitiveness, Decentralization, and Effectiveness

Degree of Decentralization:	Market Conditions		
	Highly competitive	Moderately competitive	Non-competitive
high (index 1.0-1.6)	$E_b=1.32$ $E_e=1.00$ (n=6)	$E_b=2.00$ $E_e=1.50$ (n=1)	$E_b=1.37$ $E_e=1.00$ (n=3)
medium (index 1.9-2.0)	$E_b=2.13$ $E_e=1.88$ (n=4)	$E_b=1.90$ $E_e=2.00$ (n=1)	$E_b=1.80$ $E_e=1.50$ (n=4)
low (index 2.1-3.0)	$E_b=2.60$ $E_e=2.25$ (n=2)	$E_b=2.60$ $E_e=2.00$ (n=4)	$E_b=2.25$ $E_e=1.40$ (n=5)

Notes: E_b=average of effectiveness scores on behavioral criteria.

Notes: E_e=average of effectiveness scores on behavioral criteria.

though here this increase in effectiveness was slight (see second column of matrix in Table 5-4).

These results indicate that decentralization was also found to be functional in relatively noncompetitive markets.

ORGANIZATIONAL CONCERN AND DECENTRALIZATION

Last, to examine the relationships between a firm's concern toward its publics (for example, consumers, employees, suppliers, and distributors) and the degree of decentralization in decision-making utilized by that firm, I computed Spearman's rank correlation between the raw score on organizational concern (see Chapter 2) and the decentralization index (see Chapter 3) of the firm.

As shown in Table 5-5, the correlation coefficient between these two variables is 0.81, significant at .01 level.

Translated into actual managerial practices, these results show that the firms viewing their task agents or publics in long-term perspectives (showing "high concern") are more likely to have fewer layers of hierarchy in their organizational structures. They also opt for the consultative type of decision-making regarding major policies, sales, product mix, production, standards-setting, manpower policies, executive selection, and long-range planning.

In contrast, firms viewing their publics in short-term perspectives ("moderate" and "low concern") are likely to have more layers of hierarchy, and the chief executive or owner himself is making decisions concerning major and functional policies.[48]

DECENTRALIZATION AND ORGANIZATIONAL EFFECTIVENESS

Is decentralization or "participative management" dysfunctional in developing countries? Some of the cross-cultural researchers have argued in this vein, a viewpoint not supported by my findings, however.

To explore the relationship between decentralization and organizational effectiveness I devised two indices for evaluating organizational effectiveness: (1) a behavioral, or social, effectiveness index and (2) an economic and financial effectiveness index.

For the behavioral effectiveness index, the following factors were examined:

(a) ability to hire and retain high-level manpower
(b) employee morale and satisfaction in work
(c) turnover and absenteeism
(d) interpersonal relationship among superordinates and sub-ordinates
(e) interdepartmental relationships
(f) utilization of high-level manpower

For the economic effectiveness index, growth in sales and net profits during the last five years were evaluated.

Table 5-5

Organizational Concern, Decentralization, and Effectiveness

Firm no.	Organizational concern score	Decentralization Index	Effectiveness Index behavioral	economic
1	100	1.2	1.1	1.0
2	95	1.6	1.4	1.0
3	100	1.2	1.1	1.0
4	59	1.8	2.1	2.0
5	71	1.9	1.9	1.5
6	42	2.0	2.5	2.5
7	54	1.7	2.0	1.5
8	22	2.8	2.5	3.0
9	59	1.4	1.9	1.0
10	46	2.4	2.7	1.5
11	100	1.2	1.1	1.0
12	100	1.3	1.3	1.0
13	49	1.8	1.9	2.0
14	22	3.0	3.0	2.0
15	25	2.9	2.5	2.0
16	22	3.0	2.9	2.0
17	51	1.6	1.4	1.0
18	25	2.5	2.5	1.5
19	46	1.8	2.4	1.5
20	90	1.8	1.3	1.0
21	46	2.2	2.3	1.0
22	100	1.1	1.1	1.0
23	59	1.5	1.6	1.0
24	69	2.2	2.1	1.0
25	43	2.3	2.1	1.5
26	54	2.0	2.0	1.5
27	46	2.1	2.0	2.0
28	51	1.6	2.0	1.5
29	40	1.7	1.9	2.5
30	72	1.8	1.7	1.0

Spearman Rank Correlation Coefficient Results:

1. Scope of concern vs. Decentralization: 0.81
2. Decentralizing vs. effectiveness behavioral: 0.89
   economic: 0.62
   (all significant at p 0.01)

Details on the ranking of these measures and construction of indices are given in Table 3-8.

As is shown in Table 5-5, Spearman's Rank Correlation Coefficient between the decentralization index and the social or behavioral effectiveness index is 0.89, while between decentralization and economic effectiveness the index is 0.62. Both are significant as 0.01 level.

The lesser degree of relationship between decentralization and economic effectiveness underscores the influence of the existing seller's market in India. In such a situation it is easier to expand sales and generate profits in a desired manner. In spite of such market conditions, however, my results show that the decentralized firms are more effective in generating higher sales and profits than are the centralized enterprises.

SUMMARY

This chapter analyzed various aspects of the organizational set-up in American subsidiaries and local firms in the six developing countries. These include: grouping of activities, formalization and documentation of policies and procedures, authority definition and uses of organization charts, layers of hierarchy, allegation of authority, and decentralization in decision-making.

My findings indicate that both the American subsidiaries and local firms in these countries are organized on a functional basis (for example, production, sales, personnel). Line types of organizations are more popular in the local firms; only the American subsidiaries make use of specialized staff personnel.

Similarly, higher levels of formalization and documentation were quite evident among American subsidiaries in both Latin America and the Far East. Local companies, on the other hand, rely on verbal communication and informal relationships.

It was especially noticeable that an overlap in authority and a bypassing of authority frequently occurred in the local companies in both regions.

Relatively speaking, the degree of decentralization in decision-making is higher among American subsidiaries in the Far East. Local firms in both regions are more centralized than are the U.S. subsidiaries.

Notwithstanding the impact of such environmental factors as owner-manager situations, seller's-market conditions, governmental controls on prices and availability of raw materials, and foreign exchange on the delegation of authority, my findings suggest that the decentralization is more of a function of the firm's policy than the socio-cultural variables in those countries. Results also show that decentralization is not necessarily dysfunctional in developing countries.

Notes

1. Ernest Dale, *Organizations,* New York: American Management Association, 1967, p. 9.

2. James March and Herbert A. Simon, New York: Wiley, 1958. For criticism of this approach see H. Koontz, "Management Theory Jungle," *Academy of Management Journal,* vol. 4, no. 4 (December 1961), 174-88.

3. For examples of this approach see H. Koontz and C. O'Donnel, *Principles of Management: An Analysis of Management Functions,* 4th ed., New York: McGraw-Hill, 1968, chaps. 11-19.

4. Ernest Dale, *Planning and Developing the Company Structure, Research Report No. 20,* New York: American Management Association, 1952.

5. Dale, *op. cit.,* esp. pp. 289-91.

6. P. E. Holden, C. A. Pederson, and G. E. Germane, *Top Management,* New York: McGraw-Hill, 1968, pp. 5-6.

7. For a detailed study of the role of the director in the firm's management, see H. Koontz, *The Board of Directors and Effective Management,* New York: McGraw-Hill, 1967.

8. Allen Filley and Robert House, *Management Process and Organizational Behavior,* Glenview, Ill.: Scott, Foresman, 1969, pp. 212-320.

9. Z. H. K. Inkson et al., "A Comparison of Organization Structure and Managerial Roles: Ohio, U.S.A., and the Midlands, England," *Journal of Management Studies,* vol. 7, no. 3 (October 1970), 347-63.

10. Stephen A. Richardson, "Organizational Contrasts on British and American Ships," *Administrative Science Quarterly,* 1 (June 1956), 189-207.

11. *Ibid.,* pp. 206-207.

12. Stanley M. Davis, "Authority and Control in Mexican Enterprise," reprinted in his book, *Comparative Management: Organizational and Cultural Perspectives,* Englewood Cliffs, N.J.: Prentice-Hall, 1971, p. 181.

13. See, for example, Stanley M. Davis, "U.S. Versus Latin America: Business and Culture," *Harvard Business Review,* 47 (November-December 1969), 88-98; and M. Y. Yoshino, *Japan's Managerial System,* Cambridge, Mass.: MIT Press, 1968, pp. 9-11.

14. For the advantages of such a system of decision-making, see Peter Drucker, "What We Can Learn from Japanese Management," *Harvard Business Review,* vol. 49, no. 2 (March-April 1971), 110-22.

15. Elton Mayo, *The Social Problems of Industrial Organizations,* Cambridge, Mass.: Harvard Univ. Press, 1945.

16. See, for example, Rensis Likert, *The Human Organization: Its Management and Value,* New York: McGraw-Hill, 1967 and D. McGregor, *The Human Side of Enterprise,* New York: McGraw-Hill, 1960.

17. Joan Woodward, *Industrial Organizations: Theory and Practice,* London: Oxford Univ. Press, 1965.

18. Joan Woodward, "Technology, Material Control, and Organizational Behavior," in *Organizational Behavior Models,* ed. A. R. Negandhi and J. P. Schwitter, Kent, Ohio: Center for Business and Economic Research, Kent State University, 1971, p. 21.

19. Thomas Burns and G. M. Stalker, *Management of Innovation,* London: Tavistock Publications, 1961.

20. P. R. Lawrence and J. W. Lorsch, *Organization and Environment,* Homewood, Ill.: Richard D. Irwin, 1969. For further elaboration of their work, linking environmental factors with structure and individual behavior, see Jay W. Lorsch, "Environment, Organization, and the Individual," in *Environmental Settings in Organizational Functioning,* ed. A. R. Negandhi, Kent, Ohio: Center for Business and Economic Research, Kent State University, 1971, pp. 35-48.

21. Harbison and C. A. Myers, *Management in the Industrial World,* New York: McGraw-Hill, 1959.

22. Stanley M. Davis, "Authority and Control in Mexican Enterprise" and "Politics and Organizational Underdevelopment in Chile," reprinted in his book, *Comparative Management,* Englewood Cliffs, N.J.: Prentice-Hall, 1971, pp. 173-87, 188-209.

23. Albert Lauterbach, *Enterprise in Latin America,* Ithaca, N.Y.: Cornell Univ. Press, 1966.

24. G. Peter Lauter, "Sociological-Cultural and Legal Factors Impeding Decentralization of Authority in Developing Countries," *Academy of Management Journal,* vol. 12, no. 3 (September 1969), 367-78.

25. Thomas Roberto Fillol, *Social Factors in Economic Development: The Argentine Case,* Cambridge, Mass.: MIT Press, 1963, p. 76.

26. F. C. Flores, Jr., "Applicability of American Management Know-How to Developing Countries: The Case of the Philippines," unpub. Ph. D. dissertation, Graduate School of Business Administration, University of California at Los Angeles, 1967.

27. W. F. Whyte, "Culture, Industrial Relations, and Economic Development: The Case of Peru," *Industrial and Labor Relations Review,* vol. 6, no. 2 (July 1963), 107.

28. Sagar Jain, "Old Style of Management," in *Managerialism for Economic Development,* ed. S. B. Prasad and A. R. Negandhi, The Hague: Martinus Nijhoff's, 1968, pp. 8-19.

29. Davis, *op. cit.,* p. 174.

30. *Ibid.*

31. Claude McMillan, Jr., "The American Businessman in Brazil," *MSU Business Topic* (Spring 1963), reprinted in *International Dimensions in Business,* East Lansing, Mich.: Division of Research, Graduate School of Business Administration, Michigan State University, 1966, p. 99.

32. Lauter, *op. cit.,* p. 374.

33. L. A. Zurcher et al., "Value Orientation, Role Conflict, and Alienation from Work: A Cross-Cultural Study," *American Sociological Review,* vol. 30, no. 4, pp. 539-48.

34. Vidya Josh, "Personality Profiles in Industrial and Preindustrial Cultures: A TAT Study," *Journal of Social Psychology,* 66 (1965), 101-11.

35. K. L. Sharma, "Dominance-Deference: A Cross-Cultural Study," *Journal of Social Psychology,* 79 (1969), 265-66.

36. D. Narain, "Indian National Character in the Twentieth Century," reprinted in Davis, *op. cit.,* pp. 245-54.

37. W. Oberg, "Cross-Cultural Perspectives on Management Principles," *Academy of Management Journal,* vol. 6, no. 2 (June 1963), 129-43.

38. For a detailed discussion of the impact of seller's-market conditions on management practices in developing countries, see A. R. Negandhi, "Advanced Management Know-How in Underdeveloped Countries," *California Management Review,* vol. 10, no. 3 (Spring 1968), 53-60.

39. George W. England, "Personal Value System Analysis as an Aid to Understanding Organizational Behavior: A Comparative Study in Japan, Korea, and the United States," paper presented at the Exchange Seminar on Comparative Organizations, Ersel, Netherlands, March 23-27, 1970. See also G. W. England and R. Lee, "Organizational Goals and Expected Behavior Among American, Japanese, and Korean Managers—A Comparative Study," *Academy of Management Journal,* vol. 14, no. 4 (December 1971), 425-38.

40. M. Haire, E. E. Ghiselli, and L. W. Porter, *Managerial Thinking: An International Study,* New York: Wiley, 1966, esp. p. 94.

41. David Sirota and J. Michael Greenwood, "Understanding Your Overseas Work Force," *Harvard Business Review,* vol. 49, no. 1 (January-February 1971), 53-60.

42. *Ibid.,* p. 60.

43. *Ibid.*

44. Through his study in Chile, Wright claims that the American subsidiaries have more hierarchical layers than those of local companies. However, in counting such layers, he seems to have included line as well as staff positions. My data on hierarchical levels refer to line positions only. See Richard W. Wright, "Organizational Ambiente: Management and Environment in Chile," *Academy of Management Journal,* March 1971, p. 71.

45. For various studies of the influence of size, technology, and market conditions on decentralization in decision-making, see papers by J. Lorsch, D. Pugh, and Joan Woodward, in A. R. Negandhi, ed., *Modern Organizational Theory, and Effectiveness,* Kent, Ohio: Kent State University Press, 1973.

46. Joan Woodward, *Industrial Organization: Theory and Practice,* London: Oxford Univ. Press, 1965.

47. For details see A. R. Negandhi and B. D. Reimann, "A Contingency Theory of Organization Reexamined in the Context of a Developing Country," *Academy of Management Journal,* vol. 15, no. 2 (June 1972), 137-46.

48. *Ibid.*

CHAPTER 6

LEADERSHIP

Both the concept and function of leadership have sustained the consuming interest of management-organization theorists, as well as practicing managers. Recent remarks by Miles and Ritchie concerning participative management underscore this concern:

> The theory of participative management has shown a remarkable facility for holding the spotlight of debate in the management literature. . . . [However] it is often clever direction and staging rather than substance which sustains audience interest.[1]

In spite of such widespread interest, the leadership concept is the least understood variable in the management-organization literature. A great deal of confusion exists on two major issues: (1) the distinction between delegation of authority and the various types of leadership roles and (2) the impact of different styles of leadership on employee satisfaction, productivity, and management effectiveness.

In this book I distinguish the concepts of delegation of authority and leadership as follows: the degree of authority delegation spells out the scope of decision-making at each organizational level. A high degree of authority delegation suggests that a greater number of organizational decisions are made at lower levels of management; a low degree of authority delegation suggests that a greater number of decisions are made at higher levels.

In management and organization theory literature, the concept of centralization and decentralization of authority is widely used to explain the degree of authority delegation in a given organization. In contrast to authority delegation, the concept of leadership conveys ways in which leaders motivate and influence the behavior of subordinates to achieve given goals or objectives.

In essence, then, delegation of authority and decentralization are the processes of decision-making, while leadership signifies the nature and kind of interpersonal relationships between the superordinate (leader) and the subordinate (follower). It is true that the line between these two concepts is thin and at times invisible, but conceptually and operationally they should be distinguished.

At the present stage of organization theory, many scholars have equated decentralized organizations with consultative leadership and centralized organizations with autocratic leadership. However, as Melcher has indicated, this may not necessarily be true.[2]

Each type of leadership role is compatible with varying degrees of authority delegation in a given organization. In other words, one can find an authoritarian leader in a decentralized organization and a consultative leader in a centralized organization.

LEADERSHIP THEORIES

As we have seen, a complex organization by its very nature necessitates the formalization of rules, policies, procedures, and processes to channel and direct diverse activities of many different individuals toward achieving overall organizational goals and objectives. In spite of such formalization, however, the need for an individual called *leader* is inevitable for influencing and motivating organizational participants. The hierarchical arrangement itself provides designated positions of the superordinate and the subordinate. As Selznick has indicated, in modern, complex organizations, leadership itself is institutionalized.[3]

Realizing the importance of a leader in the functioning of an organization, social scientists have probed into the psychological traits of individuals, as well as work environment situations, to find the "right" qualities of a leader. There are three types of leadership theories generally recognized in the literature: trait theory, behavioral theory, and situational theory.[4] Trait theorists look for the identifiable and distinguishable characteristics, or personality profile of the leader. Behavioral theorists emphasize the behavior patterns of the leaders and typify leaders as autocratic, supportive, participative, etc.[5] The situational theorists attempt to combine both situational factors (task requirements and environmental conditions surrounding a given task) and the traits of the leaders.[6]

A leader's behavior can be classified in various ways. A leader may be authoritarian, persuasive, participative,[7] or as Jennings[8] has typified him, he may be autocrat, democrat, or bureaucrat. Perhaps Sirota's classification of leadership behavior is simple and yet more expressive.[9] According to him, a leader, in order to influence and motivate followers, may "tell," "sell," "consult," or "join" his subordinates to undertake or execute specific tasks or activities. The actual behavior patterns of each of these types is as follows:

Manager A ("tells"): Usually makes his decisions promptly and communicates them to subordinates clearly and firmly. He expects them to carry out decisions loyally and without causing difficulty.

Manager B ("sells"): Usually makes decisions promptly, but before going ahead, tries to explain them fully to subordinates. He gives them the reasons for decisions and answers whatever questions they have.

Manager C ("consults"): Usually consults with his subordinates before he reaches his decision. He listens to their advice, considers it, and then announces his decision. He then expects all to work loyally to implement it, whether or not it is in accordance with the advice they gave.

Manager D ("joins"): Usually calls a meeting of his subordinates when there is an important decision to be made. He puts the problem before the group and invites discussion. He accepts the majority viewpoint as the decision.[10]

THE AMERICAN PERSPECTIVE

Historically the frontier world of the continental United States imbued its immigrants with a sense of egalitarianism and populist aspirations. These aspirations eventually took the form of a democracy. These lofty aspirations did not remain untouched, even in the industrial life of the nation. The Western Electric experiment,[11] McGregor,[12] Likert,[13] and Argyris,[14] to name a few, have, through their own studies, indoctrinated managers and nonmanagers alike in the virtue of democratic or participative leadership. Indeed, such indoctrination is so widespread that, as Miles and Ritchie have remarked, " . . . most managers consider [autocratic] style to be socially undesirable and few will admit adherence to it in concept or practice."[15]

Realistically, however, in the American companies all sorts of leadership styles are being used, although lip service is always given to the uses and virtues of the participative type of leadership. To quote Miles and Ritchie once again:

> Many if not most of our institutions and organizations are still so structured and operated that this style is alive and well today in our society. Many schools, hospitals, labor unions, political parties, and a substantial number of business enterprises frequently behave, particularly at the lower levels, in a manner which can only be described as autocratic. Thus even though their policy statements have been revised and some participative trappings have been hung about, the main thrust of their activity is not greatly changed from what it was twenty, thirty, perhaps fifty years ago—they behave in a traditional [autocratic] manner toward the structure and direction of work. Further, the assumptions of the traditional model are . . . still widely held and espoused in our society—the rhetoric has improved, but the intent is the same.[16]

That the participative style, as expounded by Likert, McGregor, and others, may not be universal or functional is supported by many recent studies. The situational theory of Fiedler is one example.[17] In his studies of leadership he found that certain situations demand a democratic type of leadership, while in others, autocratic leadership may be more appropriate.

A recent study by Sirota and Greenwood in 25 countries also indicates some doubt about the universality of participative leadership. Commenting on participative management, Sirota argues:

. . . This emphasis on autonomy may be little more than a projection of the theorists' own goals that stem from their own professional environments—especially those with tasks that are routinized and predictable—high degrees of autonomy may be neither desired nor appropriate.[18]

Although bureaucratic and/or autocratic styles have been associated with oppressive types of management (leadership), which may reduce the commitment, morale, satisfaction, and productivity of employees, a recent study by Kohn casts doubts on such generalizations:

Observers of bureaucracy, impressed by its need to coordinate many people's activities, may assume that a primary effect of bureaucratization must be to suppress employees' individuality. We have grounds, to the contrary, that bureaucratization is consistently, albeit not strongly, associated with greater intellectual flexibility, higher evaluation of self-direction, greater openness to new experience, and more personally responsible moral standards.[19]

In emphasizing the advantages of bureaucracy, Kohn goes on to say:

[In] bureaucracies . . . superordinates cannot dismiss subordinates at will, and questionable actions can be appealed to adjudicatory agencies. [On the other hand] the power of non-bureaucratic organizations over their employees is more complete and may be more capricious. Thus, the alternative to bureaucracy's circumscribed authority is likely to be not less authority, but personal, potentially arbitrary authority.[20]

Of course, countless numbers of supporters of participative or consultative leadership have provided their own impressive list of empirical findings. Space permits me to cite only a few of these studies. Likert, for example, has shown that his type IV management (leadership) style (supportive) leads to higher employee morale, satisfaction, and productivity.[21] Chris Argyris has argued that the mature and healthy individual operates more effectively with lesser amounts of bureaucratic controls.[22] Similarly, Tannenbaum has shown that the more total influence everyone has in the system, the greater the total system efficiency.[23] Fleishman and Harris have noted that "the more the leader structures, directs, and controls, the greater the probability of turnover."[24] Argyle, Gardner, and Coffee have shown that the directive (autocratic) leadership produces higher absenteeism.[25]

FINDINGS IN 15 U.S. PARENT COMPANIES

My interviews with top, middle, and lower levels of executives in 15 parent companies revealed that the language of "Y" theory of management and participative and consultative management has been learned well by all levels of executives. Their actual practices, however, especially in the eyes of their subordinates, fell below their declared commitments. Only a few (6 out of 40) of the executives interviewed openly declared dissatisfaction with the consultative leadership role and argued in favor of the autocratic style.

I found that a majority of the companies have adopted what Miles calls a "human relations approach" rather than a "human resource approach." Under the "human relations approach," as Miles argues, superordinates go through the motions of calling meetings and listening to the subordinates' views before making decisions.[26] The degree and spirit of participative leadership varies widely under this approach.

Under the "human resource approach" label, the emphasis is on developing individual employees through participative leadership. As was mentioned, only a handful of executives actually practice this approach. However, I did not come across any instances of what Kohn calls "personal and arbitrary authority" either.[27] Thus the overall leadership style practiced in the 16 U.S. parent companies can be best classified as *semi-consultative*.

CROSS-CULTURAL PERSPECTIVE

As was the case with the centralization-decentraliziation issue, the leadership function is fertile ground for cross-cultural management theorists. Leadership styles have been investigated in a wide range of countries, developed and underdeveloped. The overriding conclusion seems straightforward: leadership style in communist countries is bureaucratic-autocratic;[28] in underdeveloped countries, autocratic-paternalistic;[29] and in European countries, autocratic.[30] It is impossible and perhaps unnecessary for our purposes to review the large number of studies, mostly opinons, concerning leadership styles in these countries. Let us, however, review a few typical studies in order to provide some perspective for our own findings in six developing countries.

Clark and McCabe have argued that American managers have a more favorable attitude toward the average person's capacity for leadership and initiative than do British and Australian managers.[31] Supporting these findings, Maier and Hoffman have shown that British managers are more attuned to an authoritarian style of leadership than are American managers.[32]

Hartman has shown that German managers by and large are authoritarian.[33] Crozier has shown that French managers are bureaucratic-autocratic.[34]

Turning to the developing nations, Meade and Whittaker,[35] as well as Thiagarajan,[36] have indicated that Indian managers are more authoritarian compared to those of other countries. Meade has further argued that in India morale and productivity were higher under authoritarian leadership than under the democratic style.[37]

More systematic studies in 14 countries by Haire, Ghiselli, and Porter, also show the trend in this direction.[38] That is, developing countries are negatively inclined toward participative leadership. Similarly, Williams has shown that Peruvian managers are primarily authoritarian.[39] Davis has argued the same point for Chilean and Mexican managers.[40] Fillol has shown similar results for Argentina.[41]

THE SOCIO-CULTURAL EXPLANATION

Probing the reasons for authoritarian leadership style in many countries, mostly the underdeveloped, sociologists and cultural anthropologists have provided explanations in terms of socio-cultural variables. To a great extent, cross-cultural theorists have relied on the explanations provided by their "pure"colleagues, the sociologists and social anthropologists. It is therefore appropriate to review briefly what these scholars have to say.

Based on the value analysis, a well-respected sociologist,

Seymour Lipset has argued that American society is egalitarian and populist compared to Great Britain, which is deferential and elitist.[42] Canada and Australia, according to him, fall in between these two extremes. The reasons for these differing national values are explained through the writings of deTocqueville[43] and Bagehot.[44] For example, Lipset states:

> A society in which the historic ties of traditional legitimacy had been forcibly broken could only sustain a stable democratic policy if it emphasized equality and if it contained competitive institutions.[45]

Conversely, he argues:

> If the privileged classes perished and continued to expect ascriptive (aristocratic) and elitist rights, a society could only have a stable democracy if the lower classes accepted the status system.[46]

In characterizing American versus British national values, Lipset writes:

> More than any other modern, non-communist industrial nation, the United States emphasizes achievement, equalitarianism, universalism, and specificity. . . . Unlike America, Britain has come to accept the values of achievement in its economic and educational system but retains the assumptions inherent in elitism: Persons in high positions are given generalized deference. In Britain, moreover, it is felt that those born to a high place should retain it.[47]

In tracing the consequences of these differing national values in industrial life, Lipset says:

> In societies characterized by ascription, elitism, particularism, and diffuseness . . . men must stay in their class position and they will be treated by others and treat each other diffusely in terms of class status . . . [in contrast] American values reject treating an individual in terms of a diffuse status, but support interaction with him in terms of his role as worker in one situation, as suburban dweller in another, as a member of the American Legion in a third, and so forth.[48]

LATIN AMERICAN AND FAR EASTERN COUNTRIES

Turning to the countries studied in this book, we find Lipset's observations about Britain equally applicable to Latin America and the Far East.

Sociologist Stanley Davis suggests that the Latin culture is not based on equalitarianism, but has its own version of Britain's elitism and particularism.[49] Specifically, Davis reports:

> Both the North American and Latin American countries have a strong sense of individuality, but the word "individuality" itself means something different in each case. . . . The U.S. executive's notion of individuality stresses a basic equality of people. His belief is that each person has (or should have) equal rights, an equal job opportunity, an equal chance to find his own place in the sun . . . on the other hand, to the Latin sense of individuality, the notion that "each person is just as good as the next" is untrue, irrelevant, and contradictory.[50]

To the Latin American, individuality means, as Gillin has remarked, each individual is unique.[51] Nevertheless, this unique personality and the dignity of the individual are in harmony with the unequal status of boss-worker, master-servant relationships.

This differing sense of individuality between North and South American, according to Davis, has direct consequences for working in a group (democratic manner) situation. In North America, Davis argues, group participation is undertaken with the view of achieving harmony and developing a cooperative spirit, while in Latin America, group (mostly family) participation is viewed as "protective environment, a sanctuary in which the unique identity of each individual is valued, supported, and enhanced rather than absorbed and assimilated into a single group identity."[52]

Similarly, in the Far Eastern countries, sociologists and social and cultural anthropologists have underscored the deferential, elitist, and particularistic cultural characteristics of these societies through their analyses of caste and class systems in India and the Confucian philosophy in China and Japan.[53] As these social scientists argue, dependence on authority, reverence for age, and "boss" authority are only the outer manifestations of basic socio-cultural traits in these societies.

Against this background, let us examine the actual leadership styles being used in American subsidiaries and their local counterparts in Latin America and the Far East. Following the analysis of leadership data, we will examine the changing attitudes and expectations of both managerial and nonmanagerial personnel in these countries. Last, we will evaluate the impact of socio-cultural traits on leadership style.

LEADERSHIP STYLES USED IN THE AMERICAN SUBSIDIARIES AND LOCAL COMPANIES IN THE SIX DEVELOPING COUNTRIES

Method of Data Collection

To infer leadership style in the companies studied, I interviewed five to six pairs of superordinate-subordinates in each company, asking them a series of informal, unstructured questions about their perception of their immediate superiors' leadership styles. At the beginning of the scheduled interview, in order to arrive at a common definition of different leadership styles, we chatted informally about the interviewer's notion of autocratic or authoritarian, democratic or consultative, bureaucratic and paternalistic leadership styles. At the end of this conversation, I gave the following definitions of each leadership style:

Authoritarian style is one in which the superior dominates the views of his subordinates and gives orders for carrying out specific tasks.

Democratic style is one in which the superior relies heavily on the opinion of his subordinates and encourages free discussion among subordinates.

Bureaucratic style is one in which the superior puts emphasis on the rules, regulations, procedures, and his own superior's "word" before making decisions. "Follow the book" is the motto in this style.

Paternalistic style is one in which the superior assumes the role of "father figure" and has strong personal and emotional ties to his subordinates.

I also inquired about the level of trust and confidence immediate superiors placed in their subordinates. Here I reversed the process and asked each immediate superior what he thought of the abilities and potential of his subordinates.

Leadership Style

Overall, my inquiry seems to confirm the prevailing belief that the leadership style in the local enterprises in developing countries is autocratic and paternalistic. American subsidiaries, however, appeared to be more in tune with the participative or democratic style; approximately 55 percent of the companies studied attempted to use such a leadership style. The outer manifestations of participative style were observable not only in the existing informal, cordial relationships between superordinates and subordinates, but also in the number of meetings scheduled, the agenda for such meetings, and the freedom of discussion of the issues involved.

On the other hand, the prevailing style of leadership in the local companies can best be characterized as authoritarian-paternalistic. As was mentioned earlier, an authoritarian leader attempts to influence and motivate his subordinates through issuing "order" and reserving all privileges of decision-making in his own hands. A paternalistic leader, while basically autocratic, carries a sense of family, or kindred relationship, with regard to his subordinates.

Interregional Comparison

There are some differences between the leadership approach found in the Latin American and Far Eastern countries. Such differences are more pronounced among American subsidiaries in these two regions. As Table 6-1 shows, 65 percent of the American subsidiaries in Latin America practice participative leadership. The corresponding figure for the Far Eastern nations is 48 percent.

I cannot say for sure whether differences among American companies in these two regions are due to socio-cultural differences. My observations indicate the following: First, managers of American subsidiaries in Latin American countries are still "real Americans" in two ways: (a) they are American-born and edu-

Table 6-1

Leadership Styles in American Subsidiaries and Local Companies in Two Regions

Organizational concern for publics: Latin America

Region leadership style:	Overall U.S.	local	Much U.S.	local	Moderate U.S.	local	Little U.S.	local
democratic	13	6	2	1	11	5	—	—
authoritarian	—	—	—	—	—	—	—	—
paternalistic	5	8	—	—	5	7	—	1
bureaucratic	1	1	—	—	1	1	—	—
not clear-cut	1	2	—	—	1	2	—	—
Total	20	17	2	1	18	15	0	1

Organizational concern for publics: Far East

	Overall U.S.	local	Much U.S.	local	Moderate U.S.	local	Little U.S.	local
democratic	17	9	10	6	6	3	1	—
authoritarian	—	—	—	—	—	—	—	—
paternalistic	13	22	2	2	10	11	1	9
bureaucratic	6	7	—	3	5	4	1	—
not clear-cut	—	—	—	—	—	—	—	—
Total	36	38	12	11	21	18	3	9

Summary Comparisons

Item	Percent of total firms in each category
Democratic style of leadership as perceived by the subordinates in:	
U.S. subsidiaries in both regions (n=56)	55%
U.S. subsidiaries in Latin American countries (n=20)	65
U.S. subsidiaries in Far Eastern countries (n=36)	48
Local companies in both regions (n=55)	28
Local companies in Latin American countries (n=17)	35
Local companies in Far Eastern countries (n=38)	25
"much concern" companies (n=26)	75
"moderate concern" companies (n=72)	35
"little concern" companies (n=13)	8

cated and (b) they are less influenced by Latin culture *per se*. In contrast, many managers of American subsidiaries in the Far East, especially in India (comprising roughly 50 percent of the total sample in this region), are British-born and educated.

Leadership Style and Organizational Concern

A firm's orientation toward its clientage group is more strongly associated with leadership style than with the ownership of the firm. For example, we see that approximately 75 percent of the firms manifesting "much concern" for their employees, consumers, distributors, suppliers, and other publics practice a participative style of leadership. In contrast, only 35 percent of the firms having "moderate" and 8 percent of the firms having "little concern" practice such leadership. These findings raise some interesting questions and cast doubt on the general notion held by many cross-cultural theorists that the underdeveloped countries are authoritarian societies. As we will see in a later section, the managerial attitudes, economic conditions, and employment opportunities available have much to do with the leadership style used in industrial enterprises in any society, developed or underdeveloped.

Trust and Faith in Subordinates

There are various shadings of participative leadership. It varies from a mere facade resulting in addressing subordinates by their first names and wearing a smile in even the worst situations to a genuine participation embodying the basic premise of developing individuals to their fullest physiological, psychological, and intellectual capacities. This latter type of participative leadership is referred by Argyris[54] as identifying and utilizing the "psychological energy" of employees and by Miles[55] as adopting the "human resource" (versus "human relations") approach in dealing with subordinates.

The type and degree of participative leadership can be seen in superiors' trust and confidence in the abilities of their subordinates. Many recent studies have shown that without the basic trust and confidence in subordinates, participative leadership (management) is nothing more than a hollow experience.

Haire, Ghiselli, and Porter, in their study of 14 countries, for example, show that although managers everywhere have been leaning toward participative, group-centered leadership (management), it is only in a few countries that they actually seem to have basic faith and trust in the abilities of their subordinates.[56] They state their findings in these words:

> There is universally more acceptance of what might be called higher order concepts of management [participative type] than there is of the basic conviction that the individual has initiative and leadership capacity.[57]

Further:

> Unless one believes in untapped capacity for leadership in subordinates, a classical unilateral directive management is best. Here we find a lack of basic confidence in others and at the same time a leaning toward participative group-centered management. . . . This is an unfortunate state of affairs. It is like building the techniques and practices of a Jeffersonian democracy on a basic belief in the divine rights of kings.[58]

Miles and Ritchie, in their recent study of participative management practices in American firms, found that the quantity and quality of participation are related to managers' feelings of satisfaction with their immediate superiors.[59] Managers whose superiors have relatively high trust and confidence scores are significantly more satisfied than are their colleagues whose superiors have relatively lower confidence and trust in their subordinates.

Turning to a developing country, Whyte has reported that "Peruvians are generally lacking in the trust that provides the social cement necessary for an effectively functioning organization."[60] He goes on to say:

> The prevailing pattern of centralization of control seems to be based upon beliefs that you cannot trust your subordinates to do the right things unless you watch them closely. Delegation of authority and responsibility requires a degree of faith in people that is not common in Peru.[61]

My interviews with superiors in the American subsidiaries and local firms in the six developing countries indicated considerable interfirm differences in attitudes toward subordinates' abilities. Generally the executives in American subsidiaries place much trust and confidence in their subordinates' abilities. Such trust and confidence are low in the local companies. There are no significant differences in this respect between countries in Latin American and Far Eastern regions. However, those companies (both American and local) categorized as having "much concern" toward their clientage groups are also "much" in trust and confidence. Those classified as "moderate" and "little concern" are low in trust and confidence.

The managerial leadership preferences and attitudes are not consistent, a fact also brought out in the questionnaire survey conducted in Taiwan.

Managerial Attitudes[62]

In order to assess the managerial attitudes toward participative and other leadership styles, I conducted a questionnaire survey among 75 (total universe) U.S. subsidiaries and 225 local firms in Taiwan. A series of indirect questions, patterned after Haire's, Ghiselli's, and Porter's questionnaire, were asked of the top- and middle-level executives.[63] Of the total 300 questionnaires distributed, 99 were filled out and returned. Of these, 23 were from American subsidiaries and 76 were from local firms. The questions and responses are summarized in Table 6-2.

As data in Table 6-2 show, 70 percent of the American and Chinese executives responding to the survey agree that human relations in Taiwan have an authoritarian and paternalistic flavor. It is interesting to note that a very small fraction of these managers disagree with this contention.

Similarly, a large majority of both the American (57 percent) and Chinese executives (49 percent) felt that the average human being prefers to be directed, wishes to avoid responsibility, and has relatively little ambition. In other words, these executives seem to have much less confidence and trust in the abilities and aspirations of their employees. Many executives also felt that leadership traits and abilities are basically inborn and cannot be acquired by everyone. Interestingly, more American executives (78 percent) than Chinese managers (45 percent) felt this way.

A considerable majority of the American (61 percent) and

Chinese executives (40 percent) also believed that the democratic style of mangement sounds good on paper but that, in order to achieve company goals, the executive must be assertive and dominate the views and thinking of lower-level managers. Executives interviewed in American subsidiaries in Taiwan, however, did not seem to feel this way. In fact, six of the nine U.S. subsidiaries seemed to be utilizing the consultative type of leadership.

As determined by related questions concerning the communication patterns utilized by managers and the perceived influence of subordinates on executives, more than one-third of American and Chinese executives felt that top Chinese executives communicate less to middle managers than do top-level American executives. Forty-eight percent of the American executives and 40 percent of the Chinese managers prefer interacting influences between subordinates and superordinates.

As was mentioned above, results of the questionnaire survey indicate mixed reactions. On one hand, we find confirmation of the prevailing paternalistic leadership style and philosophy in industrial enterprises in Taiwan. This is especially clear in the responses to questions 1, 2, and 5, outlined in Table 6-2. On the other hand, we also find American executives demonstrating less faith in the democratic style of leadership. This is particularly evident in the responses to questions 2, 5, and 6. At the same time, we also see the Chinese executives having second thoughts about the desirability of a paternalistic-autocratic style of management. They tend to swing on the other side of the pendulum and opt for a democratic style of leadership, or at least to agree in principle with such a leadership role.

In contrast to the survey results, companies studied through intensive interview methods show some definite patterns; American subsidiaries utilize consultative or democratic leadership style at the top level, while Japanese and Chinese managers are paternalistic and autocratic, respectively.[64]

The results from the companies studied through interviews reflect actual leadership styles being used; results obtained from the questionnaire survey show a managerial attitude toward the leadership role. The small size of my interview sample notwithstanding, I feel that differences in the two research results indicate differences between managerial attitudes and managerial practices. In other words, managerial attitudes are not consistent with their practices.

Managerial practices are ongoing phenomena and appropriate managerial attitudes must develop before they can be changed. If we interpret the survey results in this light, we can say that managerial attitudes are in a state of flux. That is, the Chinese executives are having doubts about the desirability of paternalistic leadership styles and are showing some interest in adopting consultative or democratic styles, while American executives desire adoption of the prevailing paternalistic-autocratic style. In summary, and in my opinion, these results show interacting influences at work in a cross-cultural setting where each counterpart is giving a closer look at the other's managerial system.[65]

My findings reporting the inconsistency between managerial attitudes and desired leadership style gibe with the results obtained by Haire, Ghiselli, and Porter in their 14-country study. They have argued that inconsistency may be due to the "partial digestion of 15 years of exhortation by the group-oriented consultants and professors of management."[66]

Socio-Cultural Variables and Leadership Style

In this final section, we will come back to the important question raised at the beginning of this chapter: "Is the leadership function culture-bound?" I do not pretend to have the complete answer to this question, but will attempt to raise some concern about the prevailing thesis of culture-boundness with the hope of clarifying this complicated and vital issue.

As was discussed earlier, many cross-cultural management theorists have advanced the thesis that the leadership style in developing countries is authoritarian-paternalistic and that this style is the result of their particular socio-cultural milieu. I refer to the studies of Harbison and Myers,[67] Meade and Whittaker,[68] and Haire, Ghiselli, and Porter.[69] The observation made by Barrett and Bass in their recent paper seems to typify the conclusions of these authors. They state:

> There are differences among countries in preferred styles of leadership. These differences in leadership styles appear to be

Table 6-2

**Managers' Attitudes on Leadership Role in American
Local Companies in Taiwan**

Attitude:	U.S. subsidiaries (n=23)			Local companies (n=76)		
	agree %	dis-agree %	no answer %	agree %	dis-agree %	no answer %
The human relations in Taiwan have an authoritarian and paternalistic flavor.	70	4	26	70	13	17
While democratic style of management sounds good on paper, in order to accomplish company goals year after year, top executives have to be assertive and dominate the views and thinking of other lower-level executives.	61	30	9	40	40	20
In a work situation, if the subordinates cannot influence me, then I lose some influence on them.	48	26	26	40	38	22

largely culturally based and at this point in time it would be naive to advocate one model of leadership style as being optimum for all cultural groups. The widely advocated American model of participative management may not be optimum for all cultures and in fact may be dysfunctional in some.[70]

Culture as a Residual Variable

In providing a cultural explanation, the scholars referred to above neither define "culture" as a variable nor isolate the

Table 6-2, cont'd.

Attitude:	U.S. subsidiaries (n=23)			Local companies (n=76)		
	agree %	dis-agree %	no answer %	agree %	dis-agree %	no answer %
Chinese executives communicate less to the "middle manager" than American executives and thereby save "executive time."	35	43	22	34	50	16
The average human being prefers to be directed, wishes to avoid responsibility, and has relatively little ambition.	57	39	4	49	27	24
Leadership skills can be acquired by most people regardless of their particular inborn traits and abilities.	17	78	5	43	45	12

This table reproduced from Anant R. Negandhi, *Management and Economic Development: The Case of Taiwan.* Permission of the publisher is gratefully acknowledged.

"socio-cultural" variables from the rest of the organizational and environmental variables. Even the more sophisticated and detailed study of Haire, Ghiselli, and Porter seems to have utilized culture as a residual variable. Under such circumstances it is difficult to argue for or against the cultural explanation. I would like to offer some alternative hypotheses at this stage, however, by separating environmental variables from socio-cultural variables.

My observations in the industrial enterprises—particularly

the local firms—in the six developing countries lead me to believe that the existing authoritarian-paternalistic style of leadership may be a function of the nature of the economic situation, the availability of employment opportunities, and the organizational philosophy, or concern, evidenced toward its clientage group, especially employees. The impact of organizational concern on leadership style used has already been discussed. We will now look at the impact of other factors.

The Nature of the Economic Condition

As was pointed out earlier, most of the developing countries are characterized by low per-capita income and poverty, high unemployment, excessive governmental controls, governmental interferences in the functioning of private enterprises, noncompetitive markets, and shortages of capital.

A more extensive study of managerial values by England shows that managers in all countries are pragmatic rather than idealistic.[71] Naturally, being pragmatic, they will do what in their opinion is best. Under excessive governmental controls on prices, imports, foreign exchange, etc., the manager may consider it wise to deal secretly with government officials regarding these factors and therefore not share his information with lower-level subordinates. Such a behavioral pattern will make him autocratic; nevertheless, he seems to have rationalized it on pragmatic—not cultural—grounds.

In a shortage of capital situation, it is only human to safeguard one's capital and not trust anybody, including employees. This again leads to autocratic decision-making as far as financial aspects are involved.

One might ask at this stage why employees in undeveloped countries accept this sort of managerial behavior. Cross-cultural theorists have argued that employees *prefer* such an autocratic style. For example, Haire, Ghiselli, and Porter have shown that managers in developing countries (Chile, Argentina, and India) find the concept "direct" (meaning autocratic leadership), more prestigious than the concept "persuade" (participative leadership).[72] Similarly, Williams and Whyte[73] have argued that the Peruvian employees prefer "firm" leaders.

Based on my observations in the six developing countries, I would make a distinction between what is accepted and what is preferred by the employees. Lower-level subordinates accept autocratic leaders simply because that is the only way they can hold on to their jobs. If jobs were plentiful and job security was guaranteed, most employees would prefer greater autonomy. A recent extensive study by Sirota and Greenwood[74] in 25 countries appears to support these views. They found that autonomy was ranged as one of the 10 goals of employees in all the countries studied. They also found differences in the rank-order of goals between different professions more pronounced than between different countries in a given profession.

Even Haire, Ghiselli, and Porter, who have otherwise offered a cultural explanation, found that the managerial need for autonomy was higher in Chile, Argentina, and India.[75]

In the same vein, Deasi, in his study of industrial workers in India, found that the blue-collar employees preferred cooperative, less authoritarian, supervisors.[76]

My own observations in the six developing countries are more in line with those of Sirota and Greenwood, Haire et al., and Deasi. In other words, I am of the opinion that the employees in developing countries prefer participative leadership, but that the actual leadership behavior practiced seems to be autocratic and paternalistic in nature at the present time.

Notes

1. Raymond E. Miles and J. B. Ritchie, "Participative Managements: Quality vs. Quantity," *California Management Review,* vol. 13, no. 4 (Summer 1971), 48.

2. Arlyn J. Melcher, "Participation: A Critical Review of Research Findings," unpub. manuscript, Kent State University.

3. Philip A. Selznick, *TVA and the Grass Roots,* Berkeley: Univ. of California Press, 1953.

4. For discussion on various theories on leadership see A. C. Filley and R. J. House, *Managerial Processes and Organizational Behavior,* Chicago: Scott, Foresman, 1969, pp. 392-96.

5. *Ibid.*

6. *Ibid.*

7. Thiagarajan and Deep have described these styles as follows: An *authoritarian leader* is one who uses his power of office to impose his decisions on his subordinates. The *persuasive leader* is one who uses logic and reasoning to influence subordinates, and the *participative leader* is one who is willing to share decision-making responsibilities equally with his subordinates. See K. M. Thiagarajan and Samuel D. Deep, "A Study of Supervisor-Subordinate Influence and Satisfaction in Four Cultures," *Journal of Social Psychology,* 82 (1970), 173.

8. Eugene E. Jennings, *The Executive: Autocrat, Bureaucrat, and Democrat,* New York: Harper and Row, 1962, esp. chaps. 5-7.

9. David Sirota, "International Survey of Goals and Beliefs," paper presented at the 16th International Congress of Applied Psychology, Amsterdam, Netherlands, 1968.

10. Sirota quoted from G. V. Barrett and B. M. Bass, "Comparative Surveys of Managerial Attitudes and Behavior," in *Comparative Management,* New York: Graduate School of Business Administration, New York Univ. Press, 1970, p. 183.

11. F. J. Roethlisberger and W. J. Dickson, *Management and the Worker,* Cambridge, Mass.: Harvard Univ. Press, 1939.

12. Douglas McGregor, *The Human Side of Enterprise,* New York: McGraw-Hill, 1960.

13. Rensis Likert, *Human Organization: Its Management and Value,* New York: McGraw-Hill, 1967, esp. p. 212.

14. Chris Argyris, *Personality and Organization,* New York: Harper and Row, 1957; *Integrating the Individual and the Organization,* New York: Wiley, 1964.

15. Miles and Ritchie, *op. cit.,* p. 50.

16. *Ibid.*

17. Fred E. Fiedler, *A Theory of Leadership Effectiveness,* New York: McGraw-Hill, 1967.

18. David Sirota and J. Michael Greenwood, "Understand Your Overseas Work Force," *Harvard Business Review,* vol. 49, no. 1 (January-February 1971), 60.

19. Melvin L. Kohn, "Bureaucratic Man: A Portrait and an Interpretation," *American Sociological Review,* 36 (June 1971), 472.

20. *Ibid.,* p. 473.

21. Likert, *op. cit.*

22. Argyris, *op. cit.*

23. A. S. Tannenbaum, *Control in Organizations,* New York: McGraw-Hill, 1968.

24. E. Gleishman and E. Harris, "Patterns of Leadership Behavior Related to Employee Grievances and Turnover," Department of Industrial Administration, Yale University, 1961, mimeographed.

25. M. Argyle, G. Gardner, and F. Coffee, "Supervisory Methods Related to Productivity Absenteeism and Labor Turnover," *Human Relations,* vol. 11, no. 1 (1958), 23-40.

26. R. Miles, "Human Relations or Human Resources," *Harvard Business Review,* vol. 43, no. 4 (July-August 1965), 148-63.

27. Kohn, *op. cit.*

28. See B. M. Richman, *Soviet Management,* Englewood Cliffs, N.J.: Prentice-Hall, 1965.

29. See respective chapters in F. Harbinson and C. Myers, *Management in the Industrial World,* New York: McGraw-Hill, 1959.

30. *Ibid.*

31. A. W. Clark and S. McCabe, "Leadership Beliefs of Australian Managers," *Journal of Applied Psychology,* 54 (1970), 1-6.

32. N. R. F. Maier and L. R. Hoffman, "Group Decision in England and the United States," *Personnel Psychology,* 15 (1962), 75-87.

33. H. Hartmann, *Authority and Organization in German Management,* Princeton, N.J.: Princeton Univ. Press, 1959.

34. M. Cruzier, *The Bureaucratic Phenomenon,* Chicago: University of Chicago Press, 1964; see also Cruzier's recent article, "The Cultural Determinants of Organizational Behavior," in *Environmental Settings in Organizational Functioning,* ed. A. R. Negandhi, Kent, Ohio: Kent State Univ. Press, 1970, pp. 49-58.

35. R. D. Meade and J. D. Whittaker, "A Cross-Cultural Study of Authoritarianism," *Journal of Social Psychology,* 72 (1967), 3-7.

36. Thiagarajan and Deep, *op. cit.*

37. R. D. Meade, "An Experimental Study of Leadership in India," *Journal of Social Psychology* (1967), 35–43.

38. M. Haire, E. E. Ghiselli, and L. W. Porter, *Managerial*

Thinking: An International Study, New York: Wiley, 1966.

39. L. K. Williams, W. F. Whyte, and C. S. Green, "Do Cultural Differences Affect Workers' Attitudes?", *Industrial Relations,* vol. 5, no. 3 (May 1966), 110.

40. Davis, *op. cit.*

41. Thomas R. Fillol, *Social Factors in Economic Development: The Argentine Case,* Cambridge, Mass.: MIT Press, 1963, p. 76.

42. Seymour M. Lipset, "The Value Patterns of Democracy: A Case Study in Comparative Analysis," *American Sociological Review,* vol. 28, no. 4 (August 1963), 515-31.

43. Alexis Charles de Tocqueville, *Democracy in America,* New York: Colonial Press, 1899.

44. Walter Bagehof, *The English Constitution,* London: M. W. Dunne, 1901.

45. Lipset, *op. cit.,* p. 516.

46. *Ibid.,* p. 517.

47. *Ibid.*

48. *Ibid.*

49. Stanley M. Davis, "U.S. Versus Latin America: Business and Culture," *Harvard Business Review,* 47 (November-December 1969), 88-98.

50. *Ibid.,* p. 89.

51. John Gillen, "The Middle Segments and Their Values," reprinted in Davis, *op. cit.,* pp. 130-32.

52. Davis, *op. cit.,* p. 91.

53. See various essays in *The Chinese Mind: Essentials of Chinese Philosophy and Culture; The Japanese Mind: Essentials of Japanese Philosophy and Culture; and The Indian Mind: Essentials of Indian Philosophy and Culture,* ed. Charles C. Moore, Honolulu: East-West Center Press, 1967.

54. C. Argyris, *Integrating the Individual and the Organization,* New York: Wiley, 1964, pp. 153-64.

55. R. Miles, *op. cit.*

56. Haire, Ghiselli, and Porter, *op. cit.*

57. *Ibid.*

58. *Ibid.*

59. Miles and Ritchie, *op. cit.,* p. 52.

60. William F. Whyte, "Culture, Industrial Relations, and Economic Development: The Case of Peru," *Industrial and Labor Relations Review,* vol. 16, no. 4 (July 1963), 587.

61. *Ibid.*

62. For more details on the questionnaire results, see A. R. Negandhi, *Management and Economic Development: The Case of Taiwan,* The Hague: Martinus Nijhoff's, 1972.

63. Haire, Ghiselli, and Porter, *op. cit.,* pp. 184-88.

64. Negandhi, *op. cit.,* chap. 5.

65. *Ibid.*

66. Haire, Ghiselli, and Porter, *op. cit.,* p. 98.

67. Harbison and Myers, *op. cit.*

68. Meade and Whittaker, *op. cit.*

69. Haire, Ghiselli, and Porter, *op. cit.*

70. G. V. Barrett and B. M. Bass, "Comparative Surveys of Managerial Attitudes and Behavior," in *Comparative Management: Teaching, Training, and Research,* ed. Jean Boddewyn, New York: Graduate School of Business Administration, New York Univ. Press, 1970.

71. George W. England, "Personal Value System Analysis as an Aid to Understanding Organizational Behavior: A Comparative Study in Japan, Korea, and the United States," paper presented at the Exchange Seminar on Comparative Organizations, Ersel, Netherlands, March 23-27, 1970. See also G. W. England and R. Lee, "Organizational Goals and Expected Behavior Among American, Japanese, and Korean Managers—A Comparative Study," *Academy of Management Journal,* vol. 14, no. 4 (December 1971), 425-38.

72. Haire, Ghiselli, and Porter, *op. cit.,* pp. 37-54.

73. Williams, Whyte, and Green, *op. cit.*

74. Sirota and Greenwood, *op. cit.*

75. Haire, Ghiselli, and Porter, *op. cit.,* pp. 73-113.

76. K. G. Deasi, "A Study of Worker's Expectations from Supervisors and Management," *Indian Journal of Social Work,* vol. 30, no. 2 (July 1969), 105-116.

CHAPTER 7

MANPOWER MANAGEMENT: PART I, MANPOWER PLANNING, SELECTION, AND TRAINING

Of all the factors to be considered in the operation of a business enterprise, the management of human resources is perhaps the most critical. Underscoring its importance, Schultz has argued: "It simply is not possible to have the fruits of modern agriculture and the abundance of modern industry without making large investments in human beings."[1] With respect to the United States he goes on to say: ". . . the most distinctive feature of our economic system is the growth in human capital. Without it there would be only hard, manual work and poverty . . . the man without skills and knowledge leaning terrifically against nothing."[2] A similar view is that of a leading business man in the Orient, Mr. Sadao Kumazawa, President of the Oji Paper Company in Japan:

> Human resources should be properly shown in figures as assets on the balance sheet, just as physical assets are, as an indication of corporate strength. . . . Cultivation of human resources offers a scope of promise vastly wider than that of physical resources.[3]

In recent years economic planners, government officials, and politicians in the developing nations have not only shown awareness of but ardently advocated the importance of human resources in accelerating industrial and economic development in those countries. This concern at the macro level (national and governmental levels) can be discerned in the development of various manpower institutes, councils, training schools, and even the emergence of cabinet-level ministries of manpower in many of the developing countries. As we will see, in spite of such concern at the national level, corresponding concern at the firm, or organizational, level is somewhat disturbing.

In this and the next chapter we will look at the manpower management practices of industrial enterprises in the six developing countries of Latin America and the Far East. Data on the following aspects are analyzed in this chapter:

   manpower planning and policies
   organization of personnel functions
   job analysis and employee-appraisal systems
   selection and promotion procedures
   training and development of employees
   impact of environmental factors on manpower practices

The next chapter will be devoted to the two most important aspects of manpower management, compensating and motivating employees.

Before proceeding, I will briefly describe the manpower management practices of American parent companies in the United States. This will provide a comparative perspective prior to analyzing data from the six developing countries in our study.

THE AMERICAN SCENE

Since the depression years of the 1930s and the research studies of Mayo and his colleagues,[4] many U.S. business organizations (as well as government agencies) have given considerable attention to manpower planning, recruiting, selection, training, and development. Many testing devices have been developed for selecting employees and matching the individual with specific job requirements. Recent trends among the larger U.S. corporations suggest an attempt to use such "management science" concepts as mathematical, statistical, and simulation models for the personnel functions of recruiting, selecting, testing, training, and evaluating performance.[5]

MANPOWER PRACTICES IN U.S. PARENT COMPANIES

A large majority of the U.S. parent companies in our study (12 out of 15) have formulated specific manpower policies. Many of these policies cover such concerns as how to create an atmosphere where the individual participant can contribute to the fullest of his abilities, and how to select the right individuals for the required positions. Particularly, chief executives and top-level executive committees have paid considerable attention to the formulation of manpower policies.

In all parent companies the implementation of manpower policies is undertaken by the staff of the personnel departments. These departments are well organized and have many divisions, such as management training and development, wage and salary administration, employee services, fringe benefits. The companies pay particular attention to the training and development of employees at all levels. Of course, companies use various training methods—on-the-job training, formal training inside the firm, and job rotation within the firm and its subsidiaries, or divisions. Few of the firms retain behavioral researchers from universities to conduct their management training. More than half of the parent companies prepare elaborate management succession charts and management inventories. On an average, these firms spend 1 to 5 percent of their companies' man-hours in providing training at various levels. The activities represent an expenditure of 5 to 15 percent of a firm's gross sales.

Holden and his co-researchers found a similar trend among 15 large U.S. companies:

> The identification and planned development of key personnel has become a vital part of the total long-range planning activity in all the 15 corporations. . . . Replacement charts, backup lists, and individual development plans for each executive position are the rule rather than the exception today.[6]

Table 7-1 shows the various aspects of manpower management and personnel practices observed in the 15 U.S. parent companies.

Table 7-1

Aspects of Manpower Management and Personnel Practices in the 15 U.S. Parent Companies

Item	No. of companies
Formal manpower policies	13
Organization of personnel function as separate department	15
Major divisions within personnel dept:	
Wage and salary admin. division	15
Employees' services division	12
Fringe benefits division	10
Training division	14
Management training division	12
Manpower policy group	6
Industrial relations and employee relations division	15
Major personnel practices:	
Formalized job description and evaluation	14
Formalized employee selection and appraisal	14
Employee testing devices	14
Formal dismissal and layoff status	10
Development of selection and promotion criteria	10
Formalized employee health and safety programs	14
Formalized employee recreation and vacation programs	10
Retirement plans	9
Wage and salary surveys	10
Employee suggestion systems	15
Development of management succession charts and management inventory	9
Supervisory training programs	14
Blue-collar employee training programs	14
Management training programs	12

MANPOWER MANAGEMENT PRACTICES
IN DEVELOPING COUNTRIES

As in the previous chapters, data on manpower management practices are analyzed at three levels:

1. An overall comparison between the American subsidiaries and local firms in the six developing countries (Argentina, Brazil, India, the Philippines, Taiwan, and Uruguay).
2. Regional comparisons between American subsidiaries and local firms in Latin America and the Far East.
3. Comparisons between firms showing "much concern" and "moderate" and "little concern" for their publics.

Manpower Planning and Policies

Manpower planning involves (a) anticipating a firm's demands for the different types of skills that will be required to perform future activities, and (b) programming activities for recruiting, selecting, training, and developing individuals to meet anticipated demands.[7]

On the other hand, manpower policies underscore the organizational concern for its human component. Such policies provide guidelines for the following elements of managing human resources:

Employment policy—how to obtain suitably qualified and experienced personnel.

Training policy—what types of training facilities should be organized and who should be included in each type of training.

Wage and salary policy—how wages and salaries will be determined.

Staff relations policy—how to establish cooperative relationships between people in a given department and people among different departments.

Welfare and benefits policy—how to insure the health, safety, and well-being of employees.[8]

These ideas about manpower planning and forecasting are relatively new ideas and are largely under-utilized, even among large corporations in the United States. Various surveys of manpower-planning practices undertaken in the U.S. indicate a piecemeal attempt in this regard.[9] These surveys, however, do show that corporations are becoming aware of the need for systematic manpower planning and forecasting. Such U.S. companies as the North American Rockwell Corporation, General Electric, etc., already have begun systematic manpower planning and environmental forecasting programs[10] with the aid of computers. Also, as we saw earlier, Holden et al. found similar concern among the 15 U.S. corporations they studied.

As one would expect, few firms in this study of developing countries in Latin America and the Far East pay systematic attention to manpower planning and forecasting. Approximately 12 percent of the firms in our study (n=111) undertake manpower planning. There are no appreciable differences between American subsidiaries and local firms in this regard. Relatively speaking, companies in the Far Eastern region demonstrated more concern than those in Latin America.

However, differences between "much concern" and "moderate" and "little concern" firms are marked. Some 46 percent of the "much concern" companies undertake manpower planning and forecasting on an extensive and continuous basis. In contrast, only a marginal 1 percent of the firms in the "moderate" and "little concern" categories followed this practice. This demonstrates that firms showing higher concern for their employees, consumers, and other publics also show concern for their future manpower needs, while those showing less concern for their publics prefer to operate on a day-to-day basis.

A similar picture emerges when we examine the existence of manpower policies in these firms. As can be seen from Table 7-2, more than three-fourths of the firms showing "much concern" formulate and document manpower policies, while only one-fourth of the firms in the "moderate" and "little concern" categories did.

Regional differences also seem obvious. More firms in the Far Eastern region (45 percent) formulate and document manpower policies than in the Latin American region (24 percent). There are no appreciable differences between American subsidiaries and local firms.

The underlying objectives of manpower policies are to satisfy the employee's needs, to achieve higher organizational effective-

Table 7-2
International Comparison of Manpower Planning

Organizational concern for publics: Argentina, Brazil, Uruguay

Manpower planning:	Overall U.S.	local	Much U.S.	local	Moderate U.S.	local	Little U.S.	local
Extensive, continuous	1	—	1	—	—	—	—	—
Limited, continuous	13	6	1	1	12	5		
Ad hoc, discrete	6	6	—	—	6	6	—	—
No program, not available	—	5	—	—	—	4	—	1
Total	20	17	2	1	18	15	0	1

Organizational concerns for publics: India, Philippines, Taiwan

	Overall U.S.	local	Much U.S.	local	Moderate U.S.	local	Little U.S.	local
Extensive, continuous	7	5	7	4	—	1	—	—
Limited, continuous	7	9	2	4	5	5	—	—
Ad hoc, discrete	7	10	—	1	7	9	—	—
No program, not available	15	14	3	2	9	3	3	9
Total	36	38	12	11	21	18	3	9

---

ness, to select the "right" individuals, and to provide adequate and equitable compensation to employees.

Most of the companies undertaking manpower planning and formulating manpower policies have performed these tasks in a

Table 7-2, cont'd.

Summary Comparisons:

Manpower planning is extensive and continuous:	U.S. subsidiary	Local firm	Both
	(N given in parentheses)		
In both regions	14.3% (56)	9.1% (55)	11.7% (111)
In Latin American countries	5.0% (20)	0.0% (17)	2.7% (37)
In Far Eastern countries	19.4% (36)	13.2% (38)	16.2% (74)
In "Much concern" firms	57.1% (14)	33.3% (12)	46.2% (26)
In "Moderate and Little concern" firms	0.0% (42)	2.3% (43)	1.2% (85)

collaborative or consultative manner. An executive committee composed of top-level executives and functional managers has been involved in formulating such policies.

Organization and Status of the Personnel Department

A firm's awareness and desire to preserve, develop, and utilize its human resources can also be seen in examining the organization and hierarchical status of its personnel department.

In more than two-thirds of the American subsidiaries studied in the two regions (n=56), the personnel department is organized separately and has two to three specialized units (training and development, employee benefits, industrial relations, wage and salary administration, etc.). In these companies, the personnel managers are well qualified and in many instances are trained in the United States.

Table 7-3
Documentation of Manpower Policy

Organizational concern for publics: Argentina, Brazil, Uruguay

Manpower Policy:	Overall U.S.	Overall local	Much U.S.	Much local	Moderate U.S.	Moderate local	Little U.S.	Little local
Formally stated and documented	4	5	1	—	3	4	—	1
Not formally stated or documented but generally known to employees	11	8	1	1	10	7	—	—
No policies as such	5	4	—	—	5	4	—	—
Total	20	17	2	1	18	15	0	1

Organizational concern for publics: India, Philippines, Taiwan

	Overall U.S.	Overall local	Much U.S.	Much local	Moderate U.S.	Moderate local	Little U.S.	Little local
Formally stated and documented	16	17	11	8	5	7	—	2
Not formally stated or documented but generally known to employees	14	10	1	3	13	6	—	1
No policies as such	6	11	—	—	3	5	3	6
Total	36	38	12	11	21	18	3	9

Table 7-3, cont'd.

Summary Comparisons

Personnel policies and their formulation are formally stated and documented:	U.S. subsidiary	Local firm	Both
		(N given in parentheses)	
In both regions	35.7% (56)	40.0% (55)	37.8% (111)
In Latin American countries	20.0% (20)	29.4% (17)	24.3% (37)
In Far Eastern countries	44.4% (36)	44.7% (38)	44.6% (74)
In "much concern" firms	85.7% (14)	66.7% (12)	76.9% (26)
In "moderate" and "little concern" firms	19.0% (42)	32.6% (43)	25.9% (85)

In the local companies approximately one-half of the companies (n=55) have personnel departments that are separately organized. However, in only a very few firms are there specialized units or subdivisions within the personnel department. In these firms the personnel manager, although university-educated, is not always trained to carry out the personnel function.

Hierarchical Status

Data on the organizational status of personnel departments are presented in Table 7-4. It can be seen from this table that in about one-half of the companies, the personnel function is either at the

Table 7-4
Hierarchical Status of Personnel Department

Organizational concern for publics: Argentina, Brazil, Uruguay

Hierarchical status of personnel department:	Overall U.S.	local	Much U.S.	local	Moderate U.S.	local	Little U.S.	local
Top executive level or reports to chief executive	8	8	1	1	7	7	—	—
Reports to or is part of a functional department	12	7	1	—	11	7	—	—
Ad hoc basis	—	—	—	—	—	—	—	—
Total	20	—	2	1	18	—	0	—

Organizational concern for publics: India, Philippines, Taiwan

	Overall U.S.	local	Much U.S.	local	Moderate U.S.	local	Little U.S.	local
Top executive level or reports to chief executive	22	18	10	6	11	8	1	4
Reports to or is part of a functional department	13	19	1	4	10	10	2	5
Ad hoc basis	1	—	1	—	—	—	2	5
No answer	—	1	—	1	—	—	—	—
Total	36	38	12	—	21	18	—	—

Table 7-4, cont'd.

Summary Comparisons

Personnel department is at executive level or reports to chief executive:	U.S. subsidiary	Local firm	Both
		(N given in parentheses)	
In both regions	53.5% (56)	47.3% (55)	50.5% (111)
In Latin American countries	40.0% (20)	47.1% (17)	43.2% (37)
In Far Eastern countries	61.1% (36)	47.4% (38)	54.1% (74)
In "much concern" firms	78.6% (14)	58.3% (12)	69.2% (26)
In "moderate" and "little concern" firms	45.2% (42)	44.2% (43)	44.7% (85)

---

executive level or reporting directly to the chief executive. On the surface there do not seem to be many differences between American subsidiaries and local firms in this respect. But my inquiry into the functions of these companies indicates that in many of the local companies the personnel function is carried out by the chief executive on an ad hoc basis, while in the American subsidiaries it receives systematic consideration and the personnel manager is a member of the executive committee.

Regionally, in American subsidiaries in the Far East, the personnel department occupies higher hierarchical status than in the Latin American region. There are no appreciable differences among the local firms in these two regions. However, the data reveal that the firms manifesting higher concern for their publics are more likely to identify the personnel function as crucial than those firms manifesting lower concern for their publics.

Job Analysis

Among the personnel functions, management's initial task is to gather, analyze, and record information on the duties, responsibilities, and qualifications required of persons performing given tasks. In the personnel management literature, these types of activities are subsumed under *job analysis*. Briefly, this function is composed of two interrelated activities: (a) *job description,* which records principal duties, responsibilities, and activities involved in specific jobs, and (b) *job specifications,* which outlines special qualifications the individual must possess in order to perform the assigned tasks in a specific job position.[11]

My inquiry into these functions in Latin American and Far Eastern companies suggests a dismal picture. By and large, neither the American subsidiaries nor the local firms in Latin America systematically carry on these tasks, and fewer than one-fourth of the companies in the Far East undertake job analysis in a systematic manner.

Selection and Promotion

Management's desire to treat human resources as a critical input in the functioning of an organization can also be discerned by examining a firm's selection and promotion procedures and criteria. As was noted earlier, considerable attention is devoted to these activities in the United States. Among the 15 U.S. parent companies participating in the study, I particularly noted that systematic attempts are being made to develop objective criteria and procedures for selecting and promoting employees at all levels.

The methods of selection generally follow patterns such as evaluating the educational background, training, and experience of the individual, as well as assessing the aptitudes, abilities, and attitudes of the potential employee. In this study, I concentrated on the *nature* of the selection process rather than on its various details. I also attempted to identify selection procedures and to identify the selection process as systematic and formal versus ad hoc and informal.

The data is presented in Table 7-5. Overall, I find that approximately 53 percent of the firms in both regions utilize a formal and systematic selection process. There are considerable differences between the American subsidiaries and local firms in this aspect. As can be seen in Table 7-5, more than two-thirds of the American subsidiaries have instituted a formal and systematic selection process, as opposed to only a little more than one-third of their counterpart local firms.

The informal and ad hoc selection process used by many of the local companies is vividly described by the personnel manager of a large pharmaceutical company in India. When asked, "How do you select your employees?" he quickly answered:

> I call the prospective employee into my office, ask him to sit down across from my desk, and look straight into his eyes. . . . If his eyes wink frequently, I will not give him a job; if his eyes are steady, he will be employed.

Although this selection practice may seem extreme, however, as shown in Table 7-5, ad hoc selection process existed in two-thirds of the local companies in both of the regions studied. In Taiwan, for example, my inquiry about procedures for selecting blue-collar employees reveals that frequently it amounts to no more than sending a truck to nearby villages and picking up anybody with arms, feet, and eyes who is ready to work.

Regionally, there are no significant differences between American subsidiaries and local firms. There is, however, a strong relationship between a firm's concern for its publics and its selection process. Some 81 percent of the firms in the category "much concern" have established a formal selection process, compared to 45 percent of the firms categorized as "moderate" and "little concern."

Table 7-5
Selection Process

Organizational concern for publics: Argentina, Brazil, Uruguay

Process:	Overall U.S.	local	Much U.S.	local	Moderate U.S.	local	Little U.S.	local
Formal and systemic	14	7	1	1	13	6	—	—
Ad hoc and unsystematic	6	10	1	—	5	9	—	1
Total	20	17	2	1	18	15	0	1

Organizational concern for publics: India, Philippines, Taiwan

Process:	Overall U.S.	local	Much U.S.	local	Moderate U.S.	local	Little U.S.	local
Formal and systemic	24	14	12	7	12	7	—	—
Ad hoc and unsystematic	12	24	—	4	9	11	3	9
Total	36	38	12	11	21	18	3	9

Summary Comparisons:

Use of formal and systematic selection process:	U.S. subsidiary	Local firm	Both
	(N given in parentheses)		
In both regions	67.9% (56)	38.2% (55)	53.2% (111)
In Latin American countries	70.0% (20)	41.2% (17)	56.8% (37)
In Far Eastern countries	66.7% (36)	36.9% (38)	51.4% (74)
In "much concern" firms	92.9% (14)	66.7% (12)	80.8% (26)
In "moderate" and "little concern" firms	59.5% (42)	30.2% (43)	44.7% (85)

Selection decisions, by and large, are decentralized. For example, in more than two-thirds of the companies studied, blue-collar and clerical personnel are selected by the personnel manager and/or functional manager. Yet in 62 percent of the companies, decisions concerning supervisory, technical, and managerial personnel are made either by a committee composed of functional managers or by the chief executive after extensive consultation with functional managers.

Promotion: Procedures, Criteria, and Decisions

Inquiries concerning promotion procedures, criteria, and decision-making revealed some interesting results. Although many of the companies queried rely on informal procedures for promoting employees, most of them insisted that such factors as education, training, ability, initiative, and leadership are regarded as important criteria for promoting employees. Many of the firms, however, failed to substantiate such claims in their actual practices. A larger number of American subsidiaries, for example, use periodic reports (on standardized forms) from immediate supervisors, while local companies rely on word-of-mouth information from supervisors. Specifically, 68 percent of the American subsidiaries, versus 42 percent of the local firms, use a systematic appraisal system. A larger number of U.S. subsidiaries and local firms in Far Eastern countries use formalized appraisal systems than do in Latin America.

As the data presented in Table 7-6 indicate, there is a strong correlation between a firm's concern for its publics and the nature of its appraisal system. About 92 percent of the firms categorized as "much concern" use formalized systems versus only 43 percent of the firms manifesting "moderate" and "little concern".

Decision-making in the promotional areas is generally centralized in Latin American firms but decentralized in Far Eastern ones. In Latin America 59 percent of the firms (U.S. subsidiaries and local firms combined) make promotion decisions regarding blue-collar and clerical employees above the personnel or functional manager level, while only 36 percent in the Far East make these decisions above the personnel-department level.

A similar picture emerges when we examine the data on

Table 7-6

Personnel Appraisal: Techniques Used

Organizational concern for publics: Argentina, Brazil, Uruguay

Personnel appraisal system:	Overall U.S.	local	Much U.S.	local	Moderate U.S.	local	Little U.S.	local
Periodic reports from supervisors—standard forms	12	5	2	1	10	4	—	—
Opinions of supervisors —no formal appraisal system	8	12	—	—	8	11	—	1
Top management knows every employee—no program	—	—	—	—	—	—	—	—
Ad hoc reports	—	—	—	—	—	—	—	—
No answer	—	—	—	—	—	—	—	—
Total	20	—	2	1	18	—	0	1

Organizational concern for publics: India, Philippines, Taiwan

Periodic reports from supervisors—standard forms	26	18	12	9	13	8	1	1

Table 7-6, cont'd.

	Overall U.S. local		Much U.S. local		Moderate U.S. local		Little U.S. local	
Opinions of supervisors — no formal appraisal system	8	19	—	2	6	9	2	8
Top management knows every employee — no program	—	—	—	—	—	—	—	—
Ad hoc reports	2	—	—	—	2	—	—	—
No answer	—	1	—	—	—	1	—	—
Total	36	38	12	11	21	18	3	9

Summary Comparisons:

Personnel appraisal system consists of periodic reports from supervisors using standardized forms.	U.S. subsidiary	Local firm	Both
	(N given in parentheses)		
In both regions	67.9% (56)	41.8% (55)	54.9% (111)
In Latin American countries	60.0% (20)	29.4% (17)	45.9% (37)
In Far Eastern countries	72.2% (36)	47.3% (38)	54.9% (74)
In "much concern" firms	100.0% (14)	83.3% (12)	92.3% (26)
In "moderate" and "little concern" firms	57.1% (42)	30.2% (43)	43.5% (85)

promotion decisions with respect to managerial and technical personnel. Overall, we find that in about half of the companies studied, such decisions are made by the chief executive alone. The chief executive, however, makes such decisions alone in only 23 percent of the "much concern" firms, compared to 59 percent in the firms classified as having "moderate" and "little concern."

Training and Development

It has been argued that although developing countries have vast human resources, the quality of these resources is far from satisfactory for rapid industrial and economic growth. Lack of skills, training, and education are major bottlenecks which impede using these human resources to their fullest potential.[12] Of course, experts from both developed and developing countries have realized this dilemma. As a result, in the last two decades, developed countries such as the United States, West Germany, and the United Kingdom, as well as international agencies such as the United Nations and the International Labor Organization, have helped developing countries to initiate various kinds of industrial training programs.

I was unable to collect complete data on training from the companies in Latin America. My overall evaluation of the training programs in these companies presents a gloomy picture; that is, training concepts and programs were not well developed, and the majority of companies studied followed informal and ad hoc training methods. The following analyses, therefore, are concerned mostly with the Far Eastern firms.

As can be seen in Table 7-7, 58 percent of the companies studied have instituted some sort of training program for blue-collar employees. But this high proportion is due largely to the companies in the Far East; 86 percent of the firms there have some form of formal training program for their blue-collar workers.

It is interesting that local companies outnumber the American subsidiaries in providing such formal training. This is due partly to the fact that it is the policy of American subsidiaries to hire only well-trained, qualified employees (at higher wages) who need no further training. (For the compensation practices of American subsidiaries, see Chapter 8.)

There also seems to be some relation between a firm's concern for its publics and the nature of its training program for blue-collar workers. Approximately 85 percent of the firms categorized as "much concern" provide some kind of formal training, as against 49 percent of the firms categorized as "moderate" and "little concern."

The same holds true for the data on training programs for supervisory and technical personnel. Here also companies in Latin America have informal and ad hoc training programs, while their counterparts in the Far East provide some kind of formal training. There are no significant differences between local firms and American subsidiaries in the Far Eastern region. Equal proportions of both sets of companies provide training for their supervisory and technical employees. There also appears to be a strong relationship between a firm's concern for its publics and its supervisory training programs.

Managerial training seems to be the least developed in developing countries. As Table 7-7 shows overall, only 40 percent of the firms have instituted a formal training program for their managerial personnel. Companies in the Latin American region follow informal, ad hoc practices, while 60 percent of those in the Far East conduct formal training.

Of all the training programs discussed, the correlation between a firm's concern for its publics and the nature of managerial training is the strongest. Some 77 percent of the "much concern" firms have formal training programs versus 28 percent of those classified as "moderate" and "little concern" firms.

Managerial Succession

Managerial succession has received considerable attention in recent years from both researchers and practitioners. As we saw earlier in this chapter, the study for 15 U.S. parent companies, as well as the Holden study, clearly show that the replacement charts, management inventory, and identification programs for potential managers are the rule rather than the exception.

Considering the need for and importance of managerial

Table 7-7

Training Programs for Blue-Collar, Supervisory, Technical, and Managerial Personnel

Formal training program	U.S. subsidiary	Local firm	Both
	(N given in parentheses)		
For blue-collar employees:			
In both regions	50.0% (56)	65.4% (55)	57.7% (111)
In Latin American countries	— (20)	— (17)	— (737)
In Far Eastern countries	50.0% (36)	94.7% (38)	86.4% (74)
In "much concern" firms	78.6% (14)	91.7% (12)	84.6% (26)
In "moderate" and "little concern" firms	40.5% (42)	58.1% (43)	49.4% (85)
For supervisory and technical personnel:			
In both regions	51.7% (56)	52.7% (55)	52.3% (111)
In Latin American countries	0% (20)	0% (17)	0% (37)
In Far Eastern countries	80.6% (36)	76.3% (38)	78.4% (74)
In "much concern" firms	85.7% (14)	91.7% (12)	88.5% (26)
In "moderate" and "little concern" firms	40.5% (42)	41.9% (43)	41.2% (85)
For managerial personnel:			
In both regions	41.1% (56)	38.2% (55)	39.6% (111)
In Latin American countries	0% (20)	0% (17)	0% (37)
In Far Eastern countries	63.9% (36)	55.3% (38)	59.4% (74)
In "much concern" firms	71.4% (14)	83.3% (12)	76.9% (26)
In "moderate" and "little concern" firms	31.0% (42)	25.6% (43)	28.2% (85)

input in the industrial and economic growth of developing countries, the data on managerial succession present a dark picture. Only 37 of the 111 companies have some type of managerial succession program. Of these, 27 are American subsidiaries and 10 are local firms. Here also "much concern" firms outnumber the "moderate" and "little concern" firms. The respective percentages of the firms in these two categories are 62 and 25.

Table 7-8
Managerial Succession

Use of formal procedures for managerial succession:	U.S. subsidiary	Local firm	Both
	(N given in parentheses)		
In both regions	48.2% (56)	18.2% (55)	33.3% (111)
In Latin American countries	60.0% (20)	17.6% (17)	40.5% (37)
In Far Eastern countries	41.7% (36)	18.4% (38)	29.7% (74)
In "much concern" firms	78.6% (14)	41.7% (12)	61.5% (26)
In "moderate" and "little concern" firms	38.1% (42)	11.6% (43)	24.7% (85)

Summary

In this chapter, we looked at various aspects of manpower planning, selection process, promotion procedures and criteria, appraisal systems, training programs for blue-collar, supervisory, technical, and managerial personnel, and the nature of management succession programs.

An analysis of data on these aspects indicates that the concept of manpower planning is the least developed among the companies in Latin America and the Far East. In slightly more than 50 percent of the firms studied (n=111), there is some attempt to formalize selection processes, employee appraisal systems, and training programs for blue-collar, supervisory, and technical personnel. Training and succession programs for managerial personnel are developed in approximately one-third of the companies studied.

This summary, however, conceals the real differences that exist between American subsidiaries and local firms in Latin America and the Far East. As Table 7-9 shows, formalized training programs are nonexistent among both U.S. subsidiaries and local firms in Latin American countries, while they are prevalent in the Far East.

A still more revealing aspect of the data is the strong correlation between the firms' concern for their publics and the nature of their manpower practices. Proportionally, firms in the "much concern" categories outnumber those in the "moderate" and "little concern" categories in instituting formalized and systematic manpower practices.

I readily admit that, like many other management practices, manpower management practices may be constrained by the environmental conditions in a given country. But the mere fact that more than 50 percent of the firms studied are able to utilize advanced manpower practices suggests the feasibility of transferring advanced practices to the industrial enterprises in developing countries. We will explore the feasibility of this point further in the next chapter.

Before closing this chapter, however, a discussion of the impact of environmental factors on manpower management practices is in order.

Environmental Factors and Manpower Practices

I, interviewed executives, government officials, labor leaders, labor economists, and university professors to ascertain the impact of specific environmental variables on many aspects of management practices, including manpower management practices. During these interviews, the following factors were frequently mentioned as having an impact on the manpower practices discussed in this chapter:

labor legislation
oversupply of unskilled labor and lack of skilled and trained manpower
the nature of labor unions (political in nature) and union rivalry
seller's market
lack of motivation and commitment of industrial workers

Table 7-9

Summary Results on Manpower Management Practices

Item	All companies (n=111)	Latin American region U.S. subsidiary (n=20)	Local firm (n=17)	Both (n=37)	Far Eastern region U.S. subsidiary (n=36)	Local firm (n=38)	Both (n=74)	"Much concern" firms (n=26)	"Moderate" & "Little concern" firms (n=85)
Formalized manpower planning	12	5	0	3	19	13	16	46	1.0
Formalized selection process	53	70	41	57	67	37	51	81	45
Formalized employee appraisal system	55	60	29	46	72	47	55	92	44
Formalized training program (blue-collar employee)	58	—	—	—	50	95	86	85	49
Formalized training program (supervisory and technical personnel)	52	—	—	—	81	76	78	89	41
Formalized training program (managerial personnel)	40	—	—	—	64	55	59	77	28
Formalized managerial succession program	33	60	18	41	42	18	30	62	25

The last factor, motivation and commitment of workers, is important and significant, so we will take it up in the next chapter. First, let us briefly look at the other environmental factors.

Labor Legislation

Industrial entrepreneurs in developing countries seem to have taken undue advantage of the labor situation in those countries—oversupply and a high rate of unemployment. As Fillol has remarked with respect to Argentina, "Labor tends still to be considered as just another commodity whose services are to be bought as cheaply as possible."[13]

In an attempt to remedy this situation, governments in recent years have modified their existing labor legislation and enacted more liberal labor laws, in addition to actively supporting trade union activities. This push for liberal labor legislation and the encouragement of aggressive union fronts has resulted in higher wages as well as rising expectations among the worker without a corresponding rise in productivity. In such a situation, the managers interviewed felt that it was difficult to systemize personnel practices. (The managers of companies without formalized and systematized manpower practices complained more about the environmental constraint than did those who were already using advanced manpower practices.)

Oversupply of Labor and High Unemployment

As was mentioned earlier, many of the developing countries are faced with the situation of an overly large, unskilled work force and a shortage of skilled employees, which has resulted in a high level of unemployment. Among the six developing countries —Argentina, Brazil, India, the Philippines, Taiwan, and Uruguay —Taiwan was the only country in which the unemployment rate has decreased in recent years. In India the number of people registered for work in employment agencies increased from 2.6 million in 1963 to 3.9 million in 1970. (Of course, this may be only a fraction of those unemployed.) In the Philippines, the unemployment rate increased from 6.3 percent of the labor force in 1963 to 7.8 percent in 1970. Similarly, unemployment in Uruguay increased from 5.1 percent in 1963 to 6.8 percent in 1970.

Even in Taiwan, although the overall unemployment has decreased from 5.3 percent in 1963 to 1.5 percent in 1970 (this figure was derived from the labor force sample survey rather than from the total labor force),[14] the special household surveys undertaken in recent years show that 2.2 million persons were added to the labor force during the years 1958-68, and only 729,440, or one-third, found jobs.[15] The existing sellers-market condition in developing countries has made firms insensitive to unit cost and worker productivity.[16]

The Nature of the Labor Union

Since World War II the organized labor movement has increased considerably in the developing countries. But there are many conflicting goals and ideologies being pursued by the different unions representing workers in the same firm. Labor unions in many underdeveloped countries are political; they represent political muscle and political interests instead of the interests of their members. The observations of McMillan with respect to Brazil give the picture for many developing countries:

> The American manager in Brazil finds himself in an environment where the collective interests of labor are supposedly protected by the government through legislation, but where actually unions are relatively weak, except as a political force . . . workers do not view their government-sponsored and sometimes communist-dominated unions in Brazil as agencies existing to promote their interests.[17]

Such a situation should make it easier for business firms to obtain complete support from their employees, but the executives interviewed indicated that politically-oriented union interference makes their task of implementing systematic manpower practices difficult.

Notes

1. T. W. Schultz, "Investment in Human Capital," *American Economic Review,* 51 (March 1951), 1-17, reprinted in B. F.

Kiber, *Investment in Human Capital,* Columbia, S.C.: Univ. of South Carolina Press, 1971, p. 20.

2. *Ibid.*

3. "Future Management: Effective Use of Human Resources," *Management Japan,* July-September 1971, p. 5.

4. Elton Mayo, *Human Problems of Industrial Civilization,* Cambridge, Mass.: Harvard Univ. Press, 1933.

5. P. S. Greenlaw and R. D. Smith, *Personal Management: A Management Science Approach,* Scranton, Pa.: International Textbook Company, 1970.

6. P. E. Holden et al., *Top Management,* New York: McGraw-Hill, 1968, pp. 16-18.

7. James W. Walker, "Forecasting Manpower Needs," *Harvard Business Review,* 47 (March-April 1969), 152-68.

8. *Ibid.*

9. James W. Walker, "Trends in Manpower Management Research," *Business Horizons,* 11 (August 1968), 37.

10. *Ibid.* See also "Developing Trends and Changing Institutions: Our Future Business Environment," Department of Personnel and Industrial Relations, General Electric Company, April 1968.

11. For more detailed treatment see H. J. Chruden and A. W. Sherman, Jr., *Personnel Management,* Cincinnati: South-Western Publishing Company, 1959, pp. 455-80.

12. Frederick Harbinson and Charles Myers, *Management in the Industrial World,* New York: McGraw-Hill, 1959.

13. Thomas Fillol, *Social Factors in Economic Development: The Argentine Case,* Cambridge, Mass.: MIT Press, 1963, p. 73.

14. See "Problems and Prospects of Manpower Resources in the Republic of China," *Economic Review,* November-December 1968, p. 16.

15. *Ibid.*

16. For details on the impact of seller's-market conditions on managerial practices, see A. R. Negandhi, "Advanced Management Practices in Developing Countries," *California Management Review,* (Spring 1968), 53-60.

17. Claude McMillan, Jr. et al., *International Enterprise in a Developing Economy: A Study of U.S. Business in Brazil,* East Lansing, Mich.: Bureau of Business and Economic Research, Michigan State University, 1964, p. 79.

CHAPTER 8

MANPOWER MANAGEMENT: PART II, COMPENSATION AND MOTIVATION

How to motivate people to work hard has been a perennial question ever since the Industrial Revolution. Early in the industrial era, money and mutuality of interests among employers and employees were regarded as the prime motivators for inducing people to work at their peak rates. These assumptions may be found in the writings of Adam Smith.[1] Andrew Ure,[2] and Charles Babbage.[3] These pioneering writers considered high wages, high productivity, and greater employee satisfaction and happiness as interrelated elements of industrial efficiency.[4]

The emergence of the scientific management movement and the work of Frederick Taylor,[5] Gantt,[6] and Gilbreths[7] further reinforced the concept of the money-motivation equation through greater standardization in determining "fair" wages. Taylor, Gantt, and Gilbreths argued that if the workers are honestly evaluated and paid fair wages, they will be only too happy to produce more for higher rewards.

Hawthorne's research, known as the Western Electric experiment,[8] conducted by Elton Mayo, F. J. Roethlishberger, changed the simplistic assumption about money being the prime motivator. The Hawthorne experiment demonstrated that an organization is not only a formal arrangement of managerial functions but is a social system, that human beings are not satisfied solely with financial rewards. They yearn for participation in decision-making and for recognition as individuals. The human relations theorists have argued that employees "are not rabble but individuals with psychological drives and social yearnings."[9]

During the 1930s, 40s, and 50s the findings of the human relations school received more attention from industrial managers, particularly in the United States. Since then, however, this school of thought has been criticized as being at best a pedestrian effort in research and scholarship or at worst "a cynical attempt to manipulate people."[10]

In spite of such criticisms the foundation laid by the Hawthorne research is fully ingrained in industrial practices and in later research on behavioral motivation. Many practitioners, as well as behavioral scholars, accept the notion that man is diversely motivated and has a hierarchy of needs which, according to Maslow, include: basic physiological needs (food, water, clothing, shelter, etc.), security or safety for the continuation of physiological needs, love or desire for affection and association with others, esteem or self-assertion, and self-actualization or self-fulfillment.[11]

My research on 15 U.S. parent firms, as well as studies by other scholars[12] in the United States, suggest that most of the firms have given serious thought to the varied needs of employees in designing their compensation and motivation practices. Such nonmonetary rewards as desire to participate in decision-making, self-actualization needs, and self-esteem or ego-satisfaction of employees are not merely theoretical concepts; they are incorporated in organizational philosophy and practices.

With this in mind, I collected data on a few aspects of compensation and motivation practices used by the American subsidiaries and local firms in the six developing countries. Data was collected on the following factors:

1. The nature of compensation practices for blue-collar, white-collar (clerical), supervisory, and managerial personnel.
2. The basis for determining compensation.
3. Employee benefits and service programs.
4. The nature of motivation practices.
5. The nature of nonmonetary incentives.
6. The nature of employee participation programs.
7. Other programs for improving employee morale and productivity.

In this chapter we will analyze the findings on these factors. As in the previous chapters, we will analyze the data at various levels:

Overall comparisons between the American subsidiaries and comparable local firms in the six developing countries.

Regional comparisons between the American subsidiaries and local firms in the Far East and Latin American regions.

Comparison between "much concern," "moderate concern," and "little concern" firms.

Cross-cultural management research on motivation is surrounded by many controversies. So, in order to provide a better perspective for our findings, we will briefly review the literature before analyzing the data.

CROSS-CULTURAL MANAGEMENT RESEARCH ON MOTIVATION

In recent years governmental officials, industrial leaders, politicians, and economic planners in the developing countries have realized that the key to higher economic growth is higher productivity from the industrial worker. In studies of employee morale and commitment to industrial life and productivity in underdeveloped countries, however, many researchers have written pessimistically. In his study of industrial workers in India, Ornati has concluded:

> Indian workers are not interested in factory work; they resist adjustment to the type of life which goes with industrial employment. In the value scheme of the majority of Indians, factory labor does not offer any avenue for the expression of their individual personalities; wage increase and promotions do not operate as stimulants to greater exertion, nor does greater exertion lead to changes in status.[13]

Commenting on the labor commitment in underdeveloped countries, Kerr and his co-researchers had this to say:

> Cultural factors (such as religious and ethical valuations, the

family system, class and race) all have a bearing on commitment. . . . The greater the strength of extended family, the slower the commitment of workers to industrial life.[14]

Farmer and Richman, following the work of McClelland, arrived at this conclusion:

> The importance of a country's view of achievement and work as a vital determinant of managerial performance and productivity efficiency must not be understated. . . . Prevailing religious beliefs and cultural values, in connection with parental behavior, child-rearing practices . . . traditional Hinduism, Buddhism, Islam and even Catholicism are not generally conducive to a high achievement drive in their orthodox followers.[15]

Myrdal's monumental study of South Asia also reveals the impact on labor efficiency of tradition, custom, value systems, and attitudes in these countries. Myrdal argues: "in [the] absence of simultaneous changes in institutions and attitudes, the effect on labor utilization and productivity throughout the economy may still be less consequential."[16] Similarly, scholars studying the industrial scene in Latin American countries have argued that the industrial employees in these countries are more interested in maintaining and enhancing their family status and fulfilling obligations to friends and relatives than in increasing their productivity or wages.

Zurcher, Meadow, and Zurcher, in their comparative study of Mexican, Mexican-American, and Anglo-American bank employees, found that Mexicans are more particularistic than Mexican-Americans, who are in turn more particularistic than Anglo-Americans.[17] (Particularism signified the value orientation toward institutionalized obligations of friendships; in contrast, universalism indicates a value orientation toward obligation to the society and organizations.)

More important, these authors also found that alienation from work was significantly and positively related to particularism and negatively related to job longevity, position level, satisfaction with the position, and plans to continue working in a bank.

Of course not all scholars agree with the above contention that prevailing socio-cultural factors in the Far East and Latin

American regions have a negative and dominating impact on employee commitment to industrial life. A number of researchers have cast doubts on these assertions.

Morris, for example, has pointed out:

> Much of the literature tends to base interpretation on hypothetical, psychological, and sociological propositions which themselves are highly suspect. The argument typically rests on scattered fragments of evidence taken indiscriminately. . . . It is impossible to generate a satisfactory analysis from this sort of melange.[18]

He goes on to say:

> The evidence from Bombay and Jamshedpur suggests that the creation of [a] disciplined industrial labor force in a newly developing society is not particularly difficult. . . . The difference in worker stability cannot be accounted for by any substantial differences in the psychology of the raw labor recruited. Nor can it be attributed to dissimilarities in the traditional environment from which the workers came. If there were differences in work-force behavior, these flowed from employer policy.[19]

McMillan's research in Brazil revealed that:

> [South] Americans are under less compulsion to probe the attitude of their workers than they are in the United States. . . . Enlisting the allegiance of workers is easier, and motivating employees, most Americans appear to agree, is not difficult.[20]

In his study, *Social Factors in Economic Development in Argentina,* Fillol observed:

> There is no reason to believe that Argentina workers have basically different attitudes toward their jobs from workers anywhere else in industrialized Western countries. . . . Industrialists in general do not seem to have given any thought to the fact that the productivity, motivation, and cooperation of labor are primarily determined by the management which employs it and not by the more or less enlightened social and economic policies of government.[21]

Steven Piker, who based his research on Thai peasants, has argued against the influence of religion and/or the belief system (such as reliance on fate and *Karma* principles) on worldly behavior and activities of peasants.[22] He has pointed out, for example, that although the Thai peasant's belief in *Karma* (fate) has remained strong, he is considering life-here-and-now as important, if not more so, as the life beyond. In his words: "[The Thai peasant] makes merit in the hope not of attaining *Nirvana,* but of reentering the world of humans on terms more favorable to himself . . . (this) means his being more closely placed to substantial wealth and influence."[23]

Ingersoll drove the same point home when he concluded: "[Thai] villagers may ideally regard fate as an active influence but actually acknowledge fate only after the fact."[24]

Finally, in the most comprehensive study they have yet undertaken in the cross-cultural management area, Sirota and Greenwood raise considerable doubts about the prevailing thesis of the impact of socio-cultural variables on motivation.[25] In opposition to the cross-cultural thesis, they state that such generalizations, although interesting, are "based almost entirely on the subjective impressionistic experiences of the observers."[26] They further state: "Acceptance of these conclusions must therefore depend largely on faith—faith both in the observer's objectivity and in the representativeness of the anecdotal evidence he usually presents as proof of his case."[27]

NEED HIERARCHY OF THE INDUSTRIAL EMPLOYEE IN DEVELOPING COUNTRIES

Perhaps the most critical question in determining optimal compensation and motivation practices is to ascertain the actual needs, or a need hierarchy, of the industrial worker.

As we saw earlier, there are those who believe that the industrial employee in developing countries is not interested in money, advancement, or higher achievements. The implications of such assumptions are serious, since it leaves much less hope for generating economic growth and improving the standard of living for two-thirds of the human race living in a less developed part of the world.

My research in the six developing countries, as well as the findings of some other writers, questions such a pessimistic outlook. For example, my interviews with more than 500 industrial employees in developing countries clearly indicate that these employees, like their counterparts in the industrialized countries, want higher wages, opportunity for advancement, job security, fair treatment, better working conditions and welfare, and a higher standard of living for their children. I did not find many employees looking to heaven and yearning for ultimate *Nirvana*. An increasing number of scholars in recent years have undertaken studies in these countries which support this contention. Gangulli, in his study of factory workers in India, found:

> The four most important things that the workers want are sufficient and adequate income, a sense of security, an opportunity for promotion and advancement, and finally, the opportunity to learn a more interesting trade. . . . In these and also in their aspirations and expectations, there does not seem to be any fundamental difference between this group and other groups of factory employees in other countries.[28]

Altimus, Richards, and Slocum, in their study of Mexican and American industrial workers, found that job security, esteem, autonomy, and self-actualization needs were very much in the minds of the Mexican workers.[29]

Deasi's study of blue-collar and white-collar employees in India revealed that both groups prefer higher wages, better fringe benefits such as provident fund (retirement), profit-sharing plans, etc., and impartial policies on promotion and reward systems.[30] The employees' preference (need hierarchy) reported by Deasi are summarized below.

Similarly, Sirota and Greenwood found in their study of 25 countries that the most important goal of workers everywhere is to have an opportunity for individual achievement.[31] They claim that occupational and national comparisons reveal remarkable similarities in the goals of workers.

Sirota and Greenwood go on to say that "the best predictors, by far, of whether employees . . . leave or stay with the company are job-related satisfactions (challenge, utilization of skills, etc.).[32]

The question, "How do we motivate employees?" they say, is an inane question asked by managers around the world. "These employees do not have to be motivated. They are eager and ambitious, interested in having their skills utilized on present jobs and in moving ahead to more responsible and better jobs."[33]

In light of these observations, let us now examine the actual compensation practices and motivation devices utilized by the two sets of companies in the six developing countries.

COMPENSATION PRACTICES

My inquiry into compensation practices consisted of simple but basic aspects of reward systems utilized by the companies: (a) the level of compensation in relation to the "going rate" in the given country and (b) the basis for determining wage and salary levels.

I was able to collect data on the first item only from companies in the Far East. Latin American firms were unwilling to provide such information. On the second question, however, I was able to collect data from companies in both regions.

Compensation Level

A large number of American subsidiaries and local firms in the Far Eastern region instituted a policy of compensating their blue-collar, clerical, supervisory, and managerial personnel at the "market rate," or going rate. A mere 25 percent of the subsidiaries and 16 percent of the local firms compensated their employees at a higher-than-market rate; while 10 percent of the former companies and 25 percent of the latter paid their employees a lower-than-market rate .

As one would expect, progressive firms paid higher wages than did nonprogressive firms. The same was true with respect to firms showing higher concern for their task agents (employees, consumers, suppliers, etc.). For example, 44 percent of the "much concern" firms paid higher-than-market rates, compared to 10 percent of those categorized as "moderate" and "little concern."

The practice of paying the market rate indicates the concerns of labor unions and government to equalize wages of industrial workers in different industrial enterprises.

Basis for Determining Compensation

Probably more important than the level of compensation is the method for or basis of determining wage and salary rates. As we saw earlier, employees want both higher wages and an impartial, objective basis for determining wages and promotions.

As is illustrated in Table 8-2, approximately one-third of the companies studied in the two regions used some sort of objective basis (wage surveys, job evaluation, etc.) for determining wage rates for blue-collar employees. This proportion increased to one-half with respect to clerical employees but dropped to a marginal 18 percent in the case of supervisory and managerial personnel.

Overall, a larger number of companies in Latin America used objective methods of determining compensation rates than

---

Table 8-1

**Priorities and Mean Ranks of the Various Aspects
of the Job by White-Collar Workers and
Blue-Collar Workers in India**

Aspects of the job:	White-collar workers mean rank	priority	Blue-collar workers mean rank	priority
Adequate earnings	3.50	I	3.90	I
Security of the job	3.76	II	4.80	II
Good boss	4.35	III	4.10	III
Opportunities for advancement	4.85	IV	6.10	IV
Good working hours	6.17	V	5.80	V
Other benefits	6.19	VI	5.40	VI
Comfortable working conditions	6.37	VII	5.69	VII
Type of work you like	6.45	VIII	5.68	VIII
Fair treatment of grievances	7.01	IX	6.80	IX
Good company	7.03	X	6.60	X

Table 8-2

Basis of Determining Wage and Salary Levels

Wage surveys, job evaluation, etc., used to determine compensation levels	U.S. subsidiary		Local firm		Both	
	(N given in parentheses)					
Blue-collar employees:						
In both regions	39.3%	(56)	29.1%	(55)	34.2%	(111)
In Latin American countries	55.0%	(20)	47.1%	(17)	51.4%	(37)
In Far Eastern countries	30.6%	(36)	21.1%	(38)	25.7%	(74)
In "much concern" firms	28.6%	(14)	8.3%	(12)	19.2%	(26)
In "moderate" and "little concern" firms	42.9%	(42)	34.9%	(43)	38.8%	(85)
Clerical employees:						
In both regions	50.0%	(56)	50.9%	(55)	50.5%	(111)
In Latin American countries	55.0%	(20)	47.1%	(17)	51.4%	(37)
In Far Eastern countries	47.2%	(36)	54.1%	(38)	50.0%	(74)
In "much concern" firms	64.3%	(14)	50.0%	(12)	57.7%	(26)
In "moderate" and "little concern" firms	45.2%	(42)	51.2%	(43)	48.2%	(85)
Supervisory and managerial personnel:						
In both regions	17.8%	(56)	18.1%	(55)	18.0%	(111)
In Latin American countries	30.0%	(20)	41.1%	(17)	35.1%	(37)
In Far Eastern countries	11.1%	(36)	7.8%	(38)	9.4%	(74)
In "much concern" firms	21.4%	(14)	0.0%	(12)	11.5%	(26)
In "moderate" and "little concern" firms	16.6%	(42)	25.5%	(43)	21.1%	(85)

did those in the Far Eastern region. Why? I cannot be sure, but my initial query to the companies in Latin America revealed a greater pressure on companies by labor unions to move in this direction.

There are no substantial differences among the "much concern" and "moderate" and "little concern" firms with respect to the basis for determining compensation rates. In one instance, a larger proportion of the "moderate" and "little concern" firms used more objective methods for the blue-collar employees than did those of the "much concern" firms. These somewhat unexpected findings can be explained partly by the fact that the latter firms, by and large, paid higher wages and salaries than the going rate and as a result did not find it necessary to undertake wage surveys for determining compensation levels. The former firms ("moderate" and "little concern"), in their desire to pay "as much as competitors and no more," found wage surveys essential as guidelines.

Regardless of the absolute or relative wage and salary rates, employees in most American subsidiaries studied felt they were treated fairly and honestly. The same was not true in a large number of local companies in both regions. Employees in local firms felt that they were at the mercy of their immediate supervisors and that their advancement and wage increases depended largely on their supervisors.

MOTIVATION PRACTICES

As we discussed at the beginning of this chapter, the emergence of the human relations school brought forth a concern for satisfying various employee needs, especially socio-psychological needs. Many U.S. companies have attempted to provide their employees with an opportunity for participation in decision-making, self-development, utilization of skills, and initiative in achieving both organizational and individual goals and objectives.

Although the actual practices of the U.S. industrial enterprises are still short of what many behavioral theorists (Argyris,[34] Bennis,[35] Myers,[36] Likert,[37] etc.) are advocating, movement toward this goal is more than a facade and represents a genuine desire and interest on the part of the individual enterprises in the United States.

What is the situation in developing countries? My inquiry into the nature of the motivation practices of the companies studied includes these aspects:

the nature of incentives used—monetary versus nonmonetary

the nature of nonmonetary rewards in existence

stress on individual development, initiative, and creative thinking

the existence of institutionalized participation programs

Monetary versus Nonmonetary Rewards

A large majority of U.S. subsidiaries and local firms in Latin America and the Far East placed major emphasis on monetary rewards as a way of motivating blue-collar employees. Reliance on monetary devices was stronger in the companies in Latin America, compared to Far Eastern companies. As can be seen in Table 8-3, 92 percent of the firms studied in Latin America, versus 67 percent in the Far East, placed primary emphasis on monetary rewards.

The difference between the "much concern" and "moderate" and "little concern" firms was not as pronounced as had been expected. A slightly lower proportion (65 percent) of the firms in the first category relied on monetary rewards, compared to 79 percent in the second category. However, only one-half of the American subsidiaries categorized as "much concern" used monetary reward as a major device for motivating blue-collar employees.

Similar trends emerged with respect to clerical employees, although the proportion of companies relying solely on monetary rewards was slightly lower. Significant differences were noticeable with respect to the "much concern" and "moderate" and "little concern" firms. Some 46 percent of the companies in the former category relied entirely on the money motivation equation, while an overwhelming 72 percent of the firms in the latter category placed their faith in money as the prime motivator.

For supervisory and managerial personnel, this proportion declined further. Overall, approximately one-third of the American subsidiaries studied relied on money for motivating their supervisory and managerial personnel. The local firms, especially in Latin American countries, still relied on monetary rewards. In other words, the differences between the American subsidiaries and local firms, as well as firms in Latin American regions and

Table 8-3
The Nature of the Reward System

Reward system consists of monetary incentives only	U.S. subsidiary	Local firm	Both
	(N given in parentheses)		
For blue-collar employees:			
In both regions	71.4% (56)	80.0% (55)	75.6% (111)
In Latin American countries	90.0% (20)	94.1% (17)	91.8% (37)
In Far Eastern countries	61.1% (36)	73.6% (38)	67.0% (74)
In "much concern" firms	50.0% (14)	83.4% (12)	65.3% (26)
In "moderate" and "little concern" firms	78.5% (42)	79.0% (43)	78.8% (85)
For Clerical employees:			
In both regions	60.7% (56)	70.9% (55)	65.7% (111)
In Latin American countries	70.0% (20)	88.2% (17)	78.3% (37)
In Far Eastern countries	55.5% (36)	63.1% (38)	59.4% (74)
In "much concern" firms	42.8% (14)	50.0% (12)	46.1% (26)
In "moderate" and "little concern" firms	66.6% (42)	76.7% (43)	71.7% (85)
For supervisory and managerial personnel:			
In both regions	26.7% (56)	50.9% (55)	38.7% (111)
In Latin American countries	25.0% (20)	76.4% (17)	48.6% (37)
In Far Eastern countries	27.7% (36)	39.4% (38)	33.7% (74)
In "much concern" firms	14.2% (14)	41.6% (12)	26.9% (26)
In "moderate" and "little concern" firms	30.9% (42)	53.4% (43)	42.3% (85)

those in Far Eastern countries, were quite pronounced. This can be seen in the data presented in Table 8-3.

This is not to say that the nonwage benefits were not utilized by the local companies in the two regions. As a matter of fact, historically the industrial employee has received considerable nonwage benefits such as hospitalization and medical expenses, severance pay, yearly bonuses, dependent allowances, and housing allowances. The local companies in both regions are more paternalistic and welfare-oriented than are their American-subsidiary counterparts. However, these nonwage benefits were not conceived as a means to satisfy the higher levels of employee needs. The local companies, although paternalistic in outlook, failed to provide what Herzberg calls, "job context hygiene" factors.[38]

The Nature of Nonmonetary Rewards

The most frequently used nonmonetary incentives in the companies studied were:

good working conditions (clean factories, air-conditioned work place, good ventilation, etc.)
recreation and sport programs
employee counseling programs
an opportunity to participate in decision-making

Table 8-4
The Nature of Non-monetary Rewards

Nonmonetary incentives consist of participating in decision-making, employee counseling, recreation programs, and good working conditions	U.S. subsidiary	Local firm	Both
	(N given in parentheses)		
In both regions	53.5% (56)	38.1% (55)	45.9% (111)
In Latin American countries	70.0% (20)	41.1% (17)	56.7% (37)
In Far Eastern countries	44.4% (36)	36.8% (38)	40.5% (74)
In "much concern" firms	78.5% (14)	66.7% (12)	73.0% (26)
In "moderate" and "little concern" firms	45.2% (42)	30.2% (43)	37.6% (85)

Table 8-5

Institutionalized Participation Program

Existence of suggestion box:	U.S. subsidiary	Local firm (N given in parentheses)	Both
In both regions	55.5% (56)	32.7% (55)	44.1% (111)
In Latin American countries	50.0% (20)	23.5% (17)	37.8% (37)
In Far Eastern countries	58.3% (36)	36.8% (38)	47.2% (74)
In "much concern" firms	100.0% (14)	83.3% (12)	92.3% (26)
In "moderate" and "little concern" firms	40.4% (42)	18.6% (43)	29.4% (85)

Some 46 percent of the firms studied provided one or more of the above nonmonetary incentives. Although there were no significant differences between the local companies in the two regions, a larger number of American subsidiaries in the Latin American region (70 percent) had instituted some sort of non-monetary incentive programs, compared to those (44 percent) in the Far Eastern region. Why? I cannot say for sure. Latin American executives interviewed gave the impression that it was absolutely necessary to have some sort of recreation and sport programs for enhancing employee morale.

Noticeable differences were also observable between "much concern" and the "moderate" and "little concern" firms. 73 percent of the firms in the former category used nonmonetary incentives, versus only 38 percent of the firms in the latter category.

More advanced morale-building programs such as self-development, reward for initiative and creative thinking, etc., were used by less than 15 percent of the firms studied, of which the majority were American subsidiaries.

Institutionalized, participative programs such as a suggestion box were used by more than one-third of the firms studied. Relatively speaking, the Far Eastern companies utilized these types of programs much more than did those in Latin America.

Table 8-6
Summary: Compensation and Motivation Practices

Item	All firms (n=111)	Latin American countries			Far Eastern countries			Organizational concern for publics	
		U.S. sub. (n=20)	Local firm (n=17)	Both (n=37)	U.S. sub. (n=37)	Local firm (n=38)	Both (n=74)	"Much concern" (n=26)	"Moderate & little concern" (n=85)
Blue- and white-collar employees were paid higher than "market rate"	20% (n=74)	N.A.	N.A.	N.A.	25%	16%	20%	43% (n=23)	9.0% (n=51)
"Objective" basis for determining wages for blue-collar employees	34	55%	47%	51%	31	21	26	19	39
"Objective" basis for determining wages for clerical employees	51	55	47	51	47	54	50	58	48
Use of nonmonetary incentives (participation in decision-making, employee counseling, good working conditions, etc.)	46	70	41	57	44	37	40	73	38
Institutionalized participation programs	44	50	24	38	58	37	47	92	29

"Much concern" firms paid more attention to their programs than those classified as "moderate" and "little concern" firms. Differences between these two sets of firms were significant. 92 percent of the firms in the first category ("much concern") provided and utilized effectively the suggestion box, compared to 29 percent of the firms in the second category.

Summing Up

To recap, my findings indicate:

American subsidiaries paid more than comparable local firms in both regions.

American subsidiaries used a greater number of nonmonetary incentives.

A large majority of local firms believed in money as the prime motivator of human activity but actually paid "as little as possible."

Regardless of the ownership status (American versus local), "much concern" firms paid higher than market wages and provided more nonmonetary incentives as compared to "moderate" and "much concern" firms.

TWO CRITICAL QUESTIONS

To conclude the analysis of data presented in Chapters 7 and 8, I raise two significant questions:

1. Are advanced manpower management practices transferable to developing countries?
2. Do those advanced practices lead to higher effectiveness?

The following analysis attempts to provide answers to the above two questions.

Transfer Feasibility

As was discussed at the end of the last chapter, the concept of manpower planning was least utilized by the U.S. subsidiaries and local companies studied in six developing countries. However, more than 50 percent of these firms did utilize advanced practices concerning the selection of employees, appraisal and evaluation of employees, and training programs for the blue-collar, supervisory, and technical personnel. Moreover, the proportion of American subsidiaries, as well as those firms classified as "much concern," was much greater in this regard (see Table 7-9).

With respect to compensation and motivation practices, the proportion of firms utilizing more sophisticated techniques and practices is much smaller. Here also, however, the American subsidiaries and firms categorized as "much concern" provide the lead. Particularly, the correlation between the firm's concern for its publics and the nature of manpower practices seems to be strong. In order to explore such a relationship systematically, I computed the manpower index by scoring each practice 1 to 3 and adding up the score and then dividing the total by the number of manpower practices. (A score of 1 represents "systematic and comprehensive practices," a score of 2 "somewhat systematic," and a score of 3 "ad hoc practices.")

This gave me a manpower-practices index for each company ranging from 1 to 3, 1 representing "the most sophisticated or advanced practices," and 3 indicating mostly "ad hoc practices."

As is shown in Table 8-7, the manpower-management index was correlated with the firm's concern for its publics.

Spearman's rank correlation coefficient between these two variables was 0.677, which indicates that *the higher the firm's concern for its publics, the more sophisticated or advanced are its manpower practices.*

Thus such a relationship is indicative of the transferability of advanced manpower practices to the developing countries. To put it differently, these findings show that the advanced practices are largely a function of the firm's own attitudes and policies rather than of the socio-cultural environment of the country, as has been argued by various cross-cultural theorists.

Practices and Organizational Effectiveness

The more important question is whether advanced manpower practices contribute to higher organizational effectiveness. It is obvious that if the answer to this question is negative, it is

Table 8-7
Rank Correlation Between Organizational Concern Score and Manpower Practices Index

Pair no.	Co.	Industry	Organizational concern score X	Rank (R$_x$)	Manpower practices C	Rank (R$_c$)	d = R$_x$ -R$_c$	d^2
1	U.S.	Pharma-	100	3	1.0	2.5	.5	.25
	Indian	ceutical	95	6	2.0	13	7	49
2	U.S.	Pharma-	100	3	1.0	2.5	.5	.25
	Indian	ceutical	59	12	2.3	20.5	8.5	72.25
3	U.S.	Pharma-	71	9	1.7	8	1	1
	Indian	ceutical	42	24	2.5	24.5	.5	.25
4	U.S.	Pharma-	54	14.5	2.7	28	13.5	182.25
	Indian	ceutical	22	29	2.3	20.5	8.5	72.25
5	U.S.	Consumer	59	12	1.7	8	4	16
	Indian	nondurable goods and soft drinks	46	20.5	2.5	24.5	4	16
6	U.S.	Toilet Soaps	100	3	1.0	2.5	.5	.25
	Indian		100	3	1.3	5	2	4
7	U.S.	Canned	49	18	2.5	24.5	6.5	42.25
	Indian	Products	22	29	2.7	28	1	1
8	U.S.	Cosmetics	25	26.5	2.5	24.5	2	4
	Indian		22	29	2.3	20.5	8.5	72.25

fruitless to search for the feasibility of transferring advanced management practices from industrially developed countries to developing ones.

To explore the relationship between manpower-management practices and organizational effectiveness, I evaluated seven behaviorally oriented criteria of effectiveness:

Table 8-7, cont'd.

Pair no.	Co.	Industry	Organi- zational concern score X	Rank (R_x)	Man- power prac- tices C	Rank (R_c)	d= R_x -R_c	d²
9	U.S.	Heavy en- gineering goods-	51	16.5	2.8	30	13.5	182.25
	Indian	metal ind.	25	26.5	2.7	28	1.5	2.25
10	U.S.	Elevators	46	20.5	2.3	20.5	0	0
	Indian	"	90	7	2.2	16.5	9.5	90.25
11	U.S.	Heavy ma-	56	20.5	2.0	13	7.5	56.25
	Indian	chine and tools	100	3	1.0	2.5	.5	.25
12	U.S.	Typewriters	59	12	2.0	13	1	1
	Indian		69	10	2.2	16.5	6.5	42.25
13	U.S.	Auto tires	43	23	1.7	8	15	225
	Indian		54	14.5	2.2	16.5	2	4
14	U.S.	Electric	46	20.5	1.8	10.5	10	100
	Indian	bulbs	51	16.5	2.2	16.5	0	0
15	U.S.	Sewing	40	25	1.8	10.5	14.5	210.25
	Indian	machines	72	8	1.5	6	2	4

$$r_s = 0.68 \qquad\qquad\qquad\qquad \text{Total:} \quad 1,451.00$$

$$r_s = 1 - \frac{1451}{4495} = 1 - .323 = .677$$

1. The firm's ability to hire and retain high-level manpower.
2. Employee morale and satisfaction in work.
3. Absenteeism.
4. Interpersonal relationships between the supervisor and sub- ordinate.
5. Interdepartmental relationships.

Table 8-8
Rank Correlation Between Manpower Practices Index and Organizational Effectiveness

Pair no.	Co.	Industry	Manpower practices index C	Rank (R) c	Effectiveness index E	Rank (R) e	d= R -R c e	d²
1	U.S.	Pharma-	1.0	2.5	1.0	2.5	0	0
	Indian	ceutical	2.0	13	1.5	8.5	4.5	20.25
2	U.S.	Pharma-	1.0	2.5	1.0	2.5	0	0
	Indian	ceutical	2.3	20.5	2.2	21	.5	.25
3	U.S.	Pharma-	1.7	8	1.8	14	6	36
	Indian	ceutical	2.5	24.5	2.2	21	3.5	12.25
4	U.S.	Pharma-	2.7	28	1.7	11	17	289
	Indian	ceutical	2.3	20.5	2.2	21	.5	.25
5	U.S.	Consumer	1.7	8	1.8	14	6	36
	Indian	nondurable goods and soft drinks	2.5	24.5	2.7	28	3.5	12.25
6	U.S.	Toilet	1.0	2.5	1.0	2.5	0	0
	Indian	soaps	1.3	5	1.2	5.5	.5	.25
7	U.S.	Canned	2.5	24.5	1.8	14	10.5	110.25
	Indian	products	2.7	28	3.0	30	2	4
8	U.S.	Cosmetics	2.5	24.5	2.5	26.5	2	4
	Indian	"	2.3	20.5	2.8	29	8.5	72.25
9	U.S.	Heavy en-	2.8	30	1.3	7	23	529
	Indian	gineering goods-metal ind.	2.7	28	2.5	26.5	1.5	2.25
10	U.S.	Elevators	2.3	20.5	2.3	24.5	4	16
	Indian	"	2.2	16.5	1.2	5.5	11	121
11	U.S.	Heavy ma-	2.0	13	2.3	24.5	11.5	132.25
	Indian	chine and tools	1.0	2.5	1.0	2.5	0	0
12	U.S.	Type-	2.0	13	1.5	8.5	4.5	20.25
	Indian	writers	2.2	16.5	2.2	21	4.5	20.25
13	U.S.	Auto tires	1.7	8	2.2	21	13	169
	Indian	"	2.2	16.5	2.0	17	.5	.25
14	U.S.	Electric	1.8	10.5	2.0	17	6.5	42.25
	Indian	bulbs	2.2	16.5	2.0	17	.5	.25
15	U.S.	Sewing	1.8	10.5	1.7	11	.5	.25
	Indian	machines	1.5	6	1.7	11	5	25

$$r = 0.63 \qquad\qquad \text{Total} \quad 1{,}675.00$$

$$r_s = 1 - \frac{1675}{4495} = 1 - .373 = .627$$

6. Executive's perception of the firm's overall objectives.

7. Utilization of high-level manpower.

In order to obtain an overall effectiveness index for each firm, the above seven measures were scored 1 to 3 and the total score obtained for each firm was divided by the number of measures (7), which gave me the effectiveness index ranging from 1 to 3.

Spearman's Rank Correlation Coefficient was computed between the two indexes of manpower management practices and organizational effectiveness. The correlation coefficient was 0.63, which suggests that *the more advanced* (systematic and comprehensive) *the manpower management practices, the higher the organizational effectiveness*. The details of these computations are given in Table 8-8.

This completes the analyses of organizational practices of the American subsidiaries and local firms in two regions of the world, namely Latin America and the Far East.

In Chapters 9 and 10 we will analyze in detail the organizational effectiveness of the firms studied in these two regions.

Notes

1. Adam Smith, *Wealth of Nations,* New York: Modern Library, 1917.

2. Andrew Ure, *The Philosophy of Manufacturers,* London: Charles Knight, 1835.

3. Charles Babbage, *On the Economy of Machinery and Manufacturers,* 3rd ed., London: Charles Knight, 1833.

4. For a detailed discussion on this point, see William G. Scott, *Organization Theory: A Behavioral Analysis for Management,* Homewood, Ill.: Richard D. Irwin, 1967, esp. pp. 21-39.

5. Frederick W. Taylor, *Scientific Management,* New York: Harper, 1947.

6. H. L. Gantt, "Training Workmen in the Habits of Industry and Cooperation," *Transactions ASME,* 30 (1908), 1,037-63.

7. L. M. Gilbreth, *The Psychology of Management,* New York: Sturgis and Walton, 1914.

8. Elton Mayo, *The Social Problems of an Industrial Civilization,* Boston: Division of Research, Graduate School of Business Admin., Harvard Univ., 1945; F. J. Roethlisberger and W. J. Dickson, *Management and the Worker: An Account of a Research Program Conducted by the Western Electric Company, Hawthorne Works,* Cambridge, Mass.: Harvard Univ. Press, 1939.

9. Scott, *op. cit.,* p. 34.

10. *Ibid.,* p. 59.

11. A. H. Maslow, *Motivation and Personality,* New York: Harper, 1954.

12. Chris Argyris, *Personality and Organization,* New York: Harper and Row, 1957; *Integrating the Individual and the Organization,* New York: Wiley, 1964; Warren G. Bennis, *Changing Organizations: Essays on the Development and Evaluation of Human Organization,* New York: McGraw-Hill, 1966; Rensis Likert, *The Human Organization: Its Management and Value,* New York: McGraw-Hill, 1967.

13. Oscar A. Ornati, *Jobs and Workers in India,* Ithaca, N.Y.: Institute of International Industrial Relations, Cornell University, 1955, p. 55.

14. Clark Kerr et al.. *Industrialism and Industrial Man,* Cambridge, Mass.: Harvard Univ. Press, 1960, p. 97.

15. Richard N. Farmer and Barry M. Richman, *Comparative Management and Economic Progress,* Homewood, Ill.: Richard D. Irwin, 1965, pp. 154-59.

16. Gunnar Myrdal, *Asian Drama: An Inquiry into the Poverty of Nations,* New York: The Twentieth Century Fund, 1968, p. 1,150.

17. L. A. Zurcher, Jr., A. Meadow, and S. E. Zurcher, "Value Orientation, Role Conflict and Alienation from Work: Cross-Cultural Study," *American Sociological Review,* 30 (August 1965), 539-48.

18. Morris David Morris, *The Emergence of an Industrial Labor Force in India: A Study of the Bombay Cotton Mills, 1859-1947,* Berkeley, Univ. of California Press, 1965, p. 4.

19. *Ibid.,* p. 202.

20. Claude McMillan, Jr., "The American Businessman in Brazil," *Business Topics,* Spring 1965, reprinted in *International*

Dimensions in Business, East Lansing, Mich.: Graduate School of Business Administration, Michigan State University, 1966, p. 103.

21. Thomas R. Fillol, *Social Factors in Economic Development: The Argentine Case,* Cambridge, Mass.: MIT Press, 1963, p. 76.

22. Steven Piker, "The Relationship of Belief Systems to Behavior in the Rural Thai Society," *Asian Survey,* 8 (May 1968), 386-99.

23. *Ibid.,* p. 399.

24. J. Ingersoll, "Fatalism in Rural Thailand," *Anthropological Quarterly,* 39 (1966), 217.

25. David Sirota and J. M. Greenwood, "Understand Your Overseas Work Force," *Harvard Business Review,* vol. 49, no. 1 (January-February 1971), 53-60.

26. *Ibid.,* p. 53.

27. *Ibid.*

28. H. C. Ganguli, "An Enquiry into Incentives for Workers in an Engineering Factory," *Indian Journal of Social Work,* June 1954, p. 10.

29. C. Altimus, Jr. et al., "Cross-Cultural Perspectives on Need Deficiencies of Blue-Collar Workers," *Quarterly Journal of Management Development,* 2 (June 1971), 91-103.

30. K. G. Deasi, "A Comparative Study of Motivation of Blue-Collar and White-Collar Workers," *Indian Journal of Social Work,* 28 (January 1958), 380-87.

31. Sirota and Greenwood, *op. cit.*

32. *Ibid.,* p. 55.

33. *Ibid.*

34. Argyris, *op. cit.*

35. Bennis, *op. cit.*

36. M. Scott Myers, "Who Are Your Motivated Workers?", *Harvard Business Review,* vol. 42, no. 1 (January-February 1964), 73-88.

37. Likert, *op. cit.*

38. F. Herzberg, *Work and the Nature of Man,* Cleveland, Ohio: World, 1966.

CHAPTER 9

ORGANIZATIONAL EFFECTIVENESS: THE BLUE-COLLAR EMPLOYEE

Although we have explored the relationships between management practices and organizational effectiveness, discussion of organizational effectiveness was held to a minimum. It is now time to examine this area in detail, particularly the rationale for using specific criteria of effectiveness. In this and Chapter 10 we will also examine the environmental impact on specific effectiveness measures, as well as the interfirm and interregional differences in organizational effectiveness.

In so doing, we will analyze in detail the organizational effectiveness of U.S. subsidiaries and local firms in the six developing countries under discussion. The analyses of data will again be carried out at four levels:

1. Comparative analysis between American subsidiaries and local firms in all six developing countries.
2. Comparisons between American subsidiaries in Latin American and Far Eastern countries.
3. Comparisons between local firms in Latin American and Far Eastern countries.
4. Comparisons between "much concern" and "moderate" and "little concern" firms.

CONCEPT OF EFFECTIVENESS

As yet there are no acceptable formulations of universal conceptual schemes, methodologies, and criteria for measuring organizational effectiveness. Consequently, there are various viewpoints for assessing effectiveness.

As Ghorpade has pointed out, there are two basic theoretical arguments for selecting specific criteria of effectiveness—"goalistic" and "systematic."[1] The goalistic criterion emphasizes the goals of organizations, while the systematic one underlines the importance of the organization's need for survival and existence as a living social system.[2]

The concept of management effectiveness has also been used variously in the business and management literature. Many management writers have equated management effectiveness with the economic effectiveness of an enterprise and accordingly have suggested such measures as sales, profits, stock prices, market shares, scrap loss, and productivity. On the other hand, behavioral-oriented management and organization theorists have emphasized the measures of human resource effectiveness, which include such factors as employee morale, interpersonal relationships, interdepartmental relationships, utilization of high-level manpower, and critical dimensions of the organization's health.

Bennis, for example, commenting on the inadequacy of economic or financial criteria of effectiveness, remarked:

> The present ways of thinking about and measuring organizational effectiveness are seriously inadequate and often misleading. . . . The present techniques of evaluation provide static indicators of certain output characteristics (i.e., performance and satisfaction) without illuminating the processes by which the organization searches for, adapts to, and solves its changing goals. . . . It is these dynamic processes of problem-solving that provide the critical dimensions of organizational health, and without knowledge of them, output measurements are woefully inadequate."[3]

Many other scholars, such as Argyris,[4] Likert,[5] Etzioni,[6] Georgopoulos and Tannenbaum,[7] and Selznick,[8] have argued for using behavioral measures to examine organizational effectiveness.

Selznick, who underscores the importance of achieving overall system effectiveness, lists five criteria:

1. The security of the organization as a whole in relation to social forces in its environment.

2. The stability of the lines of authority and communication.
3. The stability of informal relations within the organization.
4. The continuity of policy and of the sources of its determination.
5. A homogeneity of outlook with respect to the meaning and role of the organization.[9]

Other scholars have suggested the following measures of effectiveness:

1. Productivity.
2. Intraorganizational stress and conflict.
3. Organizational flexibility to adjust to external and internal changes.
4. Interrelationships among different parts of the organization.
5. Awareness of patterns in parts of the organization.
6. System effectiveness in influencing its own core activities.

I admit that the ultimate growth and survival of a business organization depend on its financial or economic strength and that such economic data as profit, cost per unit, sales volume are good indicators of a firm's financial strength. These outputs, however, are the result of what the entire organization does (including its technology and resources), rather than being merely the result of managerial action. Hypothetically, managers can overburden an organization, drain off its long-range potential, and in the short run compel the organization to achieve higher profits and sales. It is also a mistake to use these economic indices to measure management effectiveness in underdeveloped countries where the seller's-market condition prevails. In a captive market situation, achieving increased sales and profits is not a difficult task.

Accordingly, I attempted to collect data on both behavioral and financial measures of effectiveness in the course of my research. For the behavioral measures, I devised the following criteria:

1. Employee morale and satisfaction in work (operative level).
2. Interpersonal relationships among workers and supervisors.

3. Absenteeism.
4. Employee turnover.
5. Ability to hire and retain high-level manpower.
6. Interdepartmental relationships.
7. Executive's perception toward the firm's overall objectives and goals.
8. Utilization of high-level manpower.
9. Executive responsiveness in adapting to environmental changes.

Data on employee morale, absenteeism, turnover, and interpersonal relationships will be analyzed in this chapter. We will take up other measures of effectiveness in Chapter 10.

EMPLOYEE MORALE AND SATISFACTION IN WORK

Morale is reflected in the employee's attitude toward his work, group, supervisor, and the company. It is also reflected in the gratification the employee gets in his work.

Employee morale is directly linked with productivity and with absenteeism and turnover rates. The higher employee morale, the higher productivity and the lower are absenteeism and turnover. A number of studies undertaken in the U.S. have validated this relationship between morale and productivity, absenteeism, and turnover.[10] But there is also evidence suggesting that morale and productivity are not positively related. One such finding is reported by Gouldner.[11] In his gypsum plant study, Gouldner found a high degree of employee morale and a low degree of productivity and effectiveness. As Price has noted, however, "a few negative cases [such as the one reported by Gouldner] do not invalidate the overall findings concerning the positive relationship between morale and productivity."[12]

In the present study, data on employee morale were collected by interviewing randomly selected blue-collar employees and their respective supervisors. The sample size in each company ranged from 12 to 20 employees. Open-ended, nonstructured questions were posed in an effort to gain an overall perspective on employee morale and satisfaction in work.

As is illustrated in Table 9-1, employee morale in the six

Table 9-1
Employee Morale and Satisfaction in Work

Organization concern for publics: Latin America

Employee morale:	Overall U.S.	Overall local	Much U.S.	Much local	Moderate U.S.	Moderate local	Little U.S.	Little local
Highly satisfied—excellent morale	4	4	1	—	3	4	—	—
Somewhat satisfied—Average morale	13	8	1	—	12	7	—	1
Not satisfied—poor morale	3	3	—	1	3	2	—	—
Not available	—	2	—	—	—	2	—	—
Total	20	17	2	1	18	15	0	1

Organizational concern for publics: Far East

Employee morale:	Overall U.S.	Overall local	Much U.S.	Much local	Moderate U.S.	Moderate local	Little U.S.	Little local
Highly satisfied—excellent morale	13	6	9	6	4	—	—	—
Somewhat satisfied—Average morale	20	26	3	4	16	18	1	4
Not satisfied—poor morale	2	6	—	1	1	—	1	5
Not available	1	—	—	—	—	—	1	—
Total	36	38	12	11	21	18	3	9

Summary Comparisons

Item	U.S. subsidiary	Local firm	Both
	(N given in parentheses)		
High Employee Morale and satisfaction in work:			
In both regions	30.3% (56)	18.1% (55)	24.3% (111)
In Latin American countries	20.0% (20)	23.5% (17)	21.6% (37)
In Far Eastern countries	36.1% (36)	15.7% (38)	25.3% (74)
In "much concern" firms	71.4% (14)	50.0% (12)	61.5% (26)
In "moderate concern" firms	17.9% (39)	12.1% (33)	15.2% (72)
In "little concern" firms	0.0% (3)	0.0% (10)	0.0% (13)

developing countries can hardly be classified as low. In most of the companies, employees were at least moderately satisfied with their work and manifested average morale. In only 14 of the total 111 companies studied did I find the employees very dissatisfied.

Generally speaking, American subsidiaries in both regions fared better than their local counterpart. Approximately 30 percent of the American subsidiaries were able to achieve high morale and satisfaction among their employees, compared to a mere 18 percent of the local companies. American subsidiaries in the Far East did somewhat better than those in Latin America, but there were no substantial differences among the local companies in these two regions.

Organizational Concern and Employee Morale

As we will see, environmental factors seem to have considerable impact on employee morale in developing nations. Nevertheless, a firm's concern toward its publics (consumers, employees, suppliers, etc.) has considerable impact on employee morale. As can be seen in Table 9-1, approximately 62 percent of the firms categorized as "much concern" have achieved excellent employee morale. In contrast, only 15 percent of the firms showing "moderate concern" and zero for those showing "little concern" were able to accomplish this.

Socio-Cultural and Environmental Impact on Employee Morale

In Chapter 8, we looked at various viewpoints on the impact of socio-cultural variables on employee morale and productivity. Overall, we found inconclusive evidence to support the view that these variables have had much impact on employee morale in the firms studied. Interviews with blue-collar employees, supervisors, and managerial personnel did, however, indicate the impact of the environmental factors on employee morale. Frequently mentioned factors were:

1. Government attitude toward the industrial worker and the business world.
2. Management-union relationships.

3. Climatic and working conditions.
4. Health and well-being of workers.
5. Political situation.

Industrial entrepreneurs in underdeveloped areas seem to have exploited the oversupply of the labor situation. As Fillol has observed with respect to Argentina, "Labor tends still to be considered as just another commodity whose services are to be bought as cheaply as possible."[13]

In more recent years governments in underdeveloped areas have remedied this situation by supporting the industrial worker through legislative processes, modifying existing labor legislation, and enacting more clearly defined laws. They have also actively supported trade union activities. By so doing they have greatly increased the expectations and aspirations of the industrial worker. However, actual realization of benefits has lagged behind considerably.[14] Chronic inflation, especially in Latin America, has widened the gap between a worker's gain in wages and his expectation of improving his standard of living.[15]

Caught between the rising cost of living and falling purchasing power, industrial workers in underdeveloped countries have responded to any and every outside force promising them a better deal. In their plight, they have been exploited by political parties, governments, and politically oriented labor unions alike.

On the other hand, industrialists or entrepreneurs are convinced that the lack of economic progress in a country is due to unproductive labor. As Fillol so aptly remarked, "all blame for the nation's political, economic, and social troubles is put on labor and, indirectly, on government for fomenting the workers' natural faults and indolence."[16]

Management-union relationships in most developing nations, especially in the countries I studied (except Taiwan), can best be characterized as hostile. Such attitudes, as we will see in the next section, have affected not only employee commitment and morale, but interpersonal relationships between supervisors (who are considered part of the management team) and blue-collar employees.

The climate, coupled with malnutrition and a low standard of living, have had a negative impact on employee commitment

Table 9-2[a]

Impact of Environmental Variables on Employee Morale and Satisfaction in Work in the Five Underdeveloped Countries (interview responses[b])

	Argentina (n=65)	Brazil (n=90)	India (n=272)	Philippines (n=77)	Uruguay (n=66)	Taiwan[c]	Total (n=570)
Governmental attitudes towards workers and business community	33 (51%)	55 (61%)	152 (56%)	15 (19%)	29 (45%)	— —	304 (50%)
Management-union relationship	45 (72)	51 (57)	141 (52)	36 (47)	41 (62)	— —	316 (55)
Climate	d	d	166 (61)	19 (25)	d	— —	185 (32)
Health and well-being of workers	22 (34)	31 (34)	204 (75)	31 (40)	22 (34)	— —	310 (54)
Political situation	39 (60)	37 (41)	27 (10)	15 (19)	37 (54)	— —	155 (24)

a
  This Table is reproduced from A. R. Negandhi S. B. Prasad, *Comparative Management*, New York: Appleton-Century-Crofts, 1971, p. 181. Permission of the publisher is gratefully acknowledged.

b
  Respondents include executives at all levels, supervisors, and blue-collar workers.

c
  Because of the political conditions in Taiwan, many employees, supervisors, and executives were unwilling to discuss this issue freely. However, attainment of high employee committment was not particularly difficult in Taiwan.

d
  Less than 1 percent of the total respondents. Figures in parentheses show the percentage of all respondents. Many respondents mentioned more than one factor; therefore, figures are not strictly additive.

---

and morale, particularly in the Far East. As Myrdal has pointed out:

> The sultry and oppressive climate that much of South Asia experiences all or most of the time tends to make people disinclined to work. Manual laborers, for example, habitually wield their tools with a feebler stroke and take more frequent and longer rest pauses than workers in cooler climates.[17]

To recap, my findings can be summarized in the following propositions, all other factors being the same:

1. The higher the firm's concern toward its publics, the higher will be the firm's employee morale.
2. The greater the pampering of the industrial workers by the government, the greater the degree of hostility between government and business and the poorer the employee morale.
3. The firm with a hostile union is likely to have poorer employee morale than the firm with a cooperative union.[18]

Interpersonal Relationship

The interpersonal-relationship criterion of effectiveness indicates the nature of the relationship between a blue-collar employee and his supervisor. As the reader will observe, this factor and the variable, employee morale, are closely related. Research conducted by Argyris and others has shown that the interpersonal relationship between subordinate and superordinate has a considerable effect on employee morale.[19] A supportive relationship between the leader and the follower is conducive to higher employee morale and organizational effectiveness.[20]

To collect data on this factor, I asked blue-collar employees and their supervisors to rank the following questions:

To blue-collar employee:
    My Supervisor is very:

uncooperative					business-like				cooperative	
0	1	2	3	4	5	6	7	8	9	10

To supervisor:
    My employees are:

uncooperative					business-like				cooperative	
0	1	2	3	4	5	6	7	8	9	10

As I did with previous factors, I interviewed 12 to 20 employees and supervisors in each of the companies studied. The data presented in Table 9-3 show that industrial firms in developing countries have failed to create supportive or cooperative relationships between blue-collar employees and supervisors. Of the 111 companies studied in the six developing countries, only 13 firms seem to have attained a cooperative relationship between their workers and supervisors. In contrast, in approximately two-thirds of the firms, such relationships were hostile or very uncooperative.

Firms in Taiwan apparently have had less difficulty in attaining a cooperative relationship between blue-collar employees and supervisors. This is due partly to the composition of the work force (mostly unmarried girls aged 15 to 20) and partly because of the well-disciplined Chinese work force. However, as

---

Table 9-3
Interpersonal Relationships Among
Supervisors and Blue-Collar Workers

Organizational concern for publics: Latin America

Relationship between supervisor and worker:	Overall U.S.	local	Much U.S.	local	Moderate U.S.	local	Little U.S.	local
Cooperative	—	—	—	—	—	—	—	—
Somewhat cooperative	2	2	—	—	2	1	—	1
Hostile	18	15	2	1	16	14	—	—
Total	20	17	2	1	18	15	0	1

Organizational concern for publics: Far East

Cooperative	5	5	3	4	2	—	—	1
Somewhat cooperative	17	14	5	3	12	8	—	3
Hostile	14	19	4	4	7	10	3	5
Total	36	38	12	11	21	18	3	9

Interpersonal relationships among supervisors and workers:	U.S. subsidiary	Local firm	Both
	(N given in parentheses)		
Cooperative relationships:			
In both regions	8.9% (56)	9.0% (55)	9.0% (111)
In Latin American countries	0.0% (20)	0.0% (17)	0.0% (37)
In Far Eastern countries	13.8% (36)	13.1% (38)	13.5% (74)
In "much concern" firms	21.4% (14)	33.3% (12)	26.9% (26)
In "moderate concern" firms	5.1% (39)	0.0% (33)	2.7% (72)
In "little concern" firms	0.0% (3)	10.0% (12)	7.6% (13)

we will see in the last section of this chapter, the relationship between the worker and the supervisor in Taiwan was reflected in a
high-level turnover rather than in a hostile attitude toward each
other.

The Impact of Socio-Cultural and Environmental Factors

Firms with "much concern" toward their publics were partly
successful in attaining cooperative relationships (see Table 9-3),
but here, also, the impact of this variable was not considerable.
The socio-cultural and environmental variables have largely determined the interpersonal relationships, which was borne out
in my interviews with blue-collar employees, supervisors, and
managerial personnel. The following factors were frequently
mentioned as affecting the relationship between worker and
supervisor:

1. Governmental attitudes toward businessmen and the industrial work force.
2. The political nature of trade unionism.
3. Chronic unemployment and underemployment.
4. Differences in educational levels and aspirations of younger
   and older employees.
5. Social status and the class system.
6. Inflation.

The Governmental Attitude toward Business Firms

As was pointed out in the previous section, business enterprises
in developing countries, operating in a seller's market and with
an oversupply of labor, have exploited both the consumer and
the employee. To protect workers from undue exploitation, governments in developing nations have not only activated labor
unions but also enacted much new legislation. These actions
have indeed improved wage-structure and working conditions.
However, governments and labor unions have, in turn, made
every attempt to use industrial workers to achieve their own
respective political objectives. The industrial employee, instead
of the business owner, has become a pawn in the hands of
government, political, and union leaders. To improve his wages,
working conditions, and job security, the worker still looks to the

government and the unions, thus further alienating himself from management.

Coupled with this situation are the types of relationship prevalent among government, business, and management. Both governments and unions in most developing countries are antagonistic toward business enterprises. Such an attitude was expressed by a leading businessman in India: "Government thinks we are traitors and, if they could, they would hang all of us in public parks . . . while unions think that they own our business and we are servants." Such attitudes are hardly conducive to creating cooperative relationships between management and the work force.

Inflation

Prevailing rampant inflation in developing countries,[21] particularly in Latin America, has all but wiped out any gain recorded in absolute wages. Although inflation per se is a function of many factors (the political situation, balance of payments position, international trade, etc.), the workers seem to have attached the sole responsibility for inflation to the businessman and business enterprise.

Unemployment and Underemployment

Chronic conditions of unemployment and underemployment have created a defensive attitude among laborers in developing countries.[22] Such conditions bring about much anxiety, causing the industrial worker to be perpetually afraid of losing his job—an anxiety reflected in the following statements of workers in India and Argentina, respectively:

> I dare not say anything, lest you may tell to my boss, and I will be back to my village. . . . My uncle has taught me a good lesson . . not to tell my secrets to others. . . . Mr. ———— I wish I could trust and be cooperative with my friends . . . but I am afraid to do so.

> Mr. ———— cooperation is for the birds . . . we human beings talk a lot about it, but when it comes to save your skin . . . it evaporates. . . . I felt sorry for my friend who believed in these

cooperative and sympathetic attitudes toward each other, so forth . . . he is still looking for a job.

Indeed, such anxieties seem to be founded on the employment situation. Even the management personnel of many companies supported this contention. The personnel manager of an American subsidiary in Brazil asserted: "Our management does not believe in training workers because, as a policy, we let the workers go after 8 years of service . . . of 196 workers, only 5 are our permanent employees."

Young and Old Workers

Western society does not hold a monopoly on the generation gap; it seems to be a universal phenomenon. A striking gap between younger and older employees was evident in the developing countries studied. As in Western nations, the younger employees are more revolutionary and defend the liberal views of governments, unions, and political parties. Older employees are more conservative and tend to be more pro-business. These differences in perceptions and aspirations are the basis of considerable hostility among the workers themselves, hostility which unfortunately is carried forward in their attitudes toward supervisors and higher levels of management.[23]

Difference in Social Status

Additional problems in developing a cooperative relationship between workers and supervisors result from the wide differences in social status. In industrial countries, particularly the United States, the supervisor or foreman represents high skills in both the technical and human relations areas. He gets a higher salary on the basis of that knowledge and his ability to make decisions. In developing areas, the supervisor is generally in a higher class. In Taiwan the supervisor is usually a mainland Chinese, while the blue-collar employee is Taiwanese. This in itself has caused strained relationships, resulting in a higher turnover among blue-collar employees.* The supervisor identifies himself with the

*For further elaboration on this point, see the next section and A. R. Negandhi, *Management and Economic Development: The Case of Taiwan*, The Hague: Martinus-Nijhoff's, 1973.

Table 9-4
Impact of Environmental Variables on Interpersonal Relationships in Industrial Firms in the Five Underdeveloped Countries
(interview responses [a])

	Argentina[b] (n=65)	Brazil[b] (n=90)	India[b] (n=272)	Philippines[b] (n=77)	Uruguay[b] (n=66)	Total (n=570)
Employment situation	39 (60)[c]	30 (33)	144 (53)	42 (54)	30 (46)	285 (50)
Differences in education and aspirations of younger and older employees	45 (69)	56 (62)	122 (45)	35 (45)	41 (62)	299 (52)
Nature of trade unionism	31 (47)	61 (68)	120 (44)	20 (26)	40 (60)	272 (48)
Social status and class system	33 (51)	29 (32)	111 (41)	51 (66)	46 (66)	270 (47)
Governmental attitudes toward workers and business	53 (81)	51 (57)	92 (34)	32 (42)	32 (48)	260 (46)
Inflation	32 (48)	41 (46)	22 (9)	8 (10)	27 (41)	130 (23)

a Respondents included the executives at all levels, supervisors, and blue-collar workers.

b Data for Argentina, Brazil, India, the Philippines, and Uruguay are reproduced from A. R. Negandhi and S. B. Prasad, *Comparative Management,* New York: Appleton-Century-Crofts, 1971, p. 182. Permission of the publishers is gratefully acknowledged.

c Figures in parentheses show the percentages of all respondents. Many respondents mentioned more than one factor; therefore, figures are not strictly additive.

---

managerial or entrepreneurial class even though he may not in actuality belong to it. Such identification, coupled with the lack of technical skills and knowledge of human relations, arouses the worker's antagonism. Thus employees find a good excuse for demonstrating their anxieties, frustrations and anger against management through their supervisors.

The list of factors we have analyzed is by no means all-inclusive; I have attempted to single out only the most important ones. As the reader will recognize, all of these are environmental factors over which management can exercise little control. Only a few firms in this study were able to overcome environmental constraints by pursuing permanent employment policies, offering higher wages and better opportunities for advancement and self-growth, and training supervisors and workers in technical and human relations skills.

Absenteeism and Turnover

As the reader may have observed in examining the data on employee morale and interpersonal relationships, I have ignored the impact of contextual variables such as size and technology of a firm. My detailed analyses (reported elsewhere), however, failed to indicate statistically significant differences among the firms of different sizes and technological categories.[24]

The same was not true of absenteeism and turnover. Here I found considerable differences between the firms located in different countries, as well as firms belonging to different industries. Absenteeism was higher and turnover lower in the five developing countries (the exception being Taiwan, where turnover was high), compared to the United States.[25]

To ascertain the impact of environmental and contextual variables (size, ownership, location, and technology) and a firm's concern for its publics on these two important factors, I concentrated on analyzing data from two Far Eastern countries, India and Taiwan. Indian data are from closely matched pharmaceutical firms which should enable us to determine the impact of location, ownership, and a firm's concern for its publics on absenteeism and employee turnover. Taiwan data are from three sets of companies: U.S. subsidiaries, local firms, and Japanese subsidiaries. These will provide an opportunity for intercountry comparisons.

Absenteeism

Both absenteeism and turnover have been correlated with employee morale and satisfaction in work. They have also been linked with supervisory and leadership styles.

An extensive survey of research studies by Braffield and Crockett, for example, shows that employee attitude, or morale, is negatively related to absenteeism and employee turnover.[26] However, they reported considerable doubt about the presumed relationships between employee morale and performance on the job. Similarly, Herzberg, Peterson, and Capwall, in a review of research studies, also show positive relationships between employee attitudes and output.[27] More recently, a study by Porter and Lawler has indicated a positive relationship between employee morale and productivity and a negative relationship between morale and absenteeism and turnover.[28]

Absenteeism and turnover may also be a function of economic and employment conditions. For example, one may find higher rates of absenteeism and turnover in times of economic prosperity, rising wages, and low unemployment conditions. Conversely, in an economic depression or recession, when jobs are scarce, absentee report forms gather dust. In a given socio-economic and cultural environment, differences in the number of absentees among different firms might reflect their effectiveness in providing a good working condition. Research studies by Argyris,[29] Fleishman and Harris,[30] Argyle, Gardner, and Coffee,[31] and Lindguist[32] indicate a positive relationship between absenteeism, turnover, and leadership styles. To Argyris, absenteeism is one kind of defensive mechanism the employee uses to vent his frustrations, conflicts, and failure to achieve satisfaction in his work. Fleishman and Harris related turnover, as well as grievance rates, to leadership behavior, stating: "The more the leader structures, directs, and controls, the greater the probability of turnover."[33] Argyle, Gardner, and Coffee related directive leadership to absenteeism, while Lindguist demonstrated a causal relationship between unfavorable job adjustment and absenteeism.

Indian Data

As is noted above, data for absenteeism and turnover in Indian companies were collected from five American subsidiaries and five comparable local firms. The pairs were closely matched with respect to size (number of employees) and the nature of production techniques used. They were, however, located in different places, which gave me an opportunity to examine the impact of location on these two effectiveness variables.

As data presented in Tables 9-5 and 9-6 indicate, absen-

Table 9-5[a]

Absenteeism in American Subsidiaries and Local Pharmaceutical Companies in India

Type of personnel	All U.S. companies (located in Bombay) (avg. 5)		Two Indian companies (located elsewhere) (avg. 5)		All Indian companies (located in Bombay) (avg. 3)	
	1964	1965	1964	1965	1964	1965
Operators	11.10%	12.10%	11.04%	11.68%	14.17%	14.33%
Clerical	4.50	5.00	4.88(4)[b]	3.88(4)[b]	4.75(2)[b]	3.50(2)[b]
Managerial	2.00(3)[b]	2.00(3)[b]	2.00(1)[b]	2.00(1)[b]	n.a.	n.a.

[a] Reproduced from A. R. Negandhi and S. B. Prasad, *Comparative Management*, New York: Appleton-Century-Crofts, 1971, p. 113. Permission of the publisher is gratefully acknowledged.

[b] Denotes number of companies in the figure.

Table 9-6[a]

Absenteeism in American and Local Pharmaceutical Companies in India

Pair	Company identification	Type of personnel	Location	U.S. sub. 1964	1965	Indian co. 1964	1965	Location
I	1-2 (M) (MC)	operators clerical managerial	Bombay	8.0 4.0 n.a.	8.5 5.5 n.a.	7.0 5.0 2.0	9.0 4.5 2.0	elsewhere
II	3-4 (M) (MC)	operators clerical managerial	Bombay	13.0 5.0 2.0	14.0 4.0 2.0	5.7 5.0 n.a.	6.4 4.0 n.a.	elsewhere
III	5-6 (MC) (MC)	operators clerical managerial	Bombay	14.5 8.0 2.0	15.0 10.0 2.5	15.0 n.a. n.a.	16.0 n.a. n.a.	Bombay
IV	7-8 (MC) (L)	operators clerical managerial	Bombay	13.0 3.5 2.0	15.0 3.0 1.5	15.0 4.0 n.a.	14.0 3.5 n.a.	Bombay
V	9-10 (M) (L)	operators clerical managerial	Bombay	7.0 2.0 n.a.	8.0 2.5 n.a.	12.5 5.5 n.a.	13.0 3.5 n.a.	Bombay

[a] Reproduced from A. R. Negandhi and S. B. Prasad, *Comparative Management*, New York: Appleton-Century-Crofts, 1971, p. 113. Permission of the publisher is gratefully acknowledged.

KEY: M=much concern for publics
MC=moderate concern for publics
L=little concern for publics

teeism seems to be more a function of location and ownership (American versus Indian) than anything else. For example, two Indian firms located in cities other than Bombay were characterized by consistently lower rates of absenteeism and higher quitting rates, compared to other Indian (as well as American) companies in Bombay. The average rate of absenteeism among American companies was somewhat lower than in the Indian firms. Higher wage rates, better working conditions, and fair play in promotion policies in the American companies might explain these differences. Generally, American firms in India (and in most other foreign countries, for that matter) pay double the wages paid by local firms. However, absenteeism rates in the American companies are still much higher compared to those of their sister firms located in the United States. The average rate of 12.1 percent in these companies in 1965 compares unfavorably with the 2.6 percent in the U.S.[34] As is shown in Table 9-6, a firm's concern for its publics (the organization variable) seems to have much less impact on absenteeism, while environmental factors and location seem to have considerable effect.

The higher rates of absenteeism in Indian industrial enterprises can be explained in terms of the low standard of living (which affects the health and well-being of workers), climatic conditions in industrial cities (temperature varies from 85 to 110 degrees Fahrenheit, with 80 to 100 percent humidity), working conditions in factories, and permissive labor legislation in India.

Taiwan Data

Absenteeism in Taiwan does not seem to be a major problem (see Table 9-7). Absenteeism among blue-collar employees, supervisors, clerical workers, and managerial personnel was less than 4 percent in most American and Japanese subsidiaries. Local companies, however, experienced somewhat higher absenteeism.

It is interesting to note from Table 9-7 that in the local companies, supervisory personnel stayed away from work more frequently than operatives, clerical employees, and managerial personnel. My inquiry suggests that supervisors in the local firms enjoyed many privileges, such as sick leave and causal leave, and seemed to take advantage of such preferred rights. Interviews

Table 9-7
Absenteeism at Various Levels

		Absenteeism rate/year (%)				
	Level	25 or more	15 to 24	5 to 14	4 or less	n.a.
U.S. subsidiaries (n=9)	operative level	1		2	6	
	supervisor	1		1	4	3
	junior management and clerical employees		1		3	5
	senior management				3	6
Japanese subsidiaries (n=7)	operative level	1		1	5	
	supervisor		1		3	3
	junior management and clerical employees				3	4
	senior management				3	4
Local companies (n=11)	operative level		1	6	3	1
	supervisor	3	5	1	1	1
	junior management and clerical employees				5	6
	senior management				4	4

This table is reproduced from A. R. Negandhi, *Management and Economic Development: The Case of Taiwan,* The Hague: Martinus Nijhoff's, 1972, p. 103. Permission of the publisher is gratefully acknowledged.

with these supervisors, however, indicate a high level of frustration. They seemed to feel they were "in the middle," having a great deal of responsibility but no decision-making power, and lacked the opportunity to exercise initiative in their work.

Overall, the absenteeism rate in Taiwan compares favorably with companies in India. Differences in absenteeism in India and Taiwan indicate that an oppressive climate (in India) may indeed have considerable impact. As we noted in Chapter 6, there are no measurable differences in the supervisory and leadership styles in these two countries; leadership roles in both can be characterized as autocratic-paternalistic.

Employee Turnover

The concept of labor turnover implies an employee's decision to disengage from an organization's activities. Usually in management literature, labor turnover is defined as the number of people hired per unit of time in order to maintain a work force of a given size. The most frequently used formula to measure labor turnover is: $T = R/F$, where $T =$ turnover rate, $R =$ replacements per unit of time, and $F =$ average working force. This formula includes all kinds of labor turnover—workers leaving due to death, sickness, dismissal, or to join other organizations.

For this study, I concentrated on labor turnover that arises from workers leaving to join other firms. The data, here called "voluntary turnover rate," will, I hope, suggest a better correlation between employee morale and labor turnover.

Like absenteeism, the turnover rate is related to supervisory style, working conditions, levels of compensation, economic and employment conditions, and the perceived fairness or equity in wages and treatment of employees.

In the previous section I mentioned a number of studies supporting the impact of these factors (except perceived equity) on employee absenteeism and turnover. In the last few years a number of scholars have demonstrated the relationship between employee perception of wages, treatment, working conditions, and alternative job opportunities, and job satisfaction, morale, absenteeism, and reasons for terminating employment.

More than a decade ago March and Simon postulated that such factors as conformity of job to self-image, perceived possibility of interorganizational transfer, and perceived desirability of movement have a strong bearing on an employee's decision to quit his job.[35]

A recent study by Telly, French, and Scott seems to further validate this contention.[36] In their study of an aerospace firm they found:

> . . . when an employee perceives inequitable treatment, he will feel frustrated and he will not contribute his best efforts toward the management-perceived primary goals of the organization. If the inequity is excessive, he will actually separate himself from the organization.[37]

The study, they argue, supports the theory that perceptions of inequity are associated with turnover; it also indicates some of the specific kinds of treatment perceived as inequitable in a high-turnover shop, inequity with respect to supervision, lead men, working conditions, intrinsic aspects of the job, and social aspects of the job.[38]

My findings in India and Taiwan confirm the impact of such factors as wages, working conditions, perceived opportunity for advancement and alternative job opportunity, social and class status, and geographical location of the firms.

Indian Data

The data on the voluntary turnover rates in 10 pharmaceutical firms are presented in Tables 9-8 and 9-9. Table 9-8 shows that the voluntary labor turnover in American subsidiaries was much lower than that of comparable Indian companies. The average turnover rates for blue-collar workers were 1.6 percent in the former companies, while in the latter companies the rates were 4.76 percent in 1964 and 4.86 percent in 1965. Also, for clerical and managerial personnel in the Indian companies, the rate of quitting was three times that of the American subsidiaries. The high rates in the Indian companies, however, were somewhat influenced by the differing labor market conditions for two of these companies. These two companies (No. 2 and No. 4 in Table 9-9) were in smaller cities not far from farm areas. As a result, the labor force of these companies consisted of transitory farm workers. In Bombay, where other companies were located, the labor force was drawn from far-away villages. Due to a higher rate of unemployment in big cities such as Bombay, the workers were reluctant to quit their jobs. An earlier study by Ornati indicated similar patterns in labor turnover rates in different cities of India.[39] Thus, if we exclude the two Indian companies and compare American and Indian companies in Bombay, we find that the voluntary quitting rates are considerably lower in those companies. The average quitting rates for blue-collar workers fell from 4.74 percent and 4.86 percent to 2.67 percent and 2 percent in 1964 and 1965, respectively. Similar downward trends were also observed among clerical and managerial personnel.

Voluntary turnover rates in the American subsidiaries were still lower than those of the Indian companies. Table 9-9 shows the voluntary turnover rates in each pair of American and Indian

Table 9-8

Voluntary Labor Turnover in American Subsidiaries and Local Pharmaceutical Companies in India

Type of personnel:	All U.S. companies (located in Bombay) (avg. 5)		Two Indian companies (located elsewhere) (avg. 5)		All Indian companies (located in Bombay) (avg. 3)	
	1964	1965	1964	1965	1964	1965
Operators	1.6	1.6	4.74	4.86	2.67	2.00
Clerks	0.8	0.8	2.68	3.48	1.83	2.67
Managers	0.5(1)*	0.5(1)*	2.28(4)*	2.15(4)*	1.50(2)*	2.00(2)*

*Figures in parentheses represent the total number of companies.
This table is reproduced from A. R. Negandhi and S. B. Prasad, *Comparative Management*, New York: Appleton-Century-Crofts, 1971, p. 113. Permission of the publisher is gratefully acknowledged.

Table 9-9

Voluntary Labor Turnover in American and Local Pharmaceutical Companies in India

Pair	Company identification	Type of personnel	Location	U.S. sub. 1964	U.S. sub. 1965	Indian co. 1964	Indian co. 1965	Location
I	1-2	operators	Bombay	3.5	2.0	7.0	9.0	else-where
		clerical		0.5	0.5	2.0	2.5	
		managerial		0.5*	0.5*	2.0	2.0	
II	3-4	operators	Bombay	1.0	1.0	8.7	9.3	else-where
		clerical		1.0	1.0	5.3	6.9	
		managerial		nil	nil	4.1	2.6	
III	5-6	operators	Bombay	2.0	2.0	2.5	2.5	Bombay
		clerical		1.0*	1.0	1.5	1.0	
		managerial		n.a.	n.a.	1.0	2.0	
IV	7-8	operators	Bombay	1.5	2.0	2.0	1.5	
		clerical		1.0*	1.0	2.0	2.0	
		managerial		n.a.	n.a.	1.0	2.0	Bombay
V	9-10	operators	Bombay	1.0	1.0	3.5	2.0	
		clerical		0.5*	0.5*	2.0	5.0	Bombay
		managerial		nil	nil	2.0	2.0	

n.a. Not available.
This table is reproduced from A. R. Negandhi and S. B. Prasad, *Comparative Management*, Neew York: Appleton-Century-Crofts, 1971, p. 114. Permission of the publisher is gratefully acknowledged.
*Less than.

companies. These companies were paired on the basis of their similarity in size, technology (hardware), and product lines. The companies numbered 1, 3, 5, 7, and 9 are the American subsidiaries, and 2, 4, 6, 8, and 10 are their Indian counterparts. The data reveal that the most influential factor affecting employee turnover rate was the labor-market condition and ownership of the firm. The American subsidiaries with the lowest turnover rates generally pay much higher wages and offer better opportunities for advancement and training. They also use more objective methods for deciding rate and salary raises, as well as promotions.

Taiwan Data

Employee turnover seems to be a major headache for many companies in Taiwan. A sizable number of companies had an abnormally high turnover rate among their blue-collar employees. This ranged from a low of 35 percent to a high of 150 percent of their total labor force. As can be seen in Table 9-10, more than one-third of the companies studied (11 of the 27) were in this category. The average turnover rate in Taiwan was about 40 percent.

Turnover among clerical, supervisory, and managerial personnel was not as high as it was among operative level employees. Nonetheless, about one-fourth of the companies reported 15 percent or more turnover among employees at these levels.

The high level of employee turnover observed in Taiwan prompted me to inquire further into the problem. To do so, I held additional intensive interviews with some 50 executives, supervisors, blue-collar employees, economists, government officials, planners, and university professors. The following environmental factors were mentioned frequently in these interviews and will be examined in detail: industrial boom and shortage of skilled workers; low wages and lack of wage differentials between the industrial and nonindustrial workers; and social tension.[40]

Industrial Boom and Shortage of Skilled Workers

Taiwan has experienced phenomenal industrial growth in the last decade. For example, from 1953 to 1967 industrial production increased 14 percent per year, and this trend has been continuous. In the past five years Taiwan has had a 19 percent increase per year.

It is true that Taiwan may not have a labor shortage of unskilled workers in the forseeable future, but this prospect is considerably different with respect to skilled employees and supervisory, managerial, and technical personnel. In the course of my study, personnel in many of the firms complained about the shortage of manpower in these categories. Executives of firms with a high level of employee turnover put greater emphasis on the fact that shortages give rise to chronic labor turnover.

Low Wages and Lack of Differential in Wages

Low wages, coupled with the high productivity of Chinese workers, make Taiwan attractive to foreign investors, but this is a mixed blessing.[41] The lack of a reasonable wage differential between industrial and nonindustrial sectors keeps some portions of the available labor force away from industry. At the same time, it also makes it easier for the industrial worker to shift jobs.

Government-imposed martial law, which prohibits labor strikes, further aggravates the situation. Unable to bargain for improved wages and working conditions, dissatisfied workers simply quit their jobs and return to the nonindustrial sectors or to their own small businesses.

In the electronics industry, where high turnover is particularly serious, firms try to employ girls between the ages of 16 and 19, who, although well-disciplined and hard-working, are not necessarily career-oriented.

Social Tension

Another factor contributing to the high turnover in Taiwan is social tension between supervisors and blue-collar employees. This factor was particularly stressed by executives in American and Japanese subsidiaries. Executives of these companies contended that although the government has been able to reduce tension between native Taiwanese people and the mainland Chinese, there is still considerable social distance and stress between these two groups. By and large, the mainland Chinese are better educated,

Table 9-10

Employee Turnover at Various Levels

Level	25 to 150	15 to 24	5 to 14	4 or less	na.
U.S. subsidiaries (n=9) operator	3		5	1	
supervisor	1			4	4
junior management and clerical employees	2		2	4	1
senior management			1	4	4
Japanese subsidiaries (n=7) operator	3		1	3	
supervisor		1		4	2
junior management and clerical employees	2	1	1	3	
senior management					
Local companies (n=11) operator	5	4	1	1	
supervisor		1	2	6	2
junior management and clerical employees			5	4	2
senior management				5	6

(Column header: Turnover/Year (%))

This table is reproduced from A. R. Negandhi, *Management and Economic Development: The Case of Taiwan,* The Hague: Marinus Nijhoff's, 1973, p. 105. Permission of the publisher is gratefully acknowledged.

better trained, and more experienced than their counterpart Taiwanese brothers. As a result, the mainland Chinese always find jobs at supervisory, technical, and managerial levels, while the Taiwanese must be content with lower-level jobs. The relationship between supervisor and worker not only reflects a different hierarchy in skills and authority but also reflects dormant social tensions.

In particular, executives of the companies that experienced employee turnover of 150 to 200 percent during 1966, 1967, and 1968 were quite articulate in citing social tensions as the prime cause for high turnover in Taiwanese industry. To verify this contention, a number of additional executives in the companies experiencing both high and low employee turnover were asked to answer specific questions on this issue. Unfortunately many were reluctant to commit themselves one way or the other. A few executives from the Japanese subsidiaries that have experienced less than 4 percent employee turnover did mention that their policies were to hire supervisors, blue-collar employees, and technical personnel from the socially "homogeneous" groups. What they meant was, they prefer to hire either mainland Chinese or Taiwanese, but not both.

Thus there seems to be some indication that social tension exists between the mainland Chinese supervisor and the Taiwanese worker, with a resultant high turnover. I stop short of generalizing about these relationships, however, since my data are limited. My intention in singling out this variable is simply to record what I found and to shed some light on the additional factors causing high employee turnover.

SUMMARY

In this chapter we have looked at four variables of management effectiveness as it applies to blue-collar employees: employee morale and satisfaction in work, interpersonal relationships, labor turnover, and absenteeism.

Analysis of the data from 111 industrial firms in six developing countries reveals that the majority of these companies were able to attain average or moderate employee morale and satisfaction in work.

In the case of interpersonal relationships, however, most companies failed to foster cooperative attitudes among their employees. The environmental variables affecting interpersonal relationships are underemployment and unemployment situations, governmental attitudes toward the industrial worker and the business community, politically oriented trade unions, inflation, and the differences in educational attainments and aspirations between younger and older employees.

Due to the vast differences among firms in different industrial categories, data on absenteeism and turnover were intensively analyzed with respect to 10 pharmaceutical firms in India and 27 companies located in Taiwan. Analysis of these data indicates a considerable impact of such environmental and cultural factors as location, climatic conditions, and social distance and status on absenteeism and turnover.

Notes

1. J. Ghorpade, *Assessment of Organizational Effectiveness,* Pacific Palisades, Cal.: Goodyear Publishing, 1971, pp. 85-87.

2. *Ibid.*

3. W. G. Bennis, *Changing Organizations,* New York: McGraw-Hill, 1966, quoted in Ghorpade, *op. cit.,* pp. 122-23.

4. Chris Argyris, *Personality and Organization,* New York: Harper and Row, 1957; *Integrating the Individual and the Organization,* New York: Wiley, 1964.

5. Rensis Likert, *The Human Organization: Its Management and Value,* New York: McGraw-Hill, 1967.

6. Amitai Etzioni, "Two Approaches to Organizational Analysis: A Critique and a Suggestion," *Administrative Science Quarterly,* vol. 5, no. 2 (September 1960), 257-58.

7. B. S. Georgopoulos and A. S. Tannenbaum, "A Study of Organizational Effectiveness," *American Sociological Review,* vol. 22, no. 5 (1957), 534-40.

8. Philip Selznick, "Foundations of the Theory of Organization," *American Sociological Review,* vol. 13, no. 1 (1948), 25-35.

9. *Ibid.,* pp. 29-30.

10. See Daniel Katz, Nathan Maccoby, and Nancy C. Morse, *Productivity, Supervision and Morale in an Office Situation,* Ann Arbor, Mich.: Survey Research Center, Institute for Social Research, 1950; and M. Argyle, G. Gardner, and F. Coffee, "Supervisory Methods Related to Productivity, Absenteeism and Labor Turnover," *Human Relations,* vol. 11, no. 1 (1958), 23-40.

11. Alvin W. Gouldner, *Patterns of Industrial Bureaucracy,* Glencoe, Ill.: The Free Press, 1954; see also A. H. Brayfield and W. H. Crockett, "Employee Attitudes and Employee Performance," *Psychological Bulletin,* 52 (1955), 396-424.

12. James L. Price, *Organizational Effectiveness: An Inventory of Propositions,* Homewood, Ill.: Richard D. Irwin, 1968, p. 69.

13. Thomas R. Fillol, *Social Factors in Economic Development: The Argentine Case,* Cambridge, Mass.: MIT Press, 1963,

14. H. C. Ganguli, "An Inquiry into Incentives for Workers

in an Engineering Factory," *Indian Journal of Social Work,* June 1954, p. 10.

15. Fillol, *op. cit.,* chap. 4.

16. *Ibid.,* p. 74.

17. Gunnar Myrdal, *Asian Drama: An Inquiry into the Poverty of Nations,* New York: The Twentieth Century Fund, 1968, p. 1,150.

18. For details on these propositions, see A. R. Negandhi and S. B. Prasad, *Comparative Management,* New York: Appleton-Century-Crofts, 1971, pp. 100-105.

19. Argyris, *op. cit.*

20. Likert, *op. cit.*

21. For inflation rates in various developing countries, see Negandhi and Prasad, *op. cit.,* pp. 217-21.

22. Unemployment percentages varied from 10-15 percent in Argentina to 25-35 percent in India. The precise data on underemployment are difficult to obtain, but the general consenssus was that in Latin American countries, the rate of underemployment varied from 25 to 35 percent, while in Far Eastern countries these were as high as 50 to 60 percent. For interesting and scholarly observations on "unemployment" and "underemployment" in Southeast Asia, see Myrdal, *op. cit.,* chap. 21 and appen. 16.

23. Employees in the age group of 19-30 were mostly high school graduates, while the age group 35-55 were either illiterate or had had one or two years of schooling. For similar observations concerning Japanese workers, see Arthur M. Whitehill, Jr. and Shin-ichi Takezawa, *The Other Worker: A Comparative Study of Industrial Relations in the United States and Japan,* Honolulu: East-West Center Press, 1968, pp. 352-53.

24. See A. R. Negandhi, S. B. Prasad, and Y. K. Shetty, "Manpower Management and Organizational Effectiveness: A Cross-Cultural Study," *Academy of Management Proceedings,* 1973, pp. 347-349.

25. For recent statistics on the turnover of factory workers in the United States, see *Wall Street Journal,* March 25, 1970, p. 1, column 6.

26. Brayfield and Crockett, *op. cit.*

27. F. Herzberg et al., *Job Attitudes: Review or Research and Opinion,* Pittsburgh, Pa.: Psychological Service of Pittsburgh.

28. L. W. Porter and E. E. Lawler, *Managerial Attitudes*

and Performance, Homewood, Ill. Richard D. Irwin, 1968, esp. chaps. 4, 6, 7.

29. Argyris, *op. cit.*

30. E. Fleishman and E. Harris, "Patterns of Leadership Behavior Related to Employee Grievances and Turnover," Department of Industrial Administration, Yale University, 1961, mimeographed.

31. M. Argyle, G. Gardner, and F. Coffee, "Supervisory Methods Related to Productivity, Absenteeism and Labor Turnover," *Human Relations,* vol. 2, no. 1 (1958), 23-40.

32. A. Lindquist, "Absenteeism and Job Turnover as Consequences of Unfavorable Job Adjustment," *Acta Social,* vol. 3, nos. 2 and 3 (1958), 119-31.

33. Fleishman and Harris, *loc. cit.,* quoted in Argyris, *op. cit.,* p. 60.

34. F. Harbison and C. Myers, *Management in the Industrial World,* New York: McGraw-Hill, 1959, pp. 45-54.

35. James G. March and Herbert A. Simon, *Organizations,* New York: Wiley, 1963.

36. C. Telly, W. L. French, and W. G. Scott, "The Relationship of Inequity to Turnover among Hourly Workers," *Administrative Science Quarterly,* vol. 16, no. 2 (June 1971), 164-72.

37. *Ibid.,* p. 171.

38. *Ibid.*

39. Oscar Ornati, *Jobs and Workers in India,* Ithaca, N.Y.: Cornell Univ. Press, 1955.

40. For details, see A. R. Negandhi, *Management and Economic Development: The Case of Taiwan,* The Hague: Martinus Nijhoff's, 1973, pp. 106-107.

41. For further details on this point, see A. R. Negandhi, "New Frontiers for the American Business: The Case for Taiwan," *California Management Review,* vol. 14, no. 1 (Fall 1971), 96-102.

CHAPTER 10

ORGANIZATIONAL EFFECTIVENESS: HIGH-LEVEL MANPOWER

In the last chapter we looked at four criteria of effectiveness among blue-collar employees. The analysis clearly suggests the considerable impact of environmental and socio-cultural factors. In particular, employee absenteeism, turnover, and interpersonal relationships were greatly constrained by the external conditions prevailing in developing countries. As we shall see in this chapter, however, other measures of organizational effectiveness are not as affected by environmental and socio-cultural factors. The measures discussed in this section are to a large extent within the realm of managerial control.

The following measures of effectiveness deal with high-level manpower and will be analyzed in the following pages:
the ability to hire and retain managerial and technical personnel
subsystem (interdepartmental) relationships
the executive's perception of the firm's overall objectives
utilization of high-level manpower
adaptation to environmental changes.

THE ABILITY TO HIRE AND RETAIN MANAGERIAL AND TECHNICAL PERSONNEL

A firm's overall effectiveness depends largely on its ability to secure and retain high-level manpower. Almost a decade ago Jerome M. Rosow stressed the importance of this ability (in regard to organizational growth and survival):

In the past, professionals were a select group who were a very small proportion of the total organization—now, they may be *the* organization, and they are the greatest single investment in manpower. The future of the enterprise depends increasingly upon the energy of its best minds. Brainpower is the energy source of industrial growth.[1]

At the macro level many economic development theorists have argued that a nation's economic and industrial growth are functions of the quality of its human resources, particularly at the managerial and technical levels. In the case of developing countries, it has been argued that the real bottleneck in achieving rapid economic and industrial development is the shortage of trained managerial and technical personnel.[2]

Leaders of both developed and developing nations seem to have realized this fact, which is reflected in the great surge of management education and the recent forming of business and technical schools in many of the underdeveloped nations. But, in spite of their best efforts, a shortage of trained personnel continues in these countries. These shortages notwithstanding, there are considerable differences between U.S. subsidiaries and local firms with respect to their ability to attract and retain high-level manpower.

As the data in Table 10-1 indicate, approximately 48 percent of the U.S. subsidiaries in Latin America and the Far East were able to attract and retain trained managerial and technical help. Many of the executives and technical staff in these firms were college graduates. Many had earned masters degrees from abroad, including several from the United States. High-level manpower in the American subsidiaries could be judged as professionals, both by their educational backgrounds and their attitudes. In contrast to the U.S. subsidiaries, fewer than 20 percent of the local companies were able to employ and retain trained personnel.

My findings raise some serious questions about the use of trained personnel in developing countries. By and large, only the U.S. subsidiaries have been able to utilize this valuable resource effectively.

ORGANIZATIONAL CONCERN AND THE USE OF HIGH-LEVEL MANPOWER

Despite such imbalance between the U.S. subsidiaries and local

Table 10-1
Ability to Hire and Retain Trained
Managerial and Technical Personnel

Organizational concern for publics: Latin America

Item:	Overall U.S.	Local	Much U.S.	Local	Moderate U.S.	Local	Little U.S.	Local
Able to hire and retain highly trained personnel	8	3	1	1	7	2	—	—
Able to hire and retain moderately trained personnel	4	6	—	—	4	6	—	
Unable to hire and retain even moderately trained personnel	8	8	1	—	7	7	—	1
Total	20	17	2	1	18	15	0	1

Organizational concern for publics: Far East

Item:	Overall U.S.	Local	Much U.S.	Local	Moderate U.S.	Local	Little U.S.	Local
Able to hire and retain highly trained personnel	19	7	11	7	8	—	—	—
Able to hire and retain moderately trained personnel	7	13	—	1	6	10	1	2
Unable to hire and retain even moderately trained personnel	10	18	1	3	7	8	2	7
Total	36	38	12	11	21	18	3	9

Summary Comparisons:

Able to hire and retain highly trained personnel:	U.S. sub.	Local firm	Both
	(N given in parentheses)		
In both regions	48.2% (56)	18.1% (55)	33.3% (111)
In Latin American countries	40.0% (20)	17.6% (17)	29.7% (37)
In Far Eastern countries	52.7% (36)	18.9% (38)	35.1% (74)
In "much concern" firms	85.7% (14)	66.6% (12)	76.9% (26)
In "moderate" and "little concern" firms	35.7% (42)	5.0% (43)	20.0% (85)

firms in this study, I still find that the large majority of both groups showing "much concern" toward their client groups or publics were able to lure trained managerial and technical cadre into their ranks. Eighty-six percent of the American subsidiaries and 67 percent of the local firms classified as having "much concern" fall into this category.

A firm's overall concern for its publics was generally reflected in its wage and salary policies, as well as other personnel policies and practices. "Much concern" firms consistently paid better salaries and wages and provided greater opportunities for employee training, development, and advancement. Further, they utilized objective criteria for selecting, promoting, and rewarding personnel in these categories. In contrast, firms showing "little concern" paid minimum wages and salaries and for the most part utilized personal criteria (blood relationships, friendships, age, etc.) for selecting, promoting, and rewarding their high-level manpower.

SUBSYSTEMS RELATIONSHIP

The subsystem-relationship effectiveness measure refers to the nature of the relationships between the personnel in different units, or departments. My assumption here is that the harmonious relationships between different departments can lead to higher organizational effectiveness. This is not to say that conflict and tension per se are dysfunctional for organizational effectiveness. On the contrary, studies of Barker, Dembo and Levin,[3] Goldstein,[4] Allport,[5] and Roger,[6] to name a few, suggest that a certain amount of tension and frustration may actually increase creativity, satisfaction, performance, and effectiveness.

Many organization theorists agree that the minimization of spontaneous conflict between people in different departments is essential for organizational growth and survival.

In stressing the importance of reducing interunit conflicts, Caplow states:

> Since organizations are sub-divisible, self-maintenance always involves protections against these forms of internal division which threaten the existence of the whole. Of course, many organizations encourage conflict under the name of competi-

tion . . . spontaneous and unregulated conflict, however, is a direct threat to the organization's existence.[7]

In this study information was sought on how well each department recognized its interdependence with other departments and how well the various departments got along with each other. In collecting and evaluating the data on this factor, I relied heavily on what I observed rather than on what I was told by executives themselves. My overall observations in each firm were categorized for the purpose of comparison and analysis in the following manner:

very cooperative
somewhat cooperative
not cooperative.

The nature of subsystem relationships in companies in Latin America and the Far East regions are shown in Table 10-2. Some striking observations can be made from this data. For example, we find that, overall, a little more than one-third of the companies studied in the two regions are able to achieve cooperative relationships among different units or departments. This situation is somewhat misleading when the data on the American subsidiaries and local companies are examined separately. Here we find that approximately one-half of the former companies are able to achieve a cooperative and supportive relationship between their different units or departments.

As can be seen in Table 10-2, there are substantial differences between the firms (both U.S. subsidiaries and local firms) in the two regions of Latin America and the Far East. Generally, firms in the Far Eastern countries have had less difficulty attaining a cooperative relationship than the Latin American countries. The reasons behind this are due largely to the owner-manager situation and the adverse feelings toward private U.S. investments in Latin American countries.

Organizational Concern and Intergroup Relationships

One of the most striking findings was that a firm's concern for its clientage group played an important role in attaining cooperative relationships. Firms with a positive attitude toward their public, or clientage groups, were consistently better equipped than those with negative attitudes. Some 88 percent of the firms (93 percent of the U.S. subsidiaries and 83 percent of the local firms) classified as "much concern" were able to maintain a cooperative relationship between personnel in different departments. This compares favorably with 24 percent of the firms categorized as "moderate" and "little concern" firms which were able to do the same.

Translated into actual managerial practice, "much concern" firms not only stressed the importance of serving their clientage groups, but also operationalized this service concept by providing clearer statements of objectives, policies, and procedures for attaining the company's overall goals. In contrast, "moderate" and "little concern" firms were less articulate about their responsibilities to their various publics and have diffused policies regarding their goals, objectives, and procedures for attaining these goals.

As was noted above, firms in Latin American countries have had great difficulty in attaining a cooperative relationship. My interviews with managerial and technical personnel revealed the influence of two environmental factors: (1) the owner-manager situation in local companies and (2) aversion to U.S. investment among personnel in the American subsidiaries.

Although the owner-manager situation existed in all six developing countries, this situation seems slightly more prevalent in the Latin American region. Generally, the owner-manager type of organizations are overcentralized in their authority structures, which in turn gives rise to greater frustrations among the salaried employees who are not relatives of the owner-manager. As Fillol has pointed out with respect to Argentina: "When the road upward is blocked by family barriers . . . people may look at their jobs as a mere foothold from which to launch their own business."[8] McMillan observed a similar situation in Brazil: "The Brazilian industrialist of the mid-twentieth century is the family owner-manager . . . he is less a promoter of his business interests and more a defender of his aristocratic class."[9]

Because of working environment, there seems to be a lack of interest among executives in local companies in Latin America in participating and cooperating fully with each other to achieve organizational goals and objectives.

Table 10-2
Sub-systems Relationships

Organizational concern for publics: Latin America

Item:	Overall U.S.	local	Much U.S.	local	Moderate U.S.	local	Little U.S.	local
Very cooperative	5	2	1	—	4	2	—	—
Somewhat cooperative	2	4	—	—	2	4	—	—
Not cooperative	13	11	1	1	12	9	—	1
Total	20	17	2	1	18	15	0	1

Organizational concern for publics: Far East

	Overall U.S.	local	Much U.S.	local	Moderate U.S.	local	Little U.S.	local
Very cooperative	24	12	12	10	12	2	—	—
Somewhat cooperative	10	13	—	1	9	8	1	—
Not cooperative	2	13	—	—	—	8	2	5
Total	36	38	12	11	21	18	3	5

Summary Comparisons:

Very cooperative relationship:	U.S. sub.	Local firm	Both
	(N given in parentheses)		
In both regions	51.7% (56)	25.4% (55)	37.8% (111)
In Latin American countries	25.0% (20)	11.7% (17)	18.9% (37)
In Far Eastern countries	66.6% (36)	31.5% (38)	48.6% (74)
In "much concern" firms	92.8% (14)	83.3% (12)	88.4% (26)
In "moderate" and "little concern" firms	38.0% (42)	9.3% (43)	23.5% (85)

Although the American subsidiaries were not constrained by the problems affecting the owner-manager situation, they were faced with another dilemma, namely, antipathy toward U.S. private industry in Latin American countries. This attitude was carried over into organizational life by all levels of local employees and particularly by high-level personnel working in the American subsidiaries. Many American executives interviewed in this region complained more about the political attitudes of their local employees.[10]

EXECUTIVE PERCEPTION OF THE
FIRM'S OVERALL OBJECTIVES

What are the imperative criteria for examining formal organization in a systems frame of reference? Selznick lists the following five factors:

1. The security of the organization as a whole in relation to social forces in its environment.
2. Stability of the lines of authority and communication.
3. Stability of informal relations within the organization.
4. Continuity of policy and of the sources of determination.
5. A homogeneity of outlook with respect to the meaning and role of the organization.[11]

Table 10-3

Achievement of the Firm's Objectives
(Executive's Perception)

Organizational concern for publics: Latin America

Item:	Overall U.S. local		Much U.S. local		Moderate U.S. local		Little U.S. local	
Systems optimization was perceived as the most important	6	2	—	—	6	2	—	—
Subsystems optimization was perceived as equally important	14	10	2	1	12	8	—	1
Subsystems optimization was perceived as the ultimate goal	—	5	—	—	—	5	—	—
Total	20	17	2	1	18	15	0	1

In regard to a specific criterion of effectiveness, I was more concerned with factor number 5. In stressing its importance he states:

> The minimization of disaffection requires a unity derived from a common understanding of what the character of the organization is meant to be. When this homogeneity breaks down, as in the situations of internal conflict over basic issues, the continued existence of the organization is endangered. On the other hand, one of two signs of a "healthy" organization is the ability to effectively orient new members and readily slough off those who cannot be adapted to the established outlook.[12]

Data on this variable were collected by asking top- and

Table 10-3, cont'd.

Organizational concern for publics: Far East

Systems optimization was perceived as the most important	27	16	12	10	15	6	—	—
Subsystems optimization was perceived as equally important	5	18	—	1	3	11	2	6
Subsystems optimization was perceived as the ultimate goal	4	4	—	—	3	1	1	3
Total	36	38	12	11	21	18	3	9

Summary Comparisons:

Systems optimization perceived as the most important:	U.S. sub.	Local firm	Both
	(N given in parentheses)		
In both regions	58.9% (56)	32.7% (55)	45.9% (111)
In Latin American countries	30.0% (20)	11.7% (17)	21.6% (37)
In Far Eastern countries	75.0% (36)	42.1% (38)	58.1% (74)
In "much concern" firms	85.7% (14)	83.3% (12)	84.6% (26)
In "moderate" and "little concern" firms	50.0% (42)	18.6% (43)	34.1% (85)

middle-level executives of different departments about the objectives of the firm as they saw them.

In other words, indirect questioning was directed toward ascertaining the awareness of the executive concerning the overall objectives of the firm. They were also asked whether they put more emphasis on achieving the overall objectives of the firm or the objectives of their departments. On the basis of this information, I categorized each firm as follows:

Systems optimization was perceived as the most important.
Subsystems optimization was perceived as equally important.
Subsystems optimization was perceived as the ultimate goal.

Overall, 46 percent of the firms in the six developing countries stressed the importance of the total systems' goals and objectives. Among these, however, the proportion of the American subsidiaries was much higher than that of the local companies. Some 59 percent of the latter ones considered total systems optimization as the most important.

My results also show that the executives in Latin American countries were more interested in pursuing their departmental or personal objectives than those of the firm. This was true of both American subsidiaries and local firms in Latin America although the latter experienced greater difficulty in pursuing overall objectives. The reasons may lie in the socio-cultural heritage of the Latin people themselves.

As is mentioned in Chapter 4, one of the main value characteristics of Latin Americans is personalism, which stresses the achievement and pursuit of self-oriented goals and objectives rather than group-oriented objectives. Davis has underscored the implications of this value for organizational life:

> In Latin America, the group thus tends to exist as a protective environment, a sanctuary in which the unique identity of each individual is valued, supported, and enhanced, rather than absorbed and assimilated into a single group identity.[13]

The stronger owner-manager situation, as well as a lack of clarity of organizational objectives, policies, and procedures, are adversely affecting the achievement of the firm's objectives in Latin American companies. Notwithstanding this the impact of such socio-cultural and organizational variables on executive perception of a firm's objectives—the firms with positive attitudes toward their clientage groups are more likely to emphasize the firm's objectives than those with negative attitudes. Executives of 85 percent of the firm's classified as "much concern" perceived the total systems optimization as an important goal. Executives of 34 percent of the firms classified as "moderate" and "little concern" felt the same.

Utilization of High-Level Manpower

For this measure of effectiveness, I collected data on two factors: (a) executives' work profiles (how they spend their working time) and (b) the level of the executives' motivation.

The Executives' Work Profile

Although the executive's job involves a variety of tasks, there seems to be general agreement among management scholars and practitioners that the important functions of the executives are policy-making, long-range planning, and coordination of various departmental activities. True, the relative importance assigned to various executives' functions depends on the structure and nature of the industry, the competition, and the socio-economic, political, and legal conditions in a given country. For example, in a country or a specific industry, where governmental controls and bureaucracy are excessive, senior executives may be required to spend their entire time dealing with government officials. In another case, where the labor situation is explosive, senior executives may need considerable time solving labor problems.

In spite of such contingencies, it is recognized that the policy-making, long-range planning, and external relationships with the public are of major concern to the executives. Holden, Pederson, and Germane's study of large-scale firms shows that more and more top-level executives are spending their working time in policy-making, long-range planning, and in establishing external contacts with the public.[14] Since the publication of their study in 1968, the importance of the last function—establishing external contacts—has indeed increased tremendously. Since my data were collected from companies facing more or less similar socio-economic conditions, they may provide some perspective on how well companies were utilizing their high-level manpower.

Table 10-4
Utilization of High-Level Manpower
(What Managerial Personnel Do)

Organizational concern for publics: Latin America

Item	Overall U.S.	Overall local	Much U.S.	Much local	Moderate U.S.	Moderate local	Little U.S.	Little local
Policy-making and future planning	3	2	1	1	2	1	—	—
Coordination with other departments	10	7	—	—	10	6	—	1
Routine work—supervising subordinates' work	7	8	1	—	6	8	—	—
Total	20	17	2	1	18	15	0	1

Organizational concern for publics: Far East

Item	Overall U.S.	Overall local	Much U.S.	Much local	Moderate U.S.	Moderate local	Little U.S.	Little local
Policy-making and future planning	19	7	12	7	5	2	—	—
Coordination with other departments	9	11	—	4	9	7	—	—
Routine work—supervising subordinates' work	8	20	—	—	7	9	3	9
Total	36	38	12	11	21	18	3	9

Summary Comparisons:

What executives do— Policy-making and Planning:	U.S. sub.	Local firm	Both
	(N given in parentheses)		
In both regions	39.2% (56)	16.3% (55)	27.9% (111)
In Latin American countries	15.0% (20)	11.7% (17)	13.5% (37)
In Far Eastern countries	52.7% (36)	18.4% (38)	35.1% (74)
In "much concern" firms	92.8% (14)	66.6% (12)	80.7% (26)
In "moderate" and "little concern" firms	21.4% (42)	23.2% (43)	11.7% (85)

As one would expect, particularly from our discussion of policy-making and long-range planning (Chapters 3 and 4), industrial firms in developing countries have not learned how to use their executive talent fully. A mere 28 percent of the companies studied in the six developing countries emphasized policy-making and long-range planning functions for their executive personnel. Among these, however, American subsidiaries, particularly those in the Far Eastern countries, seem more articulate about using their managerial personnel, while the local companies in the Latin American countries were the least concerned. (See Table 10-4.)

Perhaps the most revealing aspect of my findings in this respect is the difference between the "much," "moderate," and "little concern" firms. An overwhelming proportion of the "much concern" firms (81 percent) utilized their executives for policy-making and long-range planning, while a mere fraction of the "moderate" and "little concern" firms (12 percent) did the same.

As noted earlier, I also found considerable differences between American subsidiaries in Latin American and Far Eastern countries. However, more similarities existed among the local firms in these two regions; that is, only a small portion of these firms utilized their managers for policy-making and long-range planning.

Such factors as the manager-owner situation, the resulting centralization of authority structures, and belligerent attitudes toward the U.S. private investment, particularly in Latin American countries, seem to have a considerable impact on this measure of effectiveness.

Executives' Attitudes toward Work

This measure of the executives' effectiveness reflected their attitudes toward jobs and interest and enthusiasm for their work. These data were collected through observing the executives' behavior in their work and by asking questions concerning their interests, satisfaction, and the reward experienced in their work.

As can be seen in Table 10-5, companies in the developing countries have by and large failed to motivate their high-level manpower. Less than 30 percent of the firms studied in the six countries inspired their top talents to work hard and be completely absorbed in their activities. The companies that were able to do so were those manifesting a positive concern for their publics. For example, in 81 percent of the firms categorized as "much concern," compared to 14 percent of the companies in the "moderate" and "little concern" classification, executive personnel displayed enormous enthusiasm and interest in their work. In other words, except for the "much concern" firms, executive personnel in the developing countries which I studied were withdrawn, defensive individuals.

The following quotations from executives in India reveal the differences between the "high concern" and the "moderate" and "low concern" firms:

> My job offers me a great opportunity to do something for India besides sending handsome profits to stockowners back home in the U.S. I can never get tired of this work . . . and the more I work, the more I am convinced that there is much to do in this life . . . without work I would be a dead person . . . and without this opportunity from my firm I would be an empty person. . . . [an American executive in India in a "much concern" American subsidiary]

> Work is the delight of my life, and I am a happy person that I have this opportunity in this company. I have everything I need to make worthwhile contributions to my company, my country, and to my people . . . my day is never over . . . and I am glad that it is not. Life is wonderful with work, and I never want to "retire" from it, even if the company stops paying me. [an Indian executive in an American subsidiary, "much concern" firm]

> Work is worship for me, and I never get tired of work . . . I strongly believe that it is the man who makes things move . . . there is no substitute for human beings . . . life without work would be like an ocean without its excitements of tides and ebbs . . . this is Mr. ———— life . . . Nehru died working . . . I would like to do the same. [an Indian executive in an Indian company, "much concern" firm]

> Oh! I can do several things at work . . . I can help my son solve his engineering problems . . . write articles on anything and everything that will make money . . . I have much time here . . . it takes only one hour a day to give orders to my staff

Table 10-5
Utilization of High-Level Manpower
(Executives' Attitudes Toward Work)

Organizational concern for publics: Latin America

Item:	Overall U.S.	local	Much U.S.	local	Moderate U.S.	local	Little U.S.	local
Most interested in work	6	5	1	1	5	3	—	1
Somewhat interested	6	3	1	—	5	3	—	—
Working to make a living	8	9	—	—	8	9	—	—
Total	20	17	2	1	18	15	0	1

Organizational concern for publics: Far East

Item:	Overall U.S.	local	Much U.S.	local	Moderate U.S.	local	Little U.S.	local
Most interested in work	12	10	10	9	2	—	—	1
Somewhat interested	17	14	2	2	15	12	—	—
Working to make a living	7	14	—	—	4	6	3	8
Total	36	38	12	11	21	18	3	9

Summary Comparisons

Executives most interested in work:	U.S. sub.	Local firm	Both
	(N given in parentheses)		
In both regions	32.1% (56)	27.2% (55)	29.7% (111)
In Latin American countries	30.0% (20)	29.4% (17)	29.7% (37)
In Far Eastern countries	33.3% (36)	26.3% (38)	29.7% (74)
In "much concern" firms	78.5% (14)	83.3% (12)	80.7% (26)
In "moderate" and "little concern" firms	16.6% (42)	11.6% (43)	14.1% (85)

for routine production activities . . . besides, I have no work here . . . it is damn easy . . . if the company does not grow, it is the managing director's problem . . . we are only educated peons . . . even the general manager, who is my boss, spends his time helping out the managing director's children and wife in their school work and shopping . . . this is India . . . McGregor's "Y" theory [the executive was a student of the late

Professor Douglas McGregor both at M.I.T. and the Indian
Institute of Management in Calcutta] is good on paper . . . it
has no meaning for my boss and the managing director . . .
and if they do not care, why should I? [an executive,
production-manager with a Ph.D. in chemical engineering in
an Indian company, "little concern" firm.]*

In summary, I find that there is poor utilization of high-
level manpower in developing countries. This by itself raises some
serious questions about the future outlook for economic and
industrial development in these countries. It seems that not only
do underdeveloped countries suffer from a shortage of managerial
personnel, but they are incapable of utilizing even their meager
supply of trained personnel.

Although environmental factors such as the owner-manager
situation, the seller's-market condition,[15] and an adverse attitude
toward U.S. investment, have contributed to the poor use of high-
level manpower, the companies' own policies and philosophies
seem to have a considerable bearing on such utilization.

ADAPTATION TO ENVIRONMENTAL CHANGES

In recent years organization theorists have begun to pay attention
to the importance of the organization environment interface.
Indeed, many "open-systems" theorists have advanced the thesis
that the survival of any organization depends largely on how well
it is able to adapt to environmental contingencies. Arguing for the
importance of such interface as a measure of organizational
effectiveness, Bennis states:

> The main challenge confronting today's organization, whether
> it is a hospital or a business enterprise, is that of responding
> to changing conditions and adapting to external stress. . . . The
> traditional ways that are employed to measure organizational
> effectiveness do not adequately reflect the true determinants
> of organizational health and success.[16]

In the same vein, Emery and Trist have argued:

*These quotations are reproduced from A. R. Negandhi and S. B. Prasad,
Comparative Management, pp. 139-40. Permission of the publisher is gratefully acknowledged.

. . . the primary task of managing an enterprise as a whole is to relate the total system to its environment, and not internal regulations per se. If the management is to control internal growth and development, it must in the first instance control the "boundary conditions"—the forms of exchange between the enterprise and the environment.[17]

To obtain some perspective on this criterion, I observed the executive's calmness in his work and his attitudes and responses to the changes in environmental conditions. To obtain such behavioral data, I interviewed 10 to 12 top- and middle-level executives of each company studied in the six developing countries. The behavior patterns are classified as follows:

able to adapt without much difficulty
moderately able to adapt
great difficulty in adapting.

It is obvious that my data fall short of ascertaining the *process* through which organizations are able to adapt to the changing environment. As noted in the beginning of Chapter 9, such scholars as Bennis, Emery and Trist, and Argyris[18] have stressed the importance of the *process* of adapting to environmental changes.

Nonetheless, my data do provide some comparative perspectives on how well two sets of firms, American subsidiaries and local companies, are able to cope with changing environments in the developing countries.

My data raised some interesting questions. First, they show that the majority of the companies were not equipped to adapt to environmental changes. Only one-third of the firms studied seemed to be able to cope with the external changes in the society. Among these, American subsidiaries were in a favorable position. As can be seen in Table 10-6, approximately 43 percent of the American subsidiaries were able to adapt to a changing environment without much difficulty. In contrast, only 27 percent of the local firms were in this fortunate position, that is, they were able to adapt without much difficulty.

It has been argued that American subsidiaries, particularly their expatriate managers, are poorly prepared for facing the host

Table 10-6
Adaptation to Environmental Changes

Organizational concern for publics: Latin America

Item:	Overall U.S.	local	Much U.S.	local	Moderate U.S.	local	Little U.S.	local
Able to adapt without much difficulty	9	3	1	—	8	3	—	—
Somewhat able to adapt	2	1	—	—	2	1	—	—
Much difficulty in adapting	9	13	1	1	8	11	—	1
	20	17	2	1	18	15	0	1

Far East

Item:	Overall U.S.	local	Much U.S.	local	Moderate U.S.	local	Little U.S.	local
Able to adapt without much difficulty	18	19	12	11	6	7	—	1
Somewhat able to adapt	15	4	—	—	14	3	1	1
Much difficulty in adapting	3	15	—	—	1	8	2	7
Total	36	38	12	11	21	18	3	9

Summary Comparisons

Able to adapt without much difficulty:	U.S. sub.	Local firm	Both
	(N given in parentheses)		
In both regions	42.8% (56)	27.2% (55)	35.1% (111)
In Latin American countries	45.0% (20)	17.6% (17)	32.4% (37)
In Far Eastern countries	41.6% (36)	31.5% (38)	36.4% (74)
In "much concern" firms	92.8% (14)	91.6% (12)	92.3% (26)
In "moderate" and "little concern" firms	33.3% (42)	25.5% (43)	29.4% (85)

country's socio-cultural, political, and economic environments. It is frequently pointed out in the international business literature that, although a large number of the U.S. subsidiaries are able to generate large profits in their overseas operations, very few have demonstrated their skill in understanding and adapting to the host country's changing aspirations and environments.

Professor Skinner seems to have expressed the views of many when he concluded his study of the U.S. corporations in the six developing countries with these words:

> United States corporations do have a great deal to offer. But it is not ready-to-wear systems and procedures and processes. It is a state of mind, a concept . . . a sense of zeal to find answers and to achieve ever-improving total productivity. [But] few Americans were able to offer this kind of approach to overseas plants. They tended to be so wound up in their own cultural assumptions and corporate wisdom of proper ways to manage their plants that they either set up systems that were incongruent to the environment or created massive resistance.[19]

Similarly, Wright, in his recent comparative study of the Chilean local firms and the American subsidiaries, found that the American companies were the least adaptable to changing environments in Chile.[20] In pointing out the adaptability and inflexibility of the American subsidiaries, Wright quotes Chilean businessmen as follows:

> Comparing Chilean management to American management is like comparing an outboard motor boat to a modern ocean liner. As long as it is a big ocean, the liner is an enormously more efficient craft that soon leaves the motor boat far behind. But bring that same ocean liner into a small, shallow harbor and then watch it operate! The motor boat will run circles around it![21]

I do not agree with either Professor Skinner's or Professor Wright's conclusions. If anything, my study indicates the greater adaptability of the American subsidiaries. To put it another way, my study shows that American executives were by no means ignorant of the prevailing socio-economic, political, legal, and cultural environments of the host countries examined.

It is true that, in line with the American tradition, both expatriate managers and those local managers working for the U.S. subsidiaries did not feel that the existing conditions in the developing countries were God-given and unalterable. They felt, on the contrary—and rightly so—that some of the prevailing conditions in those countries were dysfunctional for business efficiency and economic growth. It is those conditions they intended to alter, thus becoming active agents of change.

My findings also show that the firms with positive attitudes toward public, or clientage, groups were more adaptable than those with negative attitudes. For example, an overwhelming 92 percent of the firms categorized as "much concern" were adapting to environmental changes without much difficulty. In comparison, only 29 percent of those classified as "moderate" and "little concern" were able to do the same.

Enterprise Effectiveness

I attempted to collect data on the following factors, to evaluate enterprise effectiveness of companies studied in two regions:
  return on sales and investment
  growth in market share
  increase in sales during the last five years
  growth in price of stock and P/E ratio
  unit costs
  utilization of plant facilities
  scrap loss.

I was not successful in obtaining these data from all the companies, particularly firms in Latin America. Partial data collected from companies in India and the Philippines and Taiwan showed no appreciable differences between American subsidiaries and local firms. The impact of organizational concern variables on the firm's growth and profitability was also minimal. In other words, the prevalent seller's-market conditions in these countries have enabled all firms to increase their sales and profits regardless of their managerial practices.

Notes

1. James M. Rosow, "The Growing Role of Professional and Scientific Personnel," *Management Record,* vol. 24, no. 2 (February 1962), 23.

2. F. Harbison and C. Myers, *Management in the Industrial World,* New York: McGraw-Hill, 1959.

3. R. Baker, T. Dembo, and K. Lewin, *Frustration and Regression: Studies in Child Welfare,* vol. 18, no. 1, Iowa City, Iowa: University of Iowa, 1941.

4. K. Goldstein, *Human Nature,* Cambridge, Mass.: Harvard Univ. Press, 1951.

5. G. W. Allport, "The Trend in Motivational Theory," *American Journal of Orthopsychiatry,* vol. 23, no. 1 (January 1953), 107-19.

6. C. Rogers, "A Theory of Therapy, Personality, and Interpersonal Relationships as Developed in the Client-Centered Framework," in *Psychology: A Study of a Science,* vol. 3, ed. S. Koch, New York: McGraw-Hill, 1959, pp. 184-256.

7. T. Caplow, "The Criteria for Organizational Success," *Sociological Forces,* vol. 32, no. 1 (October 1953), 3.

8. Thomas R. Fillol, *Social Factors in Economic Development: The Argentine Case,* Cambridge, Mass.: MIT Press, 1963, p. 61.

9. Claude McMillan, Jr., "The American Businessman in Brazil," *Business Topics,* Spring 1963, reprinted in *International Dimensions in Business,* East Lansing, Mich.: Graduate School of Business Administration, Michigan State University, 1966.

10. Similar findings are reported by McMillan in Brazil, *ibid.,* and Stanley M. Davis in Chile; see his article, "Politics and Organizational Underdevelopment in Chile," *Quarterly Journal of Management Development,* vol. 1, no. 2 (December 1970), 85-102.

11. P. Selznick, "Foundations of the Theory of Organization," reprinted in F. E. Emery, *Systems Thinking,* Middlesex, Eng.: Penguin Books, 1970, pp. 261-80.

12. *Ibid.,* p. 269.

13. Stanley M. Davis, "U.S. vs. Latin America: Business and Culture," *Harvard Business Review,* vol. 47 (November-December 1969), 91.

14. P. E. Holden, C. A. Pederson, and G. E. Germane, *Top Management,* New York: McGraw-Hill, 1968, esp. chaps. 2 and 3.

15. For the impact of the seller's market on managerial behavior, see A. R. Negandhi, "Advanced Management Know-How in Developing Countries," *California Management Review,* vol. 10, no. 3 (Spring 1968), 53-60.

16. W. G. Bennis, "Towards A 'Truly' Scientific Management: The Concept of Organization Health," reprinted in *Assessment of Organizational Effectiveness,* ed. J. Ghorpade, Pacific Palisades, Cal.: Goodyear Publishing, 1971, p. 125.

17. F. E. Emery and E. L. Trist, "Socio-Technical Systems," quoted in Bennis, *ibid.,* p. 126.

18. Chris Argyris, *Integrating the Individual and the Organization,* New York: Wiley, 1964, pp. 153-54.

19. W. Skinner, *American Industry in Developing Economics,* New York: Wiley, 1968, p. 273.

20. R. W. Wright, "Organizational Ambiente: Management and Environment in Chile," *Academy of Management Journal,* vol. 14, no. 1 (March 1971), 65-74.

21. *Ibid.,* pp. 73-74.

CHAPTER 11

SUMMARY AND CONCLUSIONS: TRANSMITTING ADVANCED MANAGEMENT PRACTICES TO DEVELOPING COUNTRIES

In this study I have reported the findings of empirical research undertaken in 126 industrial firms in seven countries: the United States, Argentina, Brazil, India, the Philippines, Taiwan and Uruguay. The study was conceived in an open-system perspective. In so doing, my purpose was to ascertain the impact of both contextual (size, ownership, location, etc.) and socio-cultural and environmental variables on organizational practices and effectiveness. The specific objectives pursued were:

1. To test the universality of organizational practices.
2. To analyze the similarities and differences in organizational practices and effectiveness of industrial enterprises in a given country and among the firms in different countries.
3. To determine, on the basis of empirical evidence, the applicability and utility of U.S. organizational practices in the industrial enterprises in developing countries.
4. To analyze the impact of both the closed and open systems' variables on organizational practices and effectiveness.

As was pointed out in Chapter 1, these four objectives are to a large extent interrelated. Accordingly, as in the previous chapters, this final chapter will explore the two following questions and in so doing analyze the other objectives mentioned above: (1) Are advanced management practices transferable to the industrial enterprises in developing countries? (2) Are advanced management practices useful, in terms of generating higher organizational effectiveness, to the industrial enterprises in developing countries?

I will first outline the management practices and effectiveness of U.S. subsidiaries and local firms in the six developing countries. The profiles are derived from statistical averages of the companies studied (n=111). I will then provide the statistical frequency distribution for each element of the management practices and effectiveness investigated. Finally, I will undertake a somewhat rigorous statistical analysis of the data from a single country—India.

PROFILES OF MANAGEMENT PRACTICES AND EFFECTIVENESS

The profile of management practices and effectiveness outlined below includes the firm's orientation toward planning, policy-making, control devices, leadership style, manpower management practices, management effectiveness in handling its human resources, and financial effectiveness.

U.S. Subsidiary

Long-range planning of 5 to 10 years' duration was common among U.S. subsidiaries in the six developing countries. The typical U.S. subsidiary formulated its long-range plans in detail and involved all levels of managerial, technical, and supervisory personnel in the planning process; policy-making was taken seriously by this type of firm. There were efforts to use *major policies* effectively, both as guidelines and as instruments of an overall control to achieve the firm's objectives. Major policies were made by top-level executives, but in their formulation, all levels of managerial and technical personnel were consulted and their views considered. These policies were concentrated in the areas of pricing, personnel selection, plant investment, and salary and wage standards.

However, employee training, employee relations, purchasing, acquisition, and expansion received much less emphasis. *Other control devices* used by the U.S. subsidiary included cost and budgetary control, quality control, the maintenance of equipment, and the setting of work standards for blue-collar, supervisory, clerical, and managerial personnel. Few U.S. subsidiaries used such techniques as periodic management audit systems.

The U.S. firms were organized on the basis of major business functions (production, sales, accounting, finance). The typical firm had five to seven departments. Specialized staff personnel were frequently found. Service and maintenance departments were well organized.

Authority definition was clear for each position in the organization. *The degree of decentralization* in decision-making was greater in the U.S. subsidiaries than in comparable local firms. Attitudes of the U.S. subsidiary's executives regarding decentralization were only partially consistent with their practices.[1]

The *leadership style* used in the U.S. subsidiaries can best be characterized as democratic or consultative. Executives of these firms manifested trust and confidence in their subordinates, but their attitudes were not wholly consistent with their leadership styles.[2]

Manpower management practices were well developed. Personnel departments were organized as separate units, with specialized, trained personnel managers. Manpower management policies were stated formally. Such personnel techniques as job evaluation, development of selection and promotion criteria for managerial and technical personnel, and training programs for blue-collar employees were used widely. However, there was not much sophistication in compensation and motivational techniques and practices.

Managerial effectiveness, in terms of handling human resources, was "excellent" in some aspects and "poor" in others. For example, while the typical U.S. subsidiary did not find it difficult to attain high employee morale, it experienced some difficulty in motivating its employees. Absenteeism, particularly, was a problem. Employee productivity was average and scrap loss was higher compared to the U.S. parent companies.

With regard to high-level manpower, the U.S. subsidiaries were able to attract and retain trained managerial and technical personnel and were able to achieve cooperative departmental relationships. They were also able to utilize high-level manpower effectively and to adopt and respond to environmental changes with little difficulty. By and large, the U.S. subsidiaries made good profits and were expanding their sales considerably (three- to five-fold on an average).

The Local Firm

The planning orientation of a typical local firm can best be characterized as medium- to short-range. The typical firm in this category planned for a one- to two-year period. The resulting plans were less comprehensive and detailed. Review procedures, as well as strict adherence to planned targets, were taken less seriously than in the U.S. subsidiaries, and there was less participation in planning activities by other echelons of managers.

Policy-making was less formalized and generally not documented. No serious attempts were made to utilize major policies as guidelines or control mechanisms, but some forms of control devices were used—quality control, cost control, maintenance of equipment.

The organizational set-up in this type of firm was not very different from that of the U.S. subsidiary. The various divisions and departments within the firm were organized on the basis of such major business functions as production, sales, and purchasing. Similar to the U.S. subsidiary, the local firm had five to seven departments. Departmental lines were not clear-cut, however. The local firm generally did not utilize specialized staff personnel, although a service department was used to some extent.

Authority definition was unclear and diffuse. The *degree of decentralization* was low compared to U.S. subsidiaries. The *leadership style* can best be characterized as autocratic. Trust and confidence in subordinates was low.

Manpower management practices were the least developed. The personnel departments themselves were not organized as separate units, and qualified, trained personnel managers were not employed. There were no attempts made to formulate manpower policies.

Job evaluation techniques were utilized in one form or another, and some attempts were made to formulate selection and promotion criteria. Training and development programs were poor and used only for blue-collar employees. Compensation and motivational techniques were simple and mainly monetary.

Management effectiveness in the local firm was poor compared to the U.S. subsidiary. Employee morale in the average firm was moderate, absenteeism high, turnover low, and productivity low.

In terms of high-level manpower, the local firms were less successful in attracting and retaining trained managerial and technical personnel. Interdepartmental relationships of different departments were "somewhat cooperative" to "poor." Managers seemed to stress suboptimization of the companies' overall goals and objectives. Also, the typical local firm in this study did not effectively utilize its high-level manpower and therefore experienced considerable difficulty in adapting to environmental changes. Growth in sales and profits, however, was average.

An overall profile of management practices and effectiveness in the U.S. subsidiaries and local firms is outlined in Table 11-1 in a very abbreviated form. It represents a dominant picture of the actual situation in the developing countries studied. As the reader will recognize, however, such generalization covers up many significant differences between the firms. Such differences will become apparent when we examine the statistical frequency tables and explore the relationships between the major variables in the following sections.

Perhaps in this aspect, my research methodology, as well as my findings, differ sharply from many other cross-cultural management studies. Whereas other researchers have attempted to outline the dominant patterns of management practices and effectiveness in developing countries, my study goes one step further. It explores the nature of similarities, as well as differences, and attempts to find an explanation for these similarities and differences.

Table 11-1

Profiles of Management Practices and
Effectiveness of the U.S. Subsidiary
and the Local Firm*

Elements of Management practices and effectiveness	U.S. subsidiary	Local firm
1. Recruitment of potential managers	Formally and systematically done. Open-minded on all potential sources for managerial personnel.	Done on ad hoc basis. Restricted to small group of family members or relatives and friends.
2. Recruitment of middle and senior managers	Formally and systematically done. Provided opportunity for advancement within the firm.	Done on ad hoc basis. No systematic attempt at providing opportunity for advancement within the firm.
3. Management education	Formally done. Regularly using outside training or personnel.	Done on irregular or ad hoc basis.
4. Attitudes toward management development	Visualized as necessary element in company's growth and survival.	Considered as unnecessary expenses.
5. Treatment of existing management	Continuous evaluation. Ready to demote or fire secondrate and promote young and qualified.	Little or no evaluation. Adherence to seniority.
6. Delegation by senior management	Delegate authority to subordinates.	Unwilling to delegate authority.
7. Management structure	Decentralized—individual positions well defined and specified. Organization charts and manuals are used.	Centralized—individual positions not well defined and authority line diffused. Organization charts not used widely.

Table 11-1, cont'd.

Elements of Management practices and effectiveness	U.S. subsidiary	Local firm
8. Management communication	Free flow of communication encouraged and demanded.	A great deal of secrecy and hoarding of information at all levels.
9. Use of management consultants	Used frequently.	Not used.
10. Interfirm comparison at home and overseas	Done on regular basis.	Not done at all or done on ad hoc basis.
11. Market share	Constant awareness of market share	Not much concern.
12. Objective of firm	Growth and profits.	Profits.
13. Assessment of performance	Measured in terms of growth, long-term potential, human resources, profits, assets, and sales.	Measured in terms of short-term profits.
14. Diversification	Considered as desired objectives.	Undertaken as necessary evil.
15. Future of firm	Evaluated on long-term basis.	Evaluated on short-term or medium-term basis.
16. Long-range planning	5- to 10-year duration. Systematic and formalized.	1- to 2-year duration. Done on ad hoc basis.
17. Use of budgetary control	Used with considerable emphasis on its importance to the firm.	Done haphazardly with less emphasis on its importance to the firm.
18. Reviewing of operations	Regularly undertaken with feedback mechanism well developed.	Done on ad hoc basis with no feedback mechanism.
19. Capital budgeting	Regularly done.	Done on ad hoc basis or not done at all.
20. Policy-making	Formally stated; utilized as guidelines and control measures.	Formally not stated; not utilized as guidelines and control measures.

Table 11-1, cont'd.

Table 11-1, cont'd.

Elements of Management practices and effectiveness	U.S. subsidiary	Local firm
21. Other control devices used	Quality control, cost and budgetary control, maintenance, setting of standards.	Quality control, maintenance.
22. Grouping of activities	On functional-area basis.	On functional-area basis.
23. Number of departments	Five to seven.	Five to seven.
24. Use of specialized staff	Some.	None.
25. Use of service department	Considerable.	Some.
26. Authority definition	Clear.	Unclear.
27. Degree of decentralization	High.	Low.
28. Leadership style	Consultative.	Paternalistic-autocratic.
29. Trust and confidence in subordinates	High.	Low.
30. Managers' attitudes toward leadership style and delegation	Would prefer autocratic style; authority should be held tight at the top.	Would prefer consultative type.
31. Manpower policies	Formally stated.	Not formally stated.
32. Organization of personnel department	Separate unit.	Not separate unit.
33. Job evaluation	Done.	Done by very few.
34. Development and selection of promotion criteria	Formally done.	Done by some.
35. Compensation and motivation	Monetary and non-monetary.	Mostly monetary.
36. Employee morale	High.	Moderate.

Table 11-1, cont'd.

Elements of Management practices and effectiveness	U.S. subsidiary	Local firm
37. Absenteeism	Average.	High.
38. Turnover	Low.	Low.
39. Productivity	Average to high.	Low.
40. Ability to attract trained personnel	Able to do so.	Somewhat able to do so.
41. Interdepartmental relationships	Very cooperative.	Somewhat cooperative to not cooperative.
42. Executives' perception of the firm's overall objectives	Systems optimization as an important goal.	Subsystems optimization as an important goal.
43. Utilization of high-level manpower	Effectively utilized.	Poor utilization.
44. Adapting to environmental changes	Able to adapt without much difficulty.	Able to adapt with some difficulty.
45. Growth in sales	Phenomenal.	Considerable to low.
46. Relationship of sales to production	Production facilities are planned on creating greater demands for the goods.	Production is based on serving short-supply market conditions (seller's market).
47. Advertising and public relations	Seen as useful in creating public image of the company.	Used only as a necessary evil.
48. Capacity, efficiency, and productivity	Assessed on regular basis.	No regular assessment.
49. Plant capacity	Utilized at the fullest possible level; regular maintenance.	Utilized as seems appropriate by top man without objective assessment. Irregular maintenance.
50. Buying function	Conceived as managerial function.	Conceived as clerical function.
51. Suppliers	Conceived as partners in progress.	Conceived as a necessary evil.

Table 11-1, cont'd.

Table 11-1, cont'd.

Elements of Management practices and effectiveness	U.S. subsidiary	Local firm
52. Operational research techniques	Uses various techniques to optimize plant capacity.	Regards various techniques as status symbols rather than optimizing devices.
53. Creation of positive labor relations	Conceived of as management responsibility.	Conceived of as government/labor union responsibility.
54. Assessment of good labor relations	Done on regular and systematic basis.	Done on ad hoc basis.
55. Grievance procedure	Carefully worked out, agreed by all parties and adhered to.	Roughly drawn up and not always followed.
56. Unions	Conceived of as having constructive role to play.	Conceived of as nuisance.
57. Workers' output	Belief that employees will give their best when treated as being responsible.	Belief that employees are lazy.
58. Personnel function	Conceived of as top priority.	Conceived of as clerical chaos.
59. Training and education of workforce	Conceived of as necessary element of organizational activities; variety of training.	Conceived of as a necessary evil. Mostly on-the-job training for the blue-collar employee.
60. Shortage of skilled labor and/or other labor	Not taken for granted. Action to train up semi-skilled and unskilled personnel.	Acceptance of shortage of skilled employees as limiting factor.
61. Method of payment	Based on objective criteria. Attempts to pay higher than market rate.	Based on what they can get by with: the minimum.
62. Employees	Conceived of as resource.	Conceived of as a necessary evil.

Table 11-1, cont'd.

Elements of Management practices and effectiveness	U.S. subsidiary	Local firm
63. Relationships of research department to production	Close cooperation between two units.	Research department usually nonexistent, or if exists, operating as separate unit.
64. Problems of firm	Conceived of as an opportunity to undertake cost-efficiency measures.	Conceived as fault of others—government, labor union, competition.
65. Unprofitable products	Ready to drop unless found useful for the long-range growth.	Unable to find out in the first place.
66. Competition	Conceived of as healthy and necesary.	Conceived of as unfair and destructive.

UTILIZATION OF ADVANCED MANAGEMENT PRACTICES

Table 11-2 indicates the proportion of the U.S. subsidiaries and local firms that are able to use certain elements of advanced management practices. Data presented in this table show that 70 percent of the U.S. subsidiaries, versus 33 percent of the counterpart local firms in the two regions, were undertaking comprehensive planning. Similarly, 58 percent of the former companies, compared to 25 percent of the latter firms, had introduced formalized quality control for all or major products they manufactured. Manpower planning, however, received the most cursory treatment, even in the U.S. subsidiaries. A mere 14 percent paid attention to this aspect. The proportion of local firms undertaking manpower planning was still smaller, only 9 percent.

By and large, a higher proportion of the U.S. subsidiaries attempted to decentralize decision-making with respect to major and functional policies. Many of these companies also used a democratic leadership style. In the same vein, a greater number of the U.S. subsidiaries paid considerable attention to the selection, promotion, training, and development of their employees.

Regional Differences

Notwithstanding such overall patterns, I was also able to detect considerable differences in certain practices between the firms in Latin America and the Far East. Data for long-range planning, for example, show that only 6 percent of the local firms in the Latin American region were undertaking long-range planning for a 5- to 10-year duration. The comparable proportion of local firms in the Far Eastern region was 45 percent. In the same manner, approximately two-thirds of the U.S. subsidiaries in the Far Eastern region formalized and documented their major policies and utilized them as control measures, as against one-fourth of those in Latin America. Standards-setting for clerical and supervisory personnel received greater attention in the U.S. subsidiaries in the Far East than in Latin America. The same was true of budgetary controls, personnel policies, decentralization in decision-making, and employee-appraisal systems. Only in the area of compensation did a larger number of Latin American firms adopt formalized practices and procedures.

In sum, this picture emerges:

1. A greater number of the U.S. subsidiaries in both regions were able to utilize advanced management practices, compared to their counterpart local firms.

2. A greater number of U.S. subsidiaries and local firms in the Far East were able to utilize advanced management practices, compared to those in Latin America.

As was noted earlier, I was not satisfied with merely documenting existing management practices in developing countries —although this task by itself was necessary and important and as yet has not been seriously considered by comparative management researchers. However, I was interested in exploring the causes of interfirm and interregional differences.

To recall, my theoretical model outlined in Diagram 2-1, as well as the hypothesis, indicates that management practices are dependent upon external environmental factors and the firm's concern toward its task agents—consumers, employees, suppliers, distributors, stockholders, community, and government.

Table 11-2
Utilization of Advanced Management Practices in
U.S. Subsidiaries and Local Firms in the Two Regions:
Summary of Findings

Elements of advanced management practices and effectiveness:	Both regions U.S. local n=56 n=55		Latin America U.S. local n=20 n=17		Far East U.S. local n=36 n=38		Organizational concern for task agents:			
							Firms with "much concern" U.S. local n=14 n=12		Firms with "moderate" and "little concern" U.S. local n=42 n=43	
	1	2	3	4	5	6	7	8	9	10
Comprehensive planning	70%	33%	65%	18%	75%	40%	94%	43%	65%	31%
Long-range planning (5 to 10 years)	66	33	75	6	62	45	95	60	57	26
Considerable participation in planning process	66	35	55	36	71	40	76	60	60	28
Formalized and documented major policies	48	22	25	18	65	23	71	57	45	16
Formalized standards-setting for production employees	73	52	60	52	83	57	82	92	73	44
Formalized standards-setting for clerical and supervisory personnel	40	24	15	18	48	28	65	50	31	17
Formalized and systematic quality control for all or major products	58	25	60	26	57	27	80	75	50	12

Table 11-2, cont'd.

Table 11-2, cont'd.

Elements of advanced management practices and effectiveness:	Both regions U.S. local n=56 n=55		Latin America U.S. local n=20 n=17		Far East U.S. local n=36 n=38		Organizational concern for task agents: Firms with "much concern" U.S. local n=14 n=12		Firms with "moderate" and "little concern" U.S. local n=42 n=43	
	1	2	3	4	5	6	7	8	9	10
Formalized and systematic cost control for all or major products	62%	37%	65%	36%	61%	36%	96%	97%	50%	17%
Formalized budgetary controls	52	37	30	23	64	45	97	97	39	24
Formalized and systematic manpower planning	14	9	5	0	19	13	57	33	0	2
Formalized personnel policies	36	40	20	29	44	45	86	67	19	33
High "status" of personnel department	54	47	40	47	61	47	79	58	45	44
Formalized selection process	68	38	70	41	67	37	93	68	60	30
Formalized and systematic appraisal system	68	42	60	29	72	47	100	83	57	30
Formalized training programs for blue-collar employees	50	65	60	n.a.	50	95	79	92	41	58
Formalized training programs—supervisory personnel	52	53	n.a.	n.a.	64	76	86	92	41	42
Formalized training programs—managerial personnel	41	38	n.a.	n.a.	64	55	71	83	31	26
Formalized managerial succession programs	48	18	60	18	42	18	79	42	38	12

Formalized and systematic means of determining wages—blue-collar employee	39%	29%	55%	47%	31%	21%	29%	8%	43%	35%
Formalized and systematic means of determining wages—clerical employee	50	51	55	47	47	54	64	50	45	51
Formalized and systematic means of determining wages—supervisory and managerial personnel	18	18	30	41	11	8	21	—	17	26
Use of both monetary and nonmonetary incentives	54	38	70	41	44	37	79	68	45	30
Institutionalized participation programs	56	33	50	24	58	37	100	83	40	19
Behavioral measure of effectiveness										
High employee morale	30%	18%	20%	24%	36%	16%	71%	50%	18%	12%
Cooperative interpersonnel relationship	9	9	—	—	14	13	21	33	5	—
Able to hire and retain highly trained personnel	48	18	40	18	53	19	86	67	36	20
Cooperative interdepartmental relationships	52	25	25	12	67	32	93	83	38	9
Firm's overall objectives perceived as important	59	33	30	12	75	42	86	83	50	19
Executives spend time on policy-making and planning	39	16	15	12	53	18	93	67	21	23
High degree of drive and enthusiasm on part of executives	32	27	30	29	33	26	79	83	17	12
Able to adapt to environmental changes without much difficulty	43	27	45	18	42	32	93	92	33	26

Table 11-2, cont'd.

Table 11-2, cont'd.

Elements of advanced management practices and effectiveness	Region/Ownership				Organizational concern for task agents		
	Latin America		Far East		much	mod-erate	little
	U.S.	local	U.S.	local			
	n=20	n=17	n=36	n=38	n=26	n=72	n=13
Consultative type of decision-making regarding:	25	18	65	23	65	30	0
Selection and promotion of executives	35	52	33	40	58	37	18
Long-range planning	55	36	71	40	70	52	0
Standards-setting for blue-collar employees	60	52	83	57	85	54	24
Standards-setting for clerical and supervisory personnel	15	18	48	28	60	28	0
Leadership style democratic or participative as perceived by subordinates	65	35	48	25	75	35	8

The Impact of Environmental and Socio-cultural Variables

I have argued elsewhere that it is difficult, if not impossible, to establish the link of causation between the specific elements of socio-cultural and environmental variables and the elements of management practices and effectiveness.[3] I am less sure and perhaps less ambitious than such authors as Farmer and Richman who have advocated the feasibility of establishing such cause-and-effect relationships.[4]

My inquiry was directed at assessing the overall impact of

specific environmental and socio-cultural factors on certain elements of management practices and effectiveness. It began simply by asking executives and other employees and knowledgeable persons about their views on the impact of these factors. It was a simple "nose count," to begin with; then the conversation proceeded to an in-depth inquiry. Data thus collected represent the views of specific persons working in industrial organizations in developing countries.

How close are these views to reality? I cannot say and have refrained from claiming causal relationships in this inquiry. These overall findings have been presented elsewhere in the form of working hypotheses or propositions, with the hope that they will stimulate further research in this important area. The same propositions are reproduced below to summarize my findings on the impact of socio-cultural and environmental factors on specific elements of management practices and effectiveness. Data on this material has been reported elsewhere.[5]

The Environmental Impact on Managerial Practices[6]

Planning

Proposition 1: The greater the degree of competition, the greater will be the need for long-range planning by the individual firm.

Proposition 2: The greater the degree of economic and political instability, the lesser the likelihood that private industrial enterprises will undertake systematic long-range planning.

Proposition 3: The greater the degree of governmental control over prices and the availability of raw materials, the lesser the likelihood that the firm will undertake systematic long-range planning.

Proposition 4: The greater the governmental hostility toward the business community, the lesser the likelihood that a firm will undertake systematic long-range planning.

Decentralization in Decision-Making

Proposition 5: The stronger the owner-manager situation, the less the authority is delegated and the less clear is authority definition.

Proposition 6: Companies in a weak competitive market are

more likely to be centralized than those within a strong competitive market.

Controlling

Proposition 7: The weaker the competitive situation, the lesser the concern for quality or cost of products and the lesser the comprehensive control device employed by the firm.

Leadership Style

Proposition 8: The stronger the owner-manager situation, the greater the likelihood of autocratic leadership in the industrial firm.

Environmental Impact on Managerial Effectiveness

Employee Morale

Proposition 9: All other factors being the same, the greater the pampering of the industrial workers by the government, the greater the degree of hostility between the government and the business and the poorer the employee morale.

Proposition 10: All other factors being the same, the firm with the hostile union is likely to have poorer employee morale than the firm with the cooperative union.

Interpersonal Relationships

Proposition 11: All other factors being the same, the higher the underemployment and unemployment, the greater the degree of mistrust and lack of confidence among workers and the more severely uncooperative is the attitude of blue-collar employees.

Proposition 12: The greater the difference in educational attainments of younger and older employees, the greater the hostility and uncooperative attitudes among them.

Proposition 13: The greater the difference in social status between supervisors and blue-collar workers, the lesser the cooperative attitudes among them.

The Firm's Ability to Recruit High-Level Manpower

Proposition 14: All other factors being the same, the more owner-manager situations there are, the lesser is the firm's effectiveness in hiring and retaining high-level manpower.

Not withstanding the impact of environmental and socio-cultural variables on specific elements of management practices and effectiveness, my findings indicate that in *spite of such impact* many firms were able to utilize advanced management practices. Why? To inquire why certain firms are able to utilize advanced practices and others are not, we will now turn to the second independent variable—the organizational concern toward task environmental agents—for an explanation.

Organizational Concern Variable

The independent variable of organizational concern examines attitudes and perceptions of the executives toward the firms' important task agents (employees, consumers, suppliers, distributors). The rationale for using this variable as an independent variable is explained in Chapter 2.

To infer the organizational concern toward its task agents, I first consulted published documents and manuals of the companies studied. Next, I interviewed top- and middle-level executives. On an average, I interviewed 15 to 20 executive personnel in each firm, taking from one to three full working days for interviews in each company.

The organizational concern for task agents was evaluated in terms of the degree of longitudinal and lateral interest in task agents evidenced by decision-makers in each firm. As shown in Table 2-3, scores were derived from the intensity of concern shown. Three descriptive categories were created to identify the firm's organizational concern.

Results

Examine columns 7 and 8 and compare the figures with those in columns 1 and 2 and 9 and 10 for each of the elements of advanced management practices outlined in Table 11-2. This provides an overall picture of the influence of the organizational concern variable on utilization of advanced practices. The data on long-range planning show that 95 percent of the U.S. subsidiaries and 60 percent of the local firms categorized as "high concern" firms undertook planning for a 5- to 10-year period. The corresponding percentages for U.S. and local companies were 66 and 33 percent, respectively. The figures for the firms classified as "moderate" and "low concern" were 57 and 26 percent respectively.

Similarly, 57 percent of the U.S. subsidiaries and 33 percent of the local firms classified as "high concern" did formal and systematic manpower planning, whereas only 14 and 9 percent of the U.S. subsidiaries and local firms, overall, did the same. In this respect, of those firms classified as "moderate" and "low concern," only a few undertook manpower planning.

The same pattern emerges when we examine data on control aspects, manpower management, leadership, degree of decentralization in decision-making, training programs, and managerial succession and development programs.

The results show that approximately three-fourths of the U.S. subsidiaries and two-thirds of the local companies manifesting "high concern" for their task agents used advanced management practices. By introducing "organizational concern" as an independent variable, I was able to explain the interfirm differences more comprehensively.

As the sophisticated reader may recognize, the above analysis still covers up the differences between firms, which may be attributable to: (a) regional environmental and socio-cultural differences and (b) the firm's size and technological differences. To control for these differences, I will now undertake an analysis of data from a single country—India. The reason for choosing an Indian sample for this analysis is that doing so provides an opportunity to examine firms of different sizes and technologies, while the environmental and socio-cultural settings faced by the firms remain about the same.

My sample consisted of 15 pairs of American subsidiaries and local firms operating in India. These companies represented various industrial categories—pharmaceutical products, chemicals, soft drinks, elevators, heavy machine tools, cosmetics, sewing machines, and typewriters. Size, as measured by the total number of employees of these companies, varied from 120 to 6,500.

Through an analysis of these data, we will also be able to explore the second question: Are advanced management practices useful, in terms of effectiveness, to the industrial firms in developing countries? This should enable us to explore the relationships that may exist between management practices and organizational effectiveness.

First, let us examine the relationship between the organizational concern variable and management practices.

Organizational Concern and Advanced Management Practices

To examine statistical relationships between the organizational concern variable and the elements of advanced management practices, I constructed four indices: (1) management process index; (2) decentralization index; (3) manpower management practice index; and (4) organizational practices index. Details on the construction of these indices are given elsewhere.[7] Briefly, the factors evaluated for each index and the ranking of these factors were:

The *management process index* considered planning orientations; the nature of quality, cost, and budgetary controls; standards-setting for blue-collar, clerical, and supervisory personnel; equipment maintenance; and the leader's confidence in subordinates.

A *decentralization index* was constructed on the basis of data on the layers of hierarchy, locus of decision-making with respect to major and functional policies, and the degree of participation and information-sharing in the planning process.

The *manpower management index* considered the nature of manpower planning, employee selection and promotion practices and procedures, training programs, and compensation and benefit programs.

The *organizational practices index* was computed by adding all the factors in the above three indices.

Ranking

A three-point ranking scale was devised for each of the factors evaluated for the four indices discussed above. A ranking of 1 point represented the most advanced practices (long-range planning for 5 to 10 years, considerable participation in policy-

Table 11-3
Spearman's Rank Correlation Coefficient Between the
Organizational Concern Score and Management
Process, Decentralization, Manpower, and
Organizational Practices Indices

Index	*Correlation Coefficient**
Organizational concern score and management process index	0.72
Organizational concern score and decentralization index	0.81
Organizational concern score and manpower management practices	0.68
Organizational concern score and organizational practices index	0.88

* All significant at .05 level.

making, formalized and systematic cost and quality control programs), while a ranking of 3 points represented the least
advanced practices (ad hoc or no planning, no cost and quality
control programs). The composite index for each company was
computed by adding up the total points and dividing them by
the total number of factors evaluated for each index. This gave an
index for each company ranging from a minimum of 1.0 (the
most advanced practices) to a maximum of 3.0 (least progressive practices).

Spearman's Rank Correlation Coefficient between the
firm's organizational concern score and each of the indices was
computed. Table 11-3 shows the results of the analyses.

To examine the influence of size and technology, I first
divided firms according to Woodward's technological classification
of process, mass, and unit-production categories.[8] A comparison
of various management practice indices for these three categories
by the Kruskal-Wallis test showed no significant differences among
them.

The organizational size variable was found to be significantly related to the degree of decentralization[10] and the nature
of manpower practices.[9] However, in a multiple-regression analysis,
the contribution of the size variable seems to be negligible.[11]

As can be seen in this Table, 68 to 88 percent of variation in the firms' practices can be explained by the nature of their organizational concern for task environmental agents.

Advanced Practices and Organizational Effectiveness

Having established the fact that advanced management practices are more a function of the firm's concern for its task agents and that they are transferable from developed nations to developing countries, we are now ready to take up another important and vital question: Are advanced management practices useful, in terms of effectiveness, to industrial enterprises in developing countries?

The answer is vital if a rational decision is to be made regarding the introduction of advanced practices into developing countries. For example, if the answer to this question is no, one need not bother to inquire about the feasibility of such an idea. More important, a negative answer casts doubt on the wisdom of spending millions of U.S. tax dollars on educating and training managers from developing countries in modern management methods and practices.

During the last three decades various U.S. governmental agencies and foundations such as USAID and the Ford Foundation have helped to open U.S.-style business schools in a number of developing nations. The basic assumption behind this is that modern, advanced practices lead to higher organizational effectiveness. But this is only an assumption, a hope thus far not verified by empirical evidence.

My attempt in this regard shows that this basic assumption is correct. In order to provide a systematic answer to this question, I attempted to explore the relationship between various management practice indices and the organization effectiveness index.* The results of Spearman's correlation between various

---

* A management effectiveness index took into consideration the following factors: (1) the firm's ability to hire and retain high-level manpower; (2) employee morale and satisfaction in work; (3) interpersonal relationships between subordinates and superordinates; (4) interdepartmental relationships; (5) executives' perceptions of the firm's overall objectives; (6) utilization of high-level manpower; (7) the firm's ability to adapt to the environmental conditions; (8) growth in sales and profits in the past five years. This index was constructed on a basis similar to other indices by devising a three-point ranking scale.

Table 11-4
Spearman's Rank Correlation Coefficient Between
Management Practices and Organizational
Effectiveness Indices

Index	*Spearman's Rank Correlation Coefficient**
Management process index and organizational effectiveness index	0.81
Decentralization index and organizational effectiveness index	0.91
Manpower management practices index and organizational effectiveness index	0.63
Organization practices index and organizational effectiveness index	0.88

* All significant at .05 level.

management practices and organization effectiveness is summarized in Table 11-4.

The results presented in Table 11-4 show that the 63 to 91 percent of the differences in the firm's effectiveness can be explained by the nature of their management practices. The nature of these relationships suggests that the utilization of advanced management practices does lead to higher organizational effectiveness.

In operational terms, this study shows that the firm that undertook long-range planning; formulated major policies and utilized them as guidelines and control mechanisms; administered other control devises such as quality, cost, and budgetary controls; delegated decision-making authority to subordinates; and utilized consultative type of leadership achieved higher organizational effectiveness in terms of profitability and utilization of human resources.

Universality Issue

In this final section I will briefly analyze an issue vigorously debated by countless management scholars during the last four decades: the universality of management principles and practices. This issue, as I see it, has two focal points. One concerns the debate between the "classical and process" theorists and the "human relations and behavioral" theorists; the second is the debate between management and organization theorists in general and the "cross-cultural management" theorists.

In the main, the classical and process school theorists have made claims that management principles are universal and applicable to all types of organizations in all situations. Koontz and O'Donnell, persistent and long-time defenders of this view, have said:

> The principles related to the task of managing apply to any kind of enterprise in any kind of culture. The purpose of different enterprises may vary, but all which are organized do rely on effective group operation for efficient attainment of whatever goals they have. . . . The fundamental truths (principles) are applicable elsewhere.[11]

The universalists' claim has been challenged both in terms of its restrictive assumption about human beings and its lack of rigor in testing hypothetical and normative statements, which the universalists call principles. March and Simon have scientifically summarized the voluminous criticism leveled at the classical and process schools of management:

> Perhaps the most critical failure of classical administrative science is that it does not confront theory with evidence. In part, this is a consequence of the difficulties of operationalism [of variables].[12]

As for the limitations of the classical administrative (process) theories, they outline five major limitations:

1. Motivational assumptions underlying the theories are incomplete and consequently inaccurate.
2. There is little appreciation of the role of intraorganizational conflicts of interest in defining limits of organizational behavior.
3. The constraints placed on the human being by his limitations as a complex information-processing system are given little consideration.

4. Little attention is given to the role of cognition in task idenfication and classification, as well as in decision.
5. The phenomenon of program elaboration receives little emphasis.[13]

Claims of Cross-Cultural Management Theorists

Scholars working in the area of cross-cultural management have argued principally that management and organization theorists have shown little concern for the impact of sociocultural and environmental variables on "management principles and organizational practices." In this respect, a view expressed by Oberg is shared by many cross-cultural management theorists. Oberg argues that if the ground rules under which the manager operates are different in different cultures and/or countries, then it is fruitless to search for a common set of strategies of management. He goes on to say:

> Cultural differences from one country to another are more significant than many writers now appear to recognize. . . . If management principles are to be universal . . . they must face up to the challenge of other cultures and other business climates. . . . [The universalists' claim] is hardly warranted by either evidence or institution at this stage in the development of management theory.[14]

Parenthetically, it may be noted that criticism from cross-cultural management scholars is not directed entirely at classical and process school theorists; they are also critical of human relations and behavioral scholars who advocate universal application of the "Y theory" and "participative principles."

Essentially I share the views and criticisms of both human relations and behavioral scholars on the classical administrative theory and those of cross-cultural management scholars concerning management organization theorists.

Like the behavioral theorists, I also contend that the management principles are, as explained in the literature, largely normative statements based on deductive rather than empirical reasoning. Further, like my colleagues in cross-cultural management, I am of the opinion that the impact of socio-cultural and environmental variables has not been recognized by many management-organization theorists. However, my research findings in the six developing countries provide considerable support for both the universalists and those who are critical of their claims.

For example, if we conceive of the contributions of classical administrative theory in terms of its articulation for orderliness, systematization, and routinization of various management functions, then my findings show that a large majority of the American subsidiaries (as well as a number of local companies) were not only able to approach their managerial activities in an orderly and systematic manner, but also, by so doing, were able to increase their effectiveness. In other words, the mere fact that I was able to collect data on managerial practices or functions propounded by the classical administrative theory from companies located in seemingly diverse environmental and cultural settings shows the existence of some common language, or, if you like, universal thinking about their managerial activities.

Notwithstanding the restrictive assumptions of classical school theorists about human behavior and the lack of empirical verification of management principles, my findings indicate that the many concepts advanced by this school of management thought are understood by managers of diverse backgrounds. In this respect, based on my findings reported in this volume, I tend to support the views of Lawrence and Lorsch: "The fact that its [classical school] language persists in business usage . . . is sufficient justification for a fresh look at this theory.[15]

As I stated earlier, my findings support the contention that external environmental conditions and the socio-cultural variables have considerable impact on organizational practices and effectiveness.

Specifically, my findings concerning planning practices and decentralization in decision-making show the considerable influence of market and economic conditions (see Chapters 4 and 5). Similarly, employee morale, interpersonal relationships, and absenteeism and turnover were greatly affected by the prevailing socio-cultural settings.

To conclude, I contend that the variables and factors lying outside the organizational boundaries are as important, if not more so, as the variables within the organization in understanding organizational practices, behavior, and effectiveness. I, like Lawrence and Lorsch and others, believe that the key ideas and concepts developed by various schools of management can and should be translated into operational variables for empirical validation. Without this, the goal of building comprehensive organizational theories will indeed be elusive. As Myrdal has stated:

> Theory . . . must not only be subjected to imminent criticism for logical consistency but also constantly be measured against reality and adjusted accordingly. . . . This is the crux of all sciences. It also begins a priori but must constantly strive to find an empirical basis for knowledge and thus become more adequate to the reality under study. . . . Theory is thus no more than a corrected set of questions to the social reality under study.[16]

Notes

1. For more details on this point, see, A. R. Negandhi, *Management and Economic Development: The Case of Taiwan,* The Hague: Martinus Nijhoff's, 1973; see also chap. 5 in this book.

2. *Ibid.;* see also chap. 6 in this book.

3. Negandhi and Prasad, *op. cit.,* pp. 12-17.

4. Richard Farmer and Barry Richman, "A Model for Research in Comparative Management," *California Management Review,* Winter 1964, pp. 55-68.

5. Negandhi and Prasad, *op. cit.,* pp. 169-93.

6. For detailed discussion on these propositions, see *ibid.*

7. *Ibid.,* pp. 197-208.

8. Joan Woodward, *Management and Technology,* London: Her Majesty's Stationery Office, 1958.

9. A. R. Negandhi and B. C. Reimann, "Task Environment and Decentralization in Decision-Making." in *Human Relations,* vol. 26, no. 2, 1973, pp. 203-219.

10. A. R. Negandhi and Y. K. Shatty, "Manpower Management Practices in a Developing Country." Faculty Working Paper #124, Center for Business and Economic Research: Kent State University, Kent, Ohio, 1972.

11. H. Koontz & C. O'Donnell *Principles of Management* Fourth Edition New York: McGraw-Hill Co., 1968.

12. James March and Herbert Simon, *Organizations,* New York: Wiley, 1958.

13. *Ibid.*

14. Winston Oberg, "Cross-Cultural Perspectives on Management Principles," *Journal of the Academy of Management,* vol. 6, no. 2, pp. 141-42.

15. Paul R. Lawrence and Jay W. Lorsch, *Organization and Environment: Managing Differentiation and Integration,* Boston: Division of Research, Graduate School of Business Administration, Harvard University, 1967, pp. 161-62.

16. Gunnar Myrdal, *Asian Drama: An Inquiry into the Poverty of Nations,* New York: The Twentieth Century Fund, 1968, pp. 24-25.

APPENDIX A —

COMPARATIVE MANAGEMENT RESEARCH

Interview Guide

1. *General information*
   Company's Identification _____
   Company
   (a) U.S. subsidiary _____
   (b) Taiwanese co.   _____
   (c) Japanese co.   _____

2. *Type of industry*
   (a) Chemical and pharmaceutical
   (b) Petroleum
   (c) Light engineering products
   (d) Heavy engineering products
   (e) Electrical—consumer nondurable goods
   (f) Electrical—consumer durable goods
   (g) Rubber—tires
   (h) Soaps and cosmetics
   (i) Soft drinks, canned products
   (j) Textiles
   (k) Other

3. *Size*   column
   (a) Number of employees _____   5
   (b) Sales   _____
   (c) Relative size
       large   _____
       medium   _____
       small   _____

4. *Persons Interviewed*

                                          _____
                                          _____
                                          _____

   Date

ORGANIZATIONAL CONCERN VARIABLE

5. Firm's Attitude Toward: column
   (To infer, see Appendix C)

(a) Employee			
20	10	0	6
(b) Consumer			
20	10	0	7
(c) Supplier			
15	7.5	0	8
(d) Distributor			
15	7.5	0	9
(e) Stockholder			
10	5	0	10
(f) Community			
10	5	0	11
(g) Government			
10	5	0	12
(h) Total score			
100-75	74-39	38-0	13

6. *Documentation of Policies*
   Policies documented?

   (a)_____yes   14
   (b)_____no
   (c)_____not clear

7. *Who is responsible for documentation*
   and communication?
   (a) Policy committee _____   15
   (b) Top executives _____
   (c) Divisional manager _____
   (d) Supervisor _____
   (e) Nobody _____
   (f) Not certain/unclear _____

8. *Frequency of review*
   (a) Yearly _____   16
   (b) Twice a year _____
   (c) Quarterly _____
   (d) Monthly _____
   (e) Never _____
   (f) Ad hoc _____

MANAGEMENT PROCESS VARIABLE

9. *Length of planning for the future*   column
   - (a) 5 years or more   _____   17
   - (b) 1 to 2 years   _____
   - (c) Ad hoc   _____
   - (d) No planning at all   _____
     Total score   _____

10. *Resulting plans*
    - (a) Systematic detailed   18
      plans with the
      aid of computers   _____
    - (b) Systematic detailed
      plans without the
      aid of computers   _____
    - (c) Systematic
      but limited   _____
    - (d) Limited forecasts
      randomly done   _____
    - (e) No planning at all   _____
      Total score   _____

11. *Nature of planning*
    - (a) Financial   _____   19
    - (b) Product   _____
    - (c) Plant   _____
    - (d) Combination 1 & 2   _____
    - (e) Combination 2 & 3   _____
    - (f) Combination 1 & 3   _____
    - (g) All three   _____
    - (h) none, random   _____
      Total score   _____

12. *Planning objectives: Why do you plan?*
    - (a) For long-term
      growth   _____
    - (b) For profit
      and service   _____
    - (c) To seek direction   _____
    - (d) To offer
      employment   _____
      Total score   _____

13. *Participation in the planning process*   column
    (*who plans?*)

    (a) Top-level
        executives only   _____
    (b) Top- and middle-
        level executives   _____
    (c) Top, middle- and
        lower-level
        executives   _____
        Total score   _____

14. *Information-sharing in the planning process*
    (*How do you communicate planning?*)

    (a) Confidential
        memos/verbal   _____
    (b) Special reports,
        circulated
        restrictively   _____
    (c) General/special
        reports circulated
        widely   _____
        Total score   _____

15. *Frequency of review of plans*

    (a) Monthly   _____
    (b) Quarterly   _____
    (c) Semi-annually   _____
    (d) Annually   _____
    (e) Ad hoc   _____
    (f) No information   _____
        Total score   _____

16. *What data is generated for long-range*
    planning? (See question 10.)

    (a) Detailed forecasts
        for all products   _____   24
    (b) Some departmental
        forecasts only   _____
    (c) Causal
        ideas/forecasts   _____
    (d) Not much   _____
        Total score   _____

17. *Socio-economic, political, legal, and*   column
    cultural factors affecting planning process
    (a) Economic stability   ———   **25**
    (b) Price spiral   ———
    (c) Uncertainty about
        the availability of
        raw material   ———
    (d) Government control
        of prices and raw
        material   ———
    (e) Political situation   ———
    (f) Market conditions   ———
    (g) Lack of knowledge
        on part of executives ———
    (h) Other factors   ———

GENERAL INFORMATION: ORGANIZATION STRUCTURE/ASPECT

column

18. Obtain the size of the enterprise and its sub-units

19. To infer delegation of authority
    (a) What does the manager do? (Observe activities.)
    (b) What does the assistant manager do? (Observe activities.)
    (c) What does the production manager do? (Observe activities.)
    (d) What do the supervisors and foremen do? (Observe activities.)

20. (a) Do you have an organization chart? (Obtain it and any other manuals available.)
    _____yes _____no   29
    (b) How are the activities grouped in this organization?
    _____function _____geography _____other (specify)   30
    (c) Are there any "service departments"?
    _____yes _____no   31
    (d) To whom do they report?
    _____general management   32
    _____department heads _____others

21. (a) Are ther any staff positions, as opposed to line positions, in the organization structure?
    _____yes _____no   33
    (b) How many are there and to whom do they report?
    (c) What is their authority?
    _____recommending _____gather data
    _____set policy   34
    (d) Do any supervisors in one department, line, or staff, have any direct or indirect authority in other departments? (Looking for functional authority here.)
    _____yes _____no   35

22. To whom do you report? (Further verification from the executive/personnel interviewee about overlapping of authority.)

(a) Do any other supervisors overlap your authority?
_____many _____some _____none   36
(b) How do you know what your authority is?
_____verbal _____written
_____learned on the job   37

23. (a) What use is made of committees in your organization?
_____much _____some _____none   38
(b) What authority do they have?
_____recommend _____plan
_____execute _____coordinate   39
(c) What use is made of conferences in the company?
(or in your department?)   40

24. (a) Have you been able to utilize informal groups to the benefit of the organization?
_____yes _____no _____none
If yes, how?_____   41
(b) Have they caused any problems for the company?
_____yes _____no

25. (a) Have there been any changes to the organization structure in the past five years? What are they?
_____many _____some _____none   42
(b) What caused these changes?
_____market and economic forces
_____executive personality   43
(c) Are you contemplating or considering any change? Why?
_____yes _____no
(d) Who approves the establishment of new departments or divisions?

26. How are the budgeting and cost accounting departments organized?

27. How is the personnel department organized?

28. How are the purchasing and sales depertments organized?

29. How is the production department organized?

FURTHER INFORMATION TO INFER THE DEGREE OF CENTRALIZATION-DECENTRALIZATION/ DELEGATION OF AUTHORITY

30. *Who makes major policy?*   column
    (a) Owner/top executives   _____   49
    (b) Executive committee (with top-
        level executives only)   _____
    (c) General committee, made up of
        all levels of personnel   _____
    (d) Top- and middle-level
        executives   _____
    (e) Nobody; specific policies are
        made on ad hoc basis   _____
        Total score   _____

31. *Who makes policies regarding marketing?*
    (a) Owner/top executives only   _____   50
    (b) Committee made of functional
        managers   _____
    (c) Functional managers concerned   _____
    (d) Committee made of marketing
        department personnel   _____
    (e) Not clear-cut   _____
    (f) Different for different
        departments   _____
    (g) Others   _____
        Total score   _____

32. *Policy-making for Product line*
    (a) Top-level executive only   _____   51
    (b) Executive committee of
        functional managers   _____
    (c) General executive committee   _____
    (d) Functional manager   _____
    (e) Functional manager's
        committee   _____
    (f) Ad hoc, not clear-cut   _____
        Total score   _____

33. Selection and promotion of executive personnel
    (a) Top executive/owner   _____   52
    (b) Top executive committee   _____
    (c) General committee   _____
    (d) Functional manager   _____
    (e) Ad hoc, not clear-cut   _____
        Total score   _____

34. Selection and promotion of clerical workers   column

    (a) Top executive/owner   _____   **53**
    (b) Top executive committee   _____
    (c) General committee   _____
    (d) Functional manager   _____
    (e) Supervisor   _____
    (f) Departmental committee   _____
    (g) Ad hoc   _____
        Total score   _____

35. Selection and promotion of blue-collar employees

    (a) Top executive/owner   _____   **54**
    (b) Top executive committee   _____
    (c) General committee   _____
    (d) Functional manager   _____
    (e) Supervisor   _____
    (f) Departmental committee   _____
    (g) Ad hoc   _____
        Total score   _____

36. Who sets the standards?

	(1) For production of goods/ services	(2) For executive personnel	(3) For blue-collar workers	(4) For office employees (clerical workers)
(a) Top executive/ owner	___	___	___	___
(b) Top executive committee	___	___	___	___
(c) General committee	___	___	___	___
(d) Supervisor	___	___	___	___
(e) Departmental committee	___	___	___	___
(f) Ad hoc	___	___	___	___
(g) Others	___	___	___	___
Total score	___	___	___	___

37. Further measures of decentralization
   (Schwitter-Pheysey's Project)

AUTHORITY (CENTRALIZATION:
AUTONOMY OF THE ORGANIZATION)
WHO HAS AUTHORITY TO DECIDE

(Authority = action can be taken on the decision without
waiting for confirmation from above, even if the
decision is later ratified at a higher level.)
What is the decision-making level in the organization?

Authority to Decide	Level of Authority	Score
(a) The total amount of white collar and managerial personnel that ought to be employed	___	___
(b) Appointment of supervisory staff from outside the organization (external recruitment)	___	___
(c) Promotion of supervisory staff	___	___
(d) Salaries of supervisory staff	___	___
(e) To dismiss a supervisor	___	___
(f) To determine a new product or service	___	___
(g) To determine marketing territories covered (where new or existing outputs are to be marketed)	___	___
(h) The extent of market share and type of market to be aimed for	___	___
(i) The price of the output	___	___
(j) What type, or what brand, of new equipment is to be used	___	___
(k) What types of expenditures should be recorded under various cost headings	___	___
(l) What shall be inspected (i.e., to what the inspection system, if any, shall be applied)	___	___
(m) What operations should be work-studied	___	___
(n) Which suppliers of materials are to be used	___	___
(o) Buying procedures (what procedure is to be followed when buying materials, etc.)	___	___

Authority to Decide	Authority	Score
(p) Training methods to be used (how training should be done)	———	———
(q) What and how many welfare facilities are to be provided	———	———
(r) To spend unbudgeted or unallocated money on capital items (using money not previously earmarked for a particular purpose, which would be classed as current expenditure)	———	———
(s) To spend unbudgeted or unallocated money on revenue items (using money not previously earmarked, which would be classed as current expenditure)	———	———
(t) To alter responsibilities/areas of work of specialist departments	———	———
(u) To alter responsibilities/areas of work of line departments	———	———
(v) To create a new department (functional specialist or line)	———	———
(w) To create a new job (functional specialist or line, of any status, probably signified by a new job title)	———	———
Total score:	———	59

SOME OFFSET QUESTIONS ON DECENTRALIZATION

What do the following concepts/words mean to you?
participative management —————————————— 60
"Y" theory of management ——————————————
project management ——————————————
"X" theory of management ——————————————

MANAGEMENT PROCESS VARIABLES

Controlling   column

Setting of standards. See Question 39, (1), (2), (3), (4).

38. Who usually discovers the deviations from the established standards? (X-Y theory in action) established standards?
    - (a) Top executive/owner   _____   **61**
    - (b) Executive committee   _____
    - (c) Functional manager   _____
    - (d) Departmental head   _____
    - (e) Foreman   _____
    - (f) Supervisor   _____
    - (g) Individual himself   _____

39. What types of feedback systems are being used?
    - (1) *Medium of Feedback System*
        - (a) Written memos   _____   **62**
        - (b) Verbal report   _____
        - (c) Casual hints   _____
        - (d) Private consultation   _____
        - (e) Other (specify)   _____
    - (2) The origin of the feedback system (where does it originate?)
        - (a) Top executive/owner   _____   **63**
        - (b) Executive committee   _____
        - (c) Staff department—
          accountant, controller,
          quality control, etc.   _____
        - (d) Departmental manager   _____
        - (e) Foreman/supervisor   _____
        - (f) Individual worker himself
          decides the deviation and
          corrects himself   _____
        - (g) Other (specify)   _____

CONTROL TECHNIQUES USED

40. Cost control technique:
    - (a) Cost accounting
        1. In what areas is cost accounting done?   64
           _____for all products
           _____for major products
           _____at random   _____not done

column

2. Who does cost accounting?

_____qualified personnel, separate   65
department
_____qualified personnel in
respective departments
_____unqualified personnel in
respective departments
_____unqualified personnel in separate
departments
_____manager or department head
himself
_____none

(b) Budgeting and resource allocation:

1. For what purposes is this done?

_____for entire firm   66
_____for each plant
_____for each department
_____for each product   _____none

2. Who does it?

_____department with qualified people   67
or controller
_____top management and/or committee
_____manager himself
_____department
_____others specified   _____none

(c) Job and/or time study standards

1. Production—who does it?

_____separate time and motion   68
study department
_____foreman (supervisor)
_____none   _____others (specify)

2. White-collar workers—who does it?

_____separate time and motion   69
study department
_____foreman (supervisor)
_____others (specify)
_____none

(d) Equipment maintenance—who does it?

_____separate department, skilled personnel   70
_____separate department, unskilled personnel
_____department concern
_____ad hoc

44. Research and development   column

(a) Do you spend a fixed percentage of your sales on research and development?   71

_____yes   _____no   If yes, how much?
_____0-1%
_____1-2%
_____2-3%
_____more than 3%

(b) If not, how do you determine the overall level of research and development expenditures?   72

_____what we can afford
_____percentage of profits
_____meet competitors

(c) How do you determine which research and projects will be funded within your research and development budget?   73

_____research department judgment
_____top managers' judgment
_____per requirement of consumer
_____per requirement of governmental authorities

(d) How many new products/processes have you developed in the last five years?   74

_____25 and more
_____10-24
_____1-9
_____none

(e) What is the percentage of the total sales attributed to these new products?   75

_____75-100%
_____50-74
_____25-49
_____10-24
_____0-9
_____insignificant

(f) What other innovations has the company undertaken in the last five years?   76

_____
_____
_____
_____

(g) What degree of automation and/or modernization
has taken place in the company's operations?   column
    (1) Complete overhaul of
        machinery   _____   77
    (2) Considerable overhaul of
        machinery   _____
    (3) Some overhaul of machinery _____
    (4) Complete overhaul of data
        processing (introduction of
        computer for accounting,
        budget, controlling, etc.)   _____
    (5) Some changes in data
        processing   _____
    (6) Considerable changes in
        organizational arrangements
        (what changes? Specify.)   _____
    (7) Some changes in organ-
        izational arrangements
        (what changes? Specify.)   _____
    (8) Ad hoc changes,
        uncoordinated   _____
    (9) No changes at all   _____
(h) Who decides innovation, automation, modernization?
    (1) Top executive/owner   _____   78
    (2) Executive committee   _____
    (3) General committee   _____
    (4) Ad hoc   _____
    (5) Others (specify)   _____

LEADERSHIP

Card 2: Company's Identification:

42. Types of prevailing leadership

	Top Level	Middle Level	Supervisory Level
(a) Considerably democratic			
(b) Somewhat democratic	_____	_____	_____
(c) Considerably autocratic	_____	_____	_____
(d) Somewhat autocratic	_____	_____	_____

   (e) Considerably   column
       bureaucratic   —————   —————   —————
   (f) Somewhat
       bureaucratic   —————   —————   —————
   (g) Confused, not
       clear-cut;
       depends on
       person   —————   —————   —————
  Comments (Record the impression or executives' comments about leadership role.)

43. Manager's (leader's) perception of subordinates
    A. *At top level*   9
      (a) Leader perceives subordinates
         as confident and trustworthy —————   10
      (b) Leader perceives subordinates
         as somewhat confident and
         trustworthy   —————
      (c) Leader perceives subordinates
         as not confident and
         trustworthy   —————
    B. *At middle level*
      (a) Leader perceives subordinates
         as confident and trustworthy —————   11
      (b) Leader perceives subordinates
         as somewhat confident and
         trustworthy   —————
      (c) Leader perceives subordinates
         as not confident and
         trustworthy   —————
    C. *At lower level* (supervisory level)
      (a) Leader perceives subordinates
         as confident and trustworthy —————   12
      (b) Leader perceives subordinates
         as somewhat confident and
         trustworthy   —————
      (c) Leader perceives subordinates
         as not confident and
         trustworthy   —————

MANPOWER MANAGEMENT

(Staffing Policies and Practices)

44. Are there specific policies about manpower management? (personnel policies)

    _____yes   _____no   **13**

    If yes, who formulates them?
    (a) Top executive/owner   _____   **14**
    (b) Top executive committee   _____
    (c) General committee   _____
    (d) Personnel manager   _____
    (e) Ad hoc, undiscernable   _____
    (f) Other (specify)   _____

45. Main objectives of personnel policies
    (a) To satisfy the objectives of the
         individual participant as well as
         the organizational objectives   _____
    (b) To select right individuals   _____
    (c) To avoid troublemakers   _____
    (d) No specific objectives   _____

Selection Procedures

46. What are the methods that you use to recruit your executive personnel?
    (a) Intensive interviews with the help
         of outside consultants   _____   **16**
    (b) Intensive interviews by the
         executive committee   _____
    (c) Intensive interviews by the
         personnel manager, staff,
         functional managers   _____
    (d) Simple interviews/
         questionnaire   _____
    (e) Ad hoc, depending on the
         manager's concern   _____

50. Who selects supervisory personnel?
    (a) Top executive/owner   _____   **17**
    (b) Executive committee   _____
    (c) Personnel manager   _____
    (d) Functional manager/foreman,   _____
         functional manager   _____
    (e) Personnel manager   _____
    (f) Ad hoc, not clear-cut   _____

column

47. Who selects clerical workers?
    (a) Top executive/owner   _____   18
    (b) Executive committee   _____
    (c) General staffing committee   _____
    (d) Personnel manager   _____
    (e) Functional manager   _____
    (f) Personnel manager/
        functional manager   _____
    (g) Supervisor/head clerk   _____
    (h) Others (specify)   _____

48. Who selects blue-collar workers?
    (a) Top executive/owner   _____   19
    (b) Executive committee   _____
    (c) General staffing committee   _____
    (d) Personnel manager   _____
    (e) Functional manager   _____
    (f) Personnel manager/
        functional manager   _____
    (g) Supervisor/head clerk   _____
    (h) Others (specify)   _____

49. How do the methods used in recruiting executives differ from those used to recruit lower levels of personnel? (comments)   20

50. What criteria do you use in selecting individuals who have been recruited for management positions?
    _____education   _____training and experience
    _____age   _____market contacts
    _____family ties   _____other

51. What are the criteria that you use for promoting personnel?
    education and training   _____   22
    years of experience   _____
    both   _____
    ability to get along with others   _____
    technical ability   _____
    not clear-cut   _____

52. What techniques are used in your personnel appraisal system?
    no formal appraisal system   _____   23
    standard forms   _____
    periodic reports from the supervisor   _____
    executive committee   _____
    others (specify)   _____

53. How do you provide for managerial succession?   column
    no formal method   _____   24
    management succession chart   _____
    job rotation   _____
    other   _____

54. Who makes executive promotion decisions?
    president   _____   25
    president and executive committee   _____
    president with personnel manager   _____
    president with personnel manager
      and functional manager   _____
    special promotion committee   _____
      ad hoc   _____

    A. If by a committee, who are the members of the
       committee?   26

    B. Who makes promotion decisions at lower manage-
       ment levels?
       president   _____   27
       department head or functional
         manager   _____
       department head with personnel
         manager   _____
       department head with staffing
         committee   _____
       ad hoc   _____
       others (specify)   _____

    C. Who makes promotion decisions for blue-collar
       workers?
       department head or functional
         manager   _____   28
       department head with personnel
         manager   _____
       staffing committee   _____
       supervisor   _____
       ad hoc, not clear-cut   _____

    D. Who makes hire-and-fire decisions for top-level
       executives?
       president   _____   29
       executive committee   _____
       personnel manager   _____
       special promotion committee   _____
       other   _____

    E. Who makes hire-and-fire decisions for middle man-
       agement?
       president   _____   30

· column

department head or functional
   manager   _____
department head with personnel
   manager   _____
department head with staffing
   committee   _____
others (specify)   _____

F. Who makes hire-and-fire decisions for clerical
   workers?
   department head or functional
      manager   _____   31
   department head with personnel
      manager   _____
   staffing committee   _____
   supervisor   _____
   others (specify)   _____

G. Who makes hire-and-fire decisions for blue-collar
   workers?
   department manager or functional
      manager   _____   32
   department manager with
      personnel manager   _____
   others   _____

55. What criteria are used in your personnel appraisal
    system for management positions?
    education   _____   33
    extensive experience
       (10 yrs. or more)   _____
    ability to get along with others   _____
    aggressiveness   _____
    company loyalty   _____
    other (specify)   _____

56. Do you use either written or verbal job descriptions in
    your selection process?
    written   _____   34
    written classification with no
       specific positions   _____
    verbal   _____

57. Who writes job descriptions?
    personnel department   _____   35
    motion and time study engineers   _____
    supervisors   _____
    nobody   _____
    other   _____

column

58. How do you determine the levels of compensation for various jobs within your firm?

job description	_____
recommendation of the supervisor	_____
pay goes with position	_____
going wage	_____
market forces	_____
other	_____

36

59. Do you have any type of formal traing programs?

_____yes _____no

37

For what level?

operator	_____
supervisors	_____
junior management	_____
senior management	_____

60. Which employees participate in which types of training programs?

	Operators	Supervisor	Jr. Man.	Sr. Man.
On-the-job	_____	_____	_____	_____
Formal—in company	_____	_____	_____	_____
Formal—outside	_____	_____	_____	_____
On-the-job plus in company	_____	_____	_____	_____
On-the-job plus outside	_____	_____	_____	_____
Job rotation	_____	_____	_____	_____
Training for promotion purposes	_____	_____	_____	_____

61. Who runs the training programs? _____

42

How many people are employed in running the training program at each level in question 63?

43

62. What percentage of the total average company man-hours per week are used for training purposes?

16-20%	_____
11-15%	_____
6-10%	_____
1-5%	_____

44

column

63. Do you have a layoff status for your employees?
_____yes _____no   **45**

64. Under what conditions are employees dismissed?
absence   _____
incompetence   _____
stealing   _____
insubordination   _____
market forces   _____
other   _____

65. How long does it take to dismiss employees who are no
longer needed?   **46**

66. What is the procedure for dismissal?   **47**

67. Have you experienced difficulty in recruiting and keep-
ing personnel with specific skills or abilities?   **48**
_____yes _____no
A. Which skills? _____
_____

B. For what reason?
nonavailability of skilled personnel _____   **49**
lack of training and educational
facilities in the community   _____
low wage scales   _____
low level of fringe benefits   _____
some unfavorable management
policy (specify)   _____
other   _____

68. Which skills and abilities have been the most difficult
to find and keep?
Technical personnel   _____   **50**
Managerial personnel with
special skills   _____
Managerial personnel in general _____
Blue-collar, skilled   _____
Unskilled   _____

69. Please give some estimate of your turnover rate for the
last five years.
blue-collar   _____   **51**
clerical   _____
supervisor   _____
junior management   _____
middle management   _____
top management   _____

column

70. What is your estimate of the rate of absenteeism at the various levels within your firm?

    operator   _____   52
    supervisory   _____
    junior management   _____
    senior management   _____

71. What is your personnel turnover rate among supervisors?   53

72. What are the socio-economic legal factors that in your opinion affect employee morale and satisfaction in work?   54

73. What are the factors affecting selection and promotion procedures for your high-level manpower?   55

74. What types of financial compensation do you use?

    56-58

	For workers	For executive groups	For clerical employees
salaries	_____	_____	_____
hourly wages	_____	_____	_____
bonuses	_____	_____	_____
stock options	_____	_____	_____
other	_____	_____	_____

75. How do you deal with your employees?

    through union representation   _____   59
    through first-line supervisors   _____
    both   _____

76. If you do not have a union in your firm, has there been any recent attempt by union organizers to enter your firm?

    _____yes   _____no   60

    A. What are these unions?

    B. How did you handle their attempts at organizing unions?   61

MANAGEMENT EFFECTIVENESS

(Behavioral variables)

77.

     A. Employee morale and satisfaction in work
         (to infer, interview at least 50 workers in each company)

column

    (a) Excellent morale, employee
        highly satisfied   _____   62
    (b) Average morale, employees
        somewhat satisfied   _____
    (c) Poor morale, employee
        highly dissatisfied   _____
  B. Employee productivity: obtain any measure of pro-
     ductivity available   63
    (a) Number of items produced per worker   64
    (b) Cost per unit
    (c) Scrap loss or waste material
    (d) Improvements made by the workers themselevs
    (e) Others (specify)
  C. Socio-economic, political, legal, and cultural var-
     iables affecting employee morale and satisfaction in
     work and productivity   (see 54)
     Management viewpoint   65
     Other experts' (e.g. professor, businessman, gov-
     ernment leader) viewpoints   66
     Workers' viewpoints   67
78. Interpersonal relationship: attitudes of workers among
themselves and among workers and supervisors (to
infer, interview at least 50 workers and supervisors in
each company)   67
  A. Among workers and supervisors
    (a) Very cooperative attitude
        toward each other   _____   68
    (b) Somewhat cooperative attitude
        toward each other   _____
    (c) Hostile attitude toward
        each other   _____
  B. Among workers themselves
    (a) Very cooperative   _____   69
    (b) Somewhat cooperative   _____
    (c) Hostile   _____
  C. Socio-economic, political, legal, and cultural var-
     iables affecting interpersonal relationships
     Management viewpoint   _____   70
     Other experts' viewpoints   _____
     Workers' viewpoint   _____
79. Labor absenteeism rate (percentage of total labor
force employed: average of one year)
    (a) 25% or more   _____   71
    (b) 15-24%   _____
    (c) 5-14%   _____
    (d) 4% or less   _____

column

80. Labor turnover rate (percentage of total labor force
    employed; average of one year)
    (a) 25% or more   _____   **72**
    (b) 15-24%   _____
    (c) 5-14%   _____
    (d) 4% or less   _____
81. Socio-economic, political, legal, and cultural factors
    affecting absenteeism   **73**
    A. Management viewpoint   _____
    B. Other experts' viewpoints   _____
    C. Workers' viewpoints   _____
82. Organizational effectiveness in hiring and retaining
    trained managerial and technical personnel (observe
    from executives interviewed as well as ask them about
    it)
    (a) Able to hire and retain
        highly trained personnel   _____   **74**
    (b) Able to hire and retain
        average trained personnel   _____
    (c) Not able to hire and retain
        even average trained personnel   _____
83. Environmental factors (socio-economic, political,
    legal, and cultural) affecting organizational ability to
    hire and retain trained personnel   **75**
84. Interdepartmental relationships (observe from execu-
    tives' behavior patterns, especially their viewpoints
    about other departments)
    (a) Very cooperative   _____   **76**
    (b) Somewhat cooperative   _____
    (c) Not cooperative   _____
85. Environmental factors affecting interdepartmental re-
    lationships   **77**
86. Executives' perception of the achievement of the
    firm's objectives
    (a) Total optimization (achieve-
        ment of the firm's objectives)
        is perceived as most important   _____   **78**
    (b) Suboptimization (achievement
        of the departmental objectives)
        is preferred   _____
    (c) Achievement of the departmental
        objectives as ultimate goal   _____
87. Environmental factors affecting interdepartmental re-
    lationships

column

88. Utilization of high-level manpower (interview only top executives and functional managers)
    A. What the executives do
        (1) Policy-making and planning for future _____ **79**
        (2) Coordination with other departments _____
        (3) Routine work, day-to-day work _____
        (4) Excessive supervision of subordinates' duties _____
    B. Executives' enthusiasm and drive in their work
        (1) Enormous drive and enthusiasm _____ **80**
        (2) Moderate drive and enthusiasm _____
        (3) Doing work as part of living _____

CARD 3: Company's identification 1-2

89. Environmental factors affecting the utilization of high-level manpower 6
90. Organizational effectiveness in adapting to environmental conditions
    (a) Able to adapt without much difficulty _____ 7
    (b) Able to adapt partially with some difficulty _____
    (c) Not able to adapt _____
    (d) Not discernible _____

ENTERPRISE EFFECTIVENESS

91. Obtain the following information:
    (a) Net profits of the firm for the last five years _____ 8
    (b) Gross profits of the firm for the last five years _____ 9
        Gross sales of the industry for the last five years _____ 10
    (c) Rate of return on equity of the firm for the last five years (year by year) _____ 11
        Average rate of return on equity for the industry for the last five years _____ 12
    (d) Percentage increase in profits in the last five years (year by year) _____ 13
        Average percentage increase in profits for the industry in the last five years _____ 14

column

   (e) Market share of the company in the
       main product line   _____ 15
       Percentage increase in the market share
       for the last five years   _____ 16
   (f) Market price of the company's stock   _____ 17
       Percentage increase in price of the stock
       in the last five years   _____ 18
   (g) Percentage increase in sales in the
       last five years   _____ 19
       Average percentage increase in sales for
       the industry for the last five years   _____ 20
   (h) Scrap loss   _____ 21
   (i) Workers' productivity   _____ 22
   (j) Number of new products in the
       last five years   _____ 23
   (k) Number of innovations in the
       last five years   _____ 24
92. Environmental factors affecting delegation of author-
     ity (decentralization process)   25
93. Environmental factors affecting planning
94. Environmental factors affecting control   26
95. Environmental factors affecting staffing (selecting, ap-
     praisal, promoting employees)   27
96. Environmental factors affecting leadership (including
     direction)   28
97. Environmental factors affecting adoption of advanced
     management know-how in industrial companies in
     Taiwan   29

COMMENTS

APPENDIX B —

SPECIALIZATION OF FUNCTIONS

(in order of probability of the organization having a specialist, from most likely to least likely)

	Who is responsible for: (enter job titles of employees of the unit of the organization, not contractors, consultants, HQ service departments, etc.)	Is one or more of these activities someone's sole task? (circle one)
	and equpiment	Yes No
	Buying _____ Storing _____ Inventory control _____ (or any specialized administrative work for the above) Any other jobs which may fit_____ _____ _____	
3	Carrying outputs and resources from place to place	Yes No
	Transportation: Outside (owned facilities) *or* inside (materials- handling) the organization's site Shipping/receiving _____ (or any specialized administrative work for the above _____ _____ _____	
7	Obtaining and controlling materials Any other jobs which may fit_____	
9	Recording and controlling financial resources	Yes No
	Accounting (e.g., wages officer, costs office, cashiers, ledger section, or financial accounts section) _____ Any other jobs which may fit_____ _____ _____	

	Who is responsible for: (enter job titles of employees of the unit of the organization, not contractors, consultants, HQ service departments, etc.)	Is one or more of these activities someone's sole task? (circle one)
8	Maintaining and erecting buildings and equipment	Yes No
	Maintenance (e.g., maintenance or erection of buildings, machinery, electrical fittings; surveyor or architect, etc.) _____ Any other jobs which may fit_____	
11	Controlling the quality of materials and equipment and outputs	Yes No
	final output inspection _____ raw materials and supply inspection _____ quality improvement _____ (or any specialized administrative work for the above) Any other jobs which may fit_____	
6	Maintaining human resources and promoting their identification with the organization	Yes No
	security personnel (e.g., police, uniformed gatekeepers _____ canteen services _____ welfare services _____ safety _____ fire protection _____ sports and social activities _____ magazine _____ suggestion system _____ Any other jobs which may fit_____	

	Who is responsible for: (enter job titles of employees of the unit of the organization, not contractors, consultants, HQ service departments, etc.)	Is one or more of these activities someone's sole task? (circle one)
10	Controlling workflow Day-to-day "production" planning- control _____ progress expeditors _____ longer-term production planning _____ machine-loading calculation _____ Any other jobs which may fit_____	Yes No
2	Disposing of, distributing, and servicing the output sales _____ customer service _____ pricing _____ sales records _____ Any other jobs which may fit_____	Yes No
4	Acquiring and allocating human resources Employment (i.e., recruitment and/or selection, not personnel work in general)_____ interviewing _____ (or any specialized administrative work for the above) Any other jobs which may fit_____	Yes No
13	Devising new outputs, equipment, and processes research and/or development on outputs _____ drawing office _____ (or any specialized administrative work for the above) Any other jobs which may fit_____	Yes No

	Who is responsible for: (enter job titles of employees of the unit of the organization, not contractors, consultants, HQ service departments, etc.)	Is one or more of these activities someone's sole task? (circle one)
12	Assessing and devising ways of producing the output motion study _____ method study _____ time study _____ (specialized) production engineering _____ (specialized) plant layout _____ (or any specialized administrative work for the above) Any other jobs which may fit___	Yes No
14	Developing and operating administrative procedures office methods systems or procedures _____ collection and analysis of statistics _____ records (filing) and/or post (mail) service _____ Any other jobs which may fit___	Yes No
5	Developing and transforming human resources training/education _____ Any other jobs which may fit___	Yes No
1	Developing, legitimizing, and symbolizing the organization's public image advertising _____ public relations _____ publicity work _____ display (window displays, exhibitions, etc.) _____ customer relations _____ Any other jobs which may fit___	Yes No

	Who is responsible for: (enter job titles of employees of the unit of the organization, not contractors, consultants, HQ service departments, etc.)	Is one or more of these activities someone's sole task? (circle one)
15	Dealing with legal and insurance requirements legal work _____ insurance work _____ shareholder roster _____ Any other jobs which may fit_____ _____ _____	Yes No
16	Acquiring information in the operational field market research _____ (specialized) economic analysis _____ Any other jobs which may fit_____ _____ _____	Yes No

APPENDIX C —

Figure C-1
Company's Philosophy Toward Employees

Four Factors Evaluated

1. Top management's stated policy or philosophy concerning employee development
2. Employee's perception of the company's concern toward individual development
3. Prospective employee's image of the company
4. Public image of the company

to categorize

Company's Concern toward Employee Development as

1. "much concern"
2. "moderate concern"
3. "little or no concern"

Figure C-2
Company's Philosophy Toward Consumers

Seven Factors Evaluated			*Company's Attitude toward Consumers as*
1. Company's profit and service objectives—implied, expressed, and implemented			
2. Consumer's image of the company and its products			
3. Employee's image of the company and of its profit objective		1. "consumer as the king"	
4. Supplier's image of the company, its products, and its profit objectives	to categorize	2. "consumers are necessary to make profit"	
5. Distributor's image of the company, its products, and profit objectives		3. "consumers should take what we make"	
6. Stockholder's image of the company and its profit objective			
7. Company pricing policies			

Figure C-3
Company's Philosophy Toward Distributors

Four Factors Evaluated			*Company's Attitude as*
1. Management policy statement and implementation			
2. Marketing programs and procedures		1. "honest relationship absolutely necessary"	
3. Implied and expressed attitude of marketing executives toward distributors	to categorize	2. "good relationship helpful"	
4. Distributor's attitude toward company		3. "relationship is a necessary evil"	

Figure C-4
Company's Philosophy Toward Suppliers

Five Factors Evaluated

Company's Attitude as

1. Company's policy statements
2. Implementation of policies
3. Programs and procedures of purchasing department of company
4. Purchasing agents' or executives' attitudes toward supplier
5. Supplier's evaluation of company

to categorize

1. "honest relationship absolutely necessary"
2. "good relationship helpful"
3. "relationship a necessary evil"

Figure C-5
Company's Philosophy Toward Stockholders

Five Factors Evaluated

Company's Attitude as

1. Company's policy statement and implementation of policies
2. Stockholders' evaluation of the company
3. Prospective investors' evaluation of the company
4. The company's senior executives' viewpoint towards stockholders
5. Actual programs and procedures of the stock department of the company

to categorize

1. "they are owners, masters; best public relation personnel"
2. "they are owners, masters"
3. "they are financier profit-eaters"

Figure C-6
Company's Philosophy Toward Government

Five Factors Evaluated		*Company's Attitude as*
1. Top executive's attitude toward government		
2. Company's participation in governmental policies		
3. Senior governmental official's attitude toward company	to categorize	1. "good partner" 2. "necessary evil" 3. "government be damned"
4. Program and procedure of company's public relation department		
5. Speeches and press statements made by the company's executives on governmental affairs		

Figure C-7
Company's Philosophy Toward Community

Six Factors Evaluated		*Company's Attitude as*
1. Programs and procedures of company's public relation department		
2. Top executives' attitude toward community		
3. Company's participation in community affairs		1. "very much concern"
4. Company's contribution to community chest, hospital facilities, and education	to categorize	2. "some concern" 3. "little or no concern"
5. Attitudes of selected community leaders toward the company		
6. Attitudes of selected educators toward company		

BIBLIOGRAPHY

I. Socio-Cultural and Environment Settings

Banfield, Edward. *The Moral Basis of a Backward Society.* Glencoe, Ill.: The Free Press, 1958.

Benedict, Ruth. *Patterns of Culture.* New York: Houghton Mifflin, 1962.

Bohannan, Paul. *Africa and Africans.* New York: Natural History Press, 1964.

Chowdhry, Kamala. "Social and Cultural Factors in Management Development in India and the Role of the Expert." *International Labour Review,* vol. 94, (August 1966), 132-47.

Fanon, Frantz. "The Pitfalls of National Consciousness." In *The Wretched of the Earth.* New York: Grove Press, 1966.

Fullerton, Kemper. *"Calvinism and Capitalism."* Harvard Theological Review, vol. 21 (1928), 163-91.

Grier, William H., and Price, M. Cobbs. *Black Rage.* New York: Richard N. Adams et al., *Social Change in Latin America Today.* New York: Random House, 1960.

Goldstein, K. *Human Nature.* Cambridge: Harvard Univ. Press, 1951.

Grier, William H., and Price M. Cobbs. *Black Rage.* New York: Basic Books, 1968.

Harbison, Frederick, and Meyers, Charles A. *Education, Manpower, and Economic Growth.* New York: McGraw-Hill, 1964.

Heilbroner, Robert L. "The Shackles of Backwardness." *The Great Ascent.* New York: Harper & Row, 1963.

Ingersoll, J. "Fatalism in Rural Thailand." *Anthropological Quarterly,* vol. 39 (1966), 200-25.

Josh, Vidga. "Personality Profiles in Industrial and Preindustrial Cultures: A TAT Study." *Journal of Social Psychology,* vol. 66 (1965), 101-11.

Kerr, Clark; Dunlop, John T.; Harbison, Frederick; and Meyers, Charles A. "Industrialism and World Society." *Harvard Business Review,* vol. 39, no. 1 (January-February 1961), 114-22.

Mandelbaum, David G. *Society in India. Vol. 2: Change and Continuity.* Berkeley: Univ. of California Press, 1970.

Mead, Margaret. *Cultural Patterns and Technical Change.* UNESCO, 1955.

Myrdal, Gunnar. *Asian Drama: An Inquiry into the Poverty of Nations.* New York: The Twentieth Century Fund, 1968.

Nagley, Charles. *The Latin American Tradition.* New York: Columbia Univ. Press, 1968.

Narain Dhirewdra. "Indian National Character in the Twentieth Century." *Annals* (March 1967), 124-32.

Piker, Steven. "The Relationship of Belief Systems to Behavior in the Rural Thai Society." *Asian Survey,* vol. 8 (May 1968), 386-99.

Porter, John. "Canadian Character in the Twentieth Century." *Annals* (March 1967), 48-56.

Shih, Ho. "A Chinese Philosopher Prefers the Material Civilization of the West." In *The World of Business,* ed. Edward Borsk, Donald Clark, and Ralph Hidy. New York: Simon and Schuster, 1962, pp. 1,505-10.

Stewart, Rosemary. "The Socio-Cultural Setting of Management in the United Kingdom." *International Labour Review,* vol. 94, no. 2 (August 1966), 108-31.

Turnbull, Colin M. "Something Old." *The Lonely African.* Garden City, N.Y.: Anchor Books, 1963.

Vogel, Ezra F. *Japan's New Middle Class.* Berkeley: Univ. of California Press, 1963.

Whyte, W. F. "Culture, Industrial Relations, and Economic Development: The Case of Peru." *Industrial and Labor Relations Review,* vol. 6, no. 2 (July 1963).

Whyte, F., and Braum, Robert R. "Heroes, Homework, and Industrial Growth." *Columbia Journal of World Business,* vol. 1, no. 2 (Spring 1966), 51-57.

II.   Research Designs and Models for Cross-Cultural Management Studies

Altimus, C., et al. "Cross-Cultural Perspectives on Need Deficiencies of Blue-Collar Workers." *Quarterly Journal of Management Development,* 2 (June 1971), 91-103.

Bass, B. M., and Leavitt, H. S. "Some Experiences in Planning and Operating." *Management Science,* vol. 9, no. 4 (July 1963), 574-85.

Bendix, Reinhard. "Concepts and Generalizations in Comparative

Sociological Studies." *American Sociological Review,* vol. 28 (August 4, 1963), 532-39.

Farmer, R. N., and Richman, B. M. *Comparative Management and Economic Progress.* Homewood, Ill.: Richard D. Irwin, 1965.

Farmer, R. N., and Richman, Barry. "A Model for Research in Comparative Management." *California Management Review,* vol. 4 (Winter 1964), 55-68.

Herzberg, F., et al. *Job Attitudes: Review of Research and Opinion.* Pittsburgh: Psychological Service of Pittsburgh, 1957.

Meade, R. D. "An Experimental Study of Leadership in India." *Journal of Social Psychology,* 72 (1967), 35-43.

Negandhi, A. R. "Advanced Management Know-How in Developing Countries." *California Management Review,* vol. 10, no. 3 (Spring 1968), 53-60.

Negandhi, A. R., and Estafen, B. D. "Determining Applicability of American Management Know-How in Differing Environments and Cultures." *Academy of Management Journal,* vol. 8, no. 4 (December 1965), 319-23.

Prasad, S. B. "Comparative Managerialism as an Approach to International Economic Growth." *Quarterly Journal of AIESEC International,* 2 (August 1966), 22-30.

Schollhammer, Hans. "The Comparative Management Theory Jungle." *Academy of Management Journal,* 12 (March 1969), 86-87.

Sharma, K. L. "Dominance-Deference: A Cross-Cultural Study." *The Journal of Social Psychology,* 79 (1969), 265-66.

Zurcher, L. A., et al. "Value Orientation, Role Conflict, and Alienation from Work: A Cross-Cultural Study." *American Sociological Review,* vol. 30, no. 4, pp. 539-48.

III. IMPACT OF ECONOMIC, LEGAL, AND POLITICAL FACTORS ON ORGANIZATIONAL PRACTICES AND EFFECTIVENESS

Aguilar, Francis. *Scanning the Business Environment.* New York: Macmillan, 1967.

Bennis, W. G. *Changing Organizations.* New York: McGraw-Hill, 1966.

Burns, Thomas, and Stalker, G. M. *Management of Innovation.* London: Tavistock Publications, 1961.

Caplow, T. "The Criteria for Organizational Success." *Sociological Forces,* vol. 32, no. 1 (October 1953), 1-9.

Chamberlain, Neil. *Enterprise and Environment.* New York: McGraw-Hill, 1968.

Clee, G. H., and Scipio, A. D. "Creating a World Enterprise." *Harvard Business Review,* 37 (November-December 1959), 77-89.

Davis, Keith, and Blomstrom, R. L. *Business and Its Environment.* New York: McGraw-Hill, 1966.

Dill, William R. "Environment as an Influence on Managerial Autonomy." *Administrative Science Quarterly,* 2 (March 1958), 409-43.

Emery, F. E. *Systems Thinking.* Middlesex, Eng.: Penguin Books, 1970, pp. 261-80.

Fiedler, Fred E. *A Theory of Leadership Effectiveness.* New York: McGraw-Hill, 1967.

Lawrence, Paul R., and Lorsch, Jay W. "Differentiation and Integration in Complex Organizations." *Administrative Science Quarterly,* June 1967, pp. 1-47.

Lawrence, Paul R., and Lorsch, S. W. *Organization and Environment.* Homewood, Ill.: Richard D. Irwin, 1969.

Lefton, M., and Rosengren, W. R. "Organizations and Clients: Lateral and Longitudinal Dimensions." *American Sociological Review,* 31 (1966), 802-10.

Lorsch, Jay W. "Environment, Organization and the Individual." In A. R. Negandhi, ed., *Environmental-Settings in Organizational Functioning.* Kent, Ohio: Center for Business and Economic Research, Kent State University, 1971, pp. 35-48.

Negandhi, A. R., and Reimann, B. D. "A Contingency Theory of Organization Re-Examined in the Context of a Developing Country." *Academy of Management Journal,* vol. 15, no. 2 (June 1972), 137-46.

Price, James L. *Organizational Effectiveness: An Inventory of Propositions.* Homewood, Ill.: Richard D. Irwin, 1968.

Selznick, Philip A. "Foundations of the Theory of Organization." *American Sociological Review,* vol. 13, no. 1 (1948), 25-35.

Selznick, Philip A. *TVA and the Grass Roots.* Berkeley: Univ. of California Press, 1953.

Thompson, James D. *Organizations in Action.* New York: Mc-

Graw-Hill, 1967.

Thompson, James D., and McEwen, W. J. "Organizational Goals and Environment: Goal-Setting as an Interaction Process." *American Sociological Review,* vol. 23, no. 1 (February 1968), 23-31.

Thorelli, Hans B. "Organizational Theory: An Ecological View." *Proceedings of the Academy of Management* (1967), pp. 66-84.

Woodward, Joan. *Industrial Organizations: Theory and Practice.* London: Oxford University Press, 1965.

_____. "Technology, Material Control, and Organizational Behavior." In A. R. Negandhi and J. P. Schwitter, eds., *Organizational Behavior Models.* Kent, Ohio: Center for Business and Economic Research, Kent State University, 1971, p. 21.

iv. IMPACT OF SOCIO-CULTURAL VARIABLES ON ORGANIZATIONAL PRACTICES AND EFFECTIVENESS

Abegglen, James C. *The Japanese Factory: Aspects of Its Social Organization.* New York: The Free Press, 1058, pp. 11-109.

Barrett, G. V., and Bass, B. M. "Comparative Surveys of Managerial Attitudes and Behavior." In Jean Boddewyn, ed., *Comparative Management: Teaching, Training, and Research.* New York: Graduate School of Business Administration, New York University Press, 1970.

Brown, William. "Japanese Management—The Cultural Background." *Monumenta Nipponica—Studies in Japanese Culture,* vol. 22, no. 1-2, pp. 47-60.

Clark, A. N., and McCabe, S. "Leadership Beliefs of Australian Managers." *Journal of Applied Psychology,* 54 (1970), 1-6.

Cohran, Thomas C. *The Puerto Rican Businessman: A Study in Cultural Change.* Philadelphia: Univ. of Pennsylvania Press, 1959.

_____, and Reina, R. E. *Entrepreneurship in Argentina Culture.* Philadelphia: Univ. of Pennsylvania Press, 1962.

Crozier, M. *The Bureaucratic Phenomenon.* Chicago: Univ. of Chicago Press, 1964.

_____. "The Cultural Determinants of Organizational Behavior." In A. R. Negandhi, ed., *Environmental Settings in Organizational Functioning.* Kent, Ohio: Kent State University Press, 1970, pp. 49-58.

Davis, Stanley M. "The Politics of Organizational Undevelop-

ment: Chile." *Industrial and Labor Relations Review,*
October 1970, pp. 23-83.
————. *Comparative Management: Organizational and Cultural
Perspectives.* Englewood Cliffs, N.J.: Prentice-Hall, 1971.
————. "Managerial Resource Development in Mexico." In
Robert R. Rehder, ed., *Latin American Management: De-
velopment and Performance.* Reading, Mass.: Addison-
Wesley, 1968, pp. 166-79.
————. "U.S. Versus Latin America: Business and Culture."
Harvard Business Review, 47 (November-December 1969),
88-98.
Deasi, K. G. "A Study of Workers' Expectations from Super-
visors and Management." *The Indian Journal of Social
Work,* vol. 30, no. 2 (July 1969), 105-16.
———— "A Comparative Study of Motivation of Blue-Collar and
White-Collar Workers." *The Indian Journal of Social
Work,* vol. 28, no. 4 (January 1968), 380-87.
Drucker, Peter. "What We can Learn from Japanese Manage-
ment." *Harvard Business Review,* vol. 49, no. 2 (March-
April 1971), 110-22.
Dunning, John R. "U.S. Subsidiaries in Britain and Their U.K.
Competitors." *Business Ratios,* Autumn 1966.
Eells, Richard, and Walton, Clarence C. "Business in Western
Europe." *Conceptual Foundations of Business.* Homewood,
Ill.: Richard D. Irwin, 1961.
Fayerweather, John. *The Executive Overseas.* Syracuse: Syra-
cuse Univ. Press, 1959.
Feldman, Arnold S., and Moore, Wilbert E. "Are Industrial So-
cieties Becoming Alike?" In Alvin N. Gouldner and S. M.
Miller, eds., *Applied Sociology.* New York: The Free Press
of Glencoe, 1965, pp. 260-65.
Fillol, Thomas Roberto. *Social Factors in Economic Develop-
ment: The Argentine Case.* Cambridge: MIT Press, 1963.
Gangoli, H.C. "An Enquiry into Incentives for Workers in an
Engineering Factory." *Indian Journal of Social Work,*
vol. 9, no. 2, June 1954, p. 110.
Geestz, Clifford. "Social Change and Economic Modernization
in Two Indonesian Towns: A Case in Point." In Everett
E. Hagen, ed., *On the Theory of Social Change.* Homewood, Ill.: Dorsey Press, 1962.
Gerlach, Luther P. "Traders on Bicycle: A Study of Entrepreneurship and Culture Change among the Digo and Duruma
of Kenya." *Sociologus,* vol. 13, no. 1 (1963).

Haberstroh, Chadwick. "Organization Structure: Social and Technical Elements." *Industrial Management Review,* 3 (1961), 64-77.

Haire, Mason; Ghiselli, Edwin E.; and Lyman W. Portes. "Cultural Patterns in the Role of the Manager." *Industrial Relations—A Journal of Economy and Society,* vol. 2, no. 2 (February 1963), 95-117.

————. *Managerial Thinking: An International Study.* New York: Wiley, 1966.

Harbison, F., and Myers, C. *Management in the Industrial World.* New York: McGraw-Hill, 1959.

Harbison, F., and Burgess, E. "Modern Management in Western Europe." *American Journal of Sociology,* vol. 60, no. 1 (July 1954), 15-23.

Harbon, John D. "The Dilemma of an Elite Group: The Industrialist in Latin America." *Inter-American Economic Affairs,* vol. 19, no. 2 (Autumn 1965), 43-62.

Hartmann, H. *Authority and Organization in German Management.* Princeton: Princeton Univ. Press, 1959.

Herald, David M. "Long-Range Planning and Organizational Performance: A Cross-Valuation Study." *Academy of Management Journal,* vol. 15, no. 1 (March 1972), 91-102.

Jain, Sagar. "Old Style of Management." In S. B. Prasad and A. R. Negandhi, eds., *Managerialism for Economic Development.* The Hague: Martinus Nijhoff's, 1968, pp. 8-19.

Kumazawa, Sadas. "Future Management: Effective Use of Human Resources." *Management Japan,* July-September 1971, 5-8.

Lambert, Richard D. *Workers, Factories, and Social Change in India.* Princeton: Princeton Univ. Press, 1963.

Langenderter, Harold Q. "The Egyptian Executive: A Study in Conflict." *Human Organization,* vol. 24 (Spring 1965), 89-95.

Lauter, G. Peter. "Sociological-Cultural and Legal Factors of Impending Decentralization of Authority in Developing Countries." *Academy of Management Journal,* vol. 12, no. 3 (September 1969), 367-78.

————. "Advanced Management Processes in Developing Countries: Planning in Turkey." *California Management Review,* vol. 13, no. 3 (Spring 1970), 7-12.

Lauterbach, Albert. *Enterprise in Latin America.* Ithaca: Cornell Univ. Press, 1966.

————. "Management Aims and Development Needs in Latin America." *Business History Review,* 39 (1963), 557-72.

Lindquist, A. "Absenteeism and Job Turnover as a Consequence of Unfavorable Job Adjustment." *Acta Social,* vol. 3, nos. 2 & 3 (1958), 119-31.

McCann, Eugene C. "An Aspect of Management Philosophy in the United States and Latin America." *Journal of the Academy of Management,* vol. 7, no. 2 (June 1964), 149-52.

McClelland, David. *The Achieving Society.* New York: D. Van Nostrand, 1961.

————. "Business Drive and National Achievements." *Harvard Business Review,* vol. 40, no. 4 (July-August 1962), 99-112.

McGuire, Joseph. *Business and Society.* New York: McGraw-Hill, 1963.

McMillan, Claude. "The American Businessman in Brazil." *Business Topics,* Spring, 1965.

McMillan, Claude, Jr., et al. *International Enterprise in a Developing Economy: A Study of U.S. Business in Brazil.* East Lansing: Bureau of Business and Economic Research, Michigan State University, 1964.

Maier, N.R.F., and Hoffman, L. R. "Group Decision in England and the United States." *Personnel Psychology,* 15 (1962), 75-87.

Meade, R. D., and Whittaker, J. D. "A Cross-Cultural Study of Authoritarianism." *Journal of Social Psychology,* 72 (1967), 3-7.

Morris, David. *The Emergence of an Industrial Labor Force in India: A Study of The Bombay Cotton Mills, 1859-1947.* Berkeley: Univ. of California Press, 1965.

Nash, Manning. "The Interplay of Culture and Management in a Guatemalan Textile Plant." *Machine Age Maga: The Industrialization of a Guatemalan Community.* Menasha, Wis.: American Anthropological Association, Memoirs no. 87, 1958.

Negandhi, A. R. *Management and Economic Development in Taiwan.* The Hague: Martinus Nijhoff's, 1973.

————; Prasad, S. B.; and Shetty, Y. K. "Manpower Management and Organizational Effectiveness: A Cross-Cultural Study." *Academy of Management Proceedings* (1973).

Negandhi, A. R., and Prasad, S. B. *Comparative Management.* New York: Appleton-Century-Crofts, 1970.

Nowotny, Otto .H "American vs. European Management Philosophy." *Harvard Business Review,* vol. 42, no. 2 (March-April, 1964), 101-08.

Oberg, Winston. "Cross-Cultural Perspective on Management Principles." *Academy of Management Journal,* 6 (June 1963), 141-42.

Ornati, Oscar A. *Jobs and Workers in India.* Ithaca, N.Y.: The Institute of International Relations, Cornell University, 1955.

Pelletier, Gaston. "Business Management in French Canada." *Business Quarterly,* Fall 1966, pp. 56-62.

Rawin, Solomon John. "The Manager in the Polish Enterprise: A Study of Accommodation Under Conditions of Role Conflict." *British Journal of Industrial Relations,* March 1965, pp. 1-16.

Richardson, Stephen A. "Organizational Contrasts on British and American Ships." *Administrative Science Quarterly,* vol. 1, no. 2 (September 1956).

Richman, Barry M. "Capitalists and Managers in Communist China." *Harvard Business Review,* vol. 45, no. 1 (January-February 1967), 57-71.

————. *A Firsthand Study of Industrial Management in Communist China.* Los Angeles: University of California, Division of Research, Graduate School of Business Administration, 1967.

————. *Soviet Management.* Englewood Cliffs, N.J.: Prentice-Hall, 1965.

Ryapolov, Gregory. "I Was a Soviet Manager." *Harvard Business Review,* vol. 44, no. 1 (January-February 1966), 117-25.

Singer, Milton. "Indian Joint Family in Modern Industry." In Milton Singer and Bernard S. Cohn, eds., *Structure and Change in Indian Society.* Chicago: Aldine Publishing Company, 1968, pp. 423-52.

Sirota, David, and Greenwood, S. M. "Understand Your Overseas Work Force." *Harvard Business Review,* vol. 49, no. 1 (January-February 1971), 53-60.

Strassmann, W. Paul. "The Industrialist." In John J. Johnson, ed., *Continuity and Change in Latin America.* Stanford, Cal.: Stanford Univ. Press, 1964.

Takezawa, Shinichi. "Sociocultural Aspects of Management in Japan." *International Labour Review,* 94 (August 1966), 147-74.

Thiagarajan, K. M., and Deep, S. D. "A Study of Supervisor-Subordinate Influence and Satisfaction in Four Cultures." *Journal of Social Psychology,* 82 (1970), 173-80.

Webber, Ross. *Culture and Management.* Homewood, Ill.: Richard D. Irwin, 1969.

Whitehill, Arthur M., and Takezawa, Shinichi. *The Other Worker: A Comparative Study of Industrial Relations in the United States and Japan.* Honolulu: East-West Center Press, 1968, pp. 352-53.

Whyte, William F. "Framework for the Analysis of Industrial Relations: Two Views." *Industrial and Labor Relations Review,* 3 (April 1960).

Williams, L. K.; Whyte, W. F.; and Green, C. S. "Do Cultural Differences Affect Workers' Attitudes?" *Industrial Relations,* vol. 5, no. 3 (May 1966), 105-17.

Wright, Richard W. "Organizational Ambiente: Management and Environment in Chile." *Academy of Management Journal,* vol. 14, no. 1 (March 1971), 65-74.

Yoshino, M. Y. *Japan's Managerial System.* Cambridge: M.I.T. Press, 1968.

NAME INDEX

SUBJECT INDEX